Dislocations and Multiculturalisms

Dislocations and Multiculturalisms
Essays in Homage to Professor R.K. Kaul

Edited by
Jasbir Jain

Institute for Research in Interdisciplinary Studies (IRIS)

RAWAT PUBLICATIONS
Jaipur and New Delhi

ISBN 81-7033-873-5
© Contributors, 2004

No part of this book may be reproduced or transmitted in any form or by any means, electronic or mechanical, including photocopying, recording or by any information storage and retrieval system, without permission in writing from the publishers.

Published by
Prem Rawat for *Rawat Publications*
Satyam Apts., Sector 3, Jawahar Nagar, Jaipur 302 004 (India)
Phone: 0141 265 1748 / 7006 Fax: 0141 265 1748
E-mail: info@rawatbooks.com
Website: www.rawatbooks.com

Delhi Office
4858/24, Ansari Road, Daryaganj, New Delhi 110 002
Phone: 011-23263290

Typeset by Rawat Computers, Jaipur
Printed at Chaman Enterprises, New Delhi

Contents

	In Memory of Raj Kaul — *Shiv K. Kumar*	vii
	Preface	ix
	Introduction	xi
1	Self and Multiculturalism: Towards Self-Reflection *Sudhir Chandra*	1
2	Multiculturalism and Self: Issues of Comparison Between Canada and India *Kushal Deb*	10
3	Aesthetics of Dislocation and the Dislocation of Aesthetics *Santosh Gupta*	36
4	Refugee Problem in South Asia: An Overview *B.C. Upreti*	44
5	False Consciousness and the Postcolonial Subject *Dorothy M. Figueira*	60
6	Reconstructing Time and Experience: Variations on the Theme of Dislocation *Tej N. Dhar*	69
7	Of Immigrant Writing... *Vijay Lakshmi*	90
8	Trends in Contemporary Indian Writing in English *Malashri Lal*	101
9	Lost Dreams: Intizar Husain's Search For a Nation *Veena Singh*	113

10	Imperial Narratives: Dislocation and Power in Moodie and Duncan *Supriya Agarwal*	122
11	Memory and Aesthetics: A Study of Margaret Atwood's *The Blind Assassin* *Sudha Shastri*	128
12	Journey into Memory: Signposts of Dislocation *Mini Nanda*	138
13	Alone Among Aliens *Ila Rathor*	148
14	History as Fiction: A Post-WTC Reading of Vassanji's *AMRiiKA* *Harish Narang*	160
15	Re-Configuring Identity: Suniti Namjoshi's Diasporic Journeys *Alka Kumar*	174
16	On the Edge of Animation: Pakistani Women Poets in Their Own Voice *Anisur Rahman*	190
17	Not White and Also Women: Race, Gender and Multiculturalism in South Asian Canadian Women's Poetry *Sudha Rai*	203
18	Enclaves of Otherness Within Larger Cultures: Lee Langley's *A House in Pondicherry* *Veena Jain*	214
19	Living With the Trauma of Cultural Displacement in Naipaul's *Half a Life* *Anu Celly*	222
20	Identity, Home and Culture Through Dislocations *Jasbir Jain*	230
21	A Little About Father *Nilofer Kaul*	249
	Contributors	258
	Index	260

In Memory of Raj Kaul

It will never be the same—-
Jaipur, this pink city,
for it was your presence
that lent it both colour and fragrance.

Our friendship dates back to the genesis.
In my mind's eye I see you rise again —
tall, fair and slim, embodying
grace, propriety and reason —-
values that you garnered
from your mentor, Samuel Johnson.

Wherever you are, don't forget
that you'd always reign supreme
in our hearts.
We the living, are now plunged
in sorrow and despondency.

Shiv K. Kumar
(Awardee Padma Bhushan)

Preface

This volume has been a long time in the making. Ideas are born, they develop and grow and await the right opportune moment to be articulated. The period of growth has been of interaction, exchange of ideas and views and of research. A large number of the papers are based on two seminars which IRIS had conducted in 2001 and 2002. The first of these was on "Narratives of Dislocation" and explored various kinds of dislocations. The second on the "Problematics of the Self and Multiculturalism" was a natural fallout of the first. How did the "self" develop after the act of dislocation and how did it relate to the new environment as it negotiated the past, the cultural inheritance, geographical and historical memories and the challenges of the present were the areas of our concern.

IRIS is greatly indebted to the various participants who opened out new areas for thought and exploration. It is also indebted to the Canadian Studies Development Programme (CSDP) and the Indian Association of Canadian Studies (IACS) for part support of the two seminars and for making it possible for us to host scholars from abroad and other parts of India.

We have not been able to include the presentations made by M.G. Vassanji, Rehana Ghadially and Amritjit Singh, and a few others. Over and above the seminar participants we have some papers in this volume which have been contributed by other friends and were solicited for this specific volume which is our homage to Professor R.K. Kaul, one of our very esteemed members, one who was actively present in both the seminars and presented papers in both. In the "Narratives of Dislocation", he presented a paper on Vassanji's *Ameriika* and in the "Problematics of the Self" on Rohinton Mistry's *Family Matters*. As these papers are now appearing in a posthumous publication, they are not being included in this volume.

The friends who have responded warmly to our request have all been close friends of Professor Kaul. Of these one is Professor Shiv K. Kumar, poet and novelist, whose poem forms the dedication in this volume, Professor Kumar and Professor Kaul were both together at the University College, Hoshiarpur and this association, begun in the late 50s, stretched over nearly half-a-century. Vijay Lakshmi a former student and colleague, and Malashri Lal, another former student have also contributed. We acknowledge their contribution and thank them for joining us in paying this tribute to a loved teacher and warm friend. I would specially like to thank Prof. Sudhir Chandra for his participation, his soul searching reflections and above all else, for being a warm friend. Another contribution is the fictional piece by Professor Kaul's daughter, Nilofer Kaul, which is her personal tribute to the memory of her father.

Scholars from different backgrounds and disciplines have got together to present the reader with an interdisciplinary approach to the theme of this volume. Each one of the contributors to this volume is a valued contributor and each essay opens out a new issue, a new area, and a new vision. Together they hold out a new hope.

Finally, a word of thanks to Pranit Rawat. I am fully aware I make heavy demands on him, and he always meets them with a smile.

Jasbir Jain

Introduction

Dislocations and Multiculturalisms is a volume which seeks to address the most ancient problems of human society as well as the greatest challenges of our times. Human society has developed from a nomadic culture into a rooted one. But with new capitalistic forces unleashed, migrations and dislocations have become the order of the day. The boundaries of the nation-state are getting fainter and fainter paradoxically at a time when nationalism itself is resurfacing with unprecedented aggressiveness.

No human society has been able to avoid either migration or dislocation for whatsoever reasons; and consequently none has been able to avoid multiculturalism. India, Malaysia, Singapore, UK and USA, Canada and Australia, European nations whether large or small, all have a mixed population where different languages, nationalities and races intermingle. The West Indies is a classic example of a "created" multicultural society. Even the so-called Islamic states have a mix of races or religions or of both. Dislocation is inevitable. Yet the kind of trauma which has come to be associated with it over the years needs attention. Why is it so traumatic? Why does it have to be so? History and memory are two separators. But even more than that what matters or what acquires importance is (a) the assurance required from the outer world for the inner being, in order to feel at home and (b) a sense of community. It is the absence or presence of these which determine the direction of the process of relocation.

Individuals respond in various way – through withdrawal and involvement, through submission/assimilation or through difference; through short-circuiting memory or through a hardening of identity constructs. Intercultural relationships are ordinarily placed within a power relationship which is bound to be conflictual. Race and religion are the two major areas of conflict though what they really cloak is economic inequality and exclusion from positions of power. The greatest challenge of our times is to minimize these areas of conflict without pushing society and the world towards neo-colonialism. The world has been striving very visibly, for at least more than two centuries, to achieve a sense of justice and equality and win a certain minimum respect for the human being. But as the large number of wars and civil unrest movements, and the growth of 'terrorism' as such indicate, the effort has not met with much success. The magic formula still lies undiscovered somewhere within the mind of man.

The essays in this volume address this twin question of dislocations and multicultural societies in various ways, through exploring the self, the multicultural situations and policies, the dimensions of the refugee problem, the camouflage offered by a false consciousness, the dislocation of aesthetics, the immigrant creative writer's dilemma and move on to individual studies of texts and genres and explore historical consciousness, intertextualities, cultural transformations and the difficult problem of belonging.

Both the categories which we have taken up for consideration are problematic in themselves. Dislocation can be of diverse kinds: physical, psychological, emotional, political marginalization, it can be alienation or self-alienation, or social ostracism, or a removal from familiar environments of family, kinship and cultural, it can come through political upheaval, mass migration or natural disaster. It can be individual or collective. But no dislocation is ever complete, terminal or permanent in itself. There is always a looking back in some way or the other. This may be through memory, recollection, history, parallels or differences. Cultural memories have a tendency to surface again and again and establish a connection with the future; they do not allow the individual to snap ties with the past. Histories govern power relations and intervene with the construction of the 'present'.

Similarly 'multiculturalism' works at many levels. It is not merely a coexistence of myriad cultures or a projection of multiple ethnicities. It finds itself constantly in opposition to the dual concepts of 'modernity' and 'uniformity'. It is paradoxical that while the trend towards globalisation aims at reinforcing *sameness*, for long-term cultural and existential survival 'separation' is necessary and 'difference' is a reality which demands recognition. The major movements for social change have, over the years, moved from the demand for *sameness* towards recognition of *difference*, thus seeking to redefine the meaning of equality.

Multiculturalism exists perforce of historical circumstances in many societies. In the recent decades, there have been institutionalized efforts towards defining the relationship between cultures through legal processes and official policies. Academic moves have been made to celebrate and accommodate diversity, and to provide space for it. The whole process lays itself open to suspicion. Specially as the economic scenario hasn't really changed. Nor has the politics of race relations. And nor the terms of capitalist progress. Hierarchies, control, subordination of the worker, exploitation through economic competition, make one see the incompatibility between the discourse of capitalist economy in its global dimensions and the aspirations of equality on part of the exploited of the third world economies. Outsourcing is both an open and a closed door.

Paradoxically, again while privacy, ownership, individuality are all terms which have their origin in capitalist formations, they also stand threatened by capitalist developments which through technology seek to encroach upon these areas. The individual, in his search for identity formation, has now to negotiate these paradoxes and to extricate whatever can sustain his existential sense of being through this maze of conflictual areas.

Dislocations are inevitable, perhaps necessary for the journey towards maturity, self-knowledge and recognition. Multiculturalism is a necessary fallout, desirable equally for the opportunities and choices it offers. Yet both destroy stability, often attack harmony and peace and have so far failed to create a sense of pure joy. Utopias end in dystopias. Do we need to hold on to conflict as the shaky foundation of human relationships?

The narratives of dislocation have given rise to new aesthetics, not merely in terms of postcolonial aesthetics but also by using fluidity as a new concept. Even new historicism, in the challenge it offers to reverence of the past and to the neutrality of the historian, in the manner in which it recognizes alternative versions as equally relevant, has been born out of this conflict. The shift from the privileging of language as the sole creator of meaning or at least the final arbiter of meaning, to the recognition that words depend for their meaning on their relation to other words, phrases, sentences and 'races', on temporal and spatial contexts, is also the result of this intermixing of histories and cultures. Linear histories are no longer possible. The diachronic process is always at work. I give two examples. Northrop Frye in his essay "Myth, Fiction and Displacement" emphasizes the essential need for displacement in order to create newness. Again, no writing is possible without reference to worlds outside the immediate present and location. There are always references, direct or indirect, subtle and intended, implicit and explicit which take the reader to other geographies, locations, histories, parallels and differences. Discourse does not function only between two points; and it is never the same. It is multi-directional and subject to constant revisions and renewals.

The two categories, thus work at multiple levels of aesthetic and semiotic meaning, have social and psychological dimensions and contain within them opposites like desire and fear, adventure and disaster, trauma and hope. It is an unending journey which we have merely begun. At the same time it is uncertain and exciting. But as the wide range of issues raised in the essays in this volume testify, there is need to focus on the relationship between self, dislocation and multiculturalism from multiple perspectives: through a ruthlessly honest introspection, sociological and historical background, literary movements and reactions, as well as through the different ways human beings relate to these problems – flight and refuge, persecution and violence, assertion and defiance, and also by redefining cultures and priorities. The act of writing, in itself, is a definition of the self, both spatially and temporally.

1

Self and Multiculturalism
Towards Self-Reflection

Sudhir Chandra

Multiculturalism is the other name of culture, an essential condition of civilised existence in today's world. And it is faced with an uncertain prospect. Fast becoming a global village following the ever accelerating shrinkage of space and time, objectively the world has never been more propitious for multiculturalism. It is also, paradoxically, the scene of a growing intolerance of, and demonic readiness to destroy, the 'other'. On how this paradox unfolds will hinge the fate of multiculturalism and, as a sequel, of humankind.

At stake in this unfolding is each one of us. Hence the significance of 'self' in the discussion of multiculturalism, as also the urgency of the theme. The coupling of 'self' and 'multiculturalism' is unlikely to have been meant as a call for us to strip ourselves. The expectation, more likely, is that we shall follow our academic wont and discuss the theme within an impersonal general context. Yet I feel compelled to talk about it in personal terms. Academic analysis for far too long has tended to be concerned with the external world without simultaneously being turned inward. It has, thus, grappled to understand the recent resurfacing of hatred and violence that we had innocently believed lay buried in the past. It has, almost invariably, located the problem in a guilty 'other', rarely, if ever, in the 'self'. It has, moreover, felt baffled by the ineffectuality of its own prescriptions in the face of a crisis threatening to engulf the whole world.

My decision to speak about self and multiculturalism in a personal context is particularly inspired by Gandhi's injunction: Let everyone examine themselves. A pivotal article of faith though it was for him, Gandhi reiterated the injunction, significantly enough, at a time when, weeks before the country's independence, he was desperate to restore sanity among people who seemed seized by inhumanity. What had happened to the non-violence that everyone, including Gandhi himself, believed had brought Indians their freedom? How could he, the seeker of truth, have failed to detect the lie and avoid the resultant disaster? What could now be done? The reiteration – 'let everyone examine themselves' – was in answer to the last question.

Gandhi's injunction is not without academic provenance. Even if not formalised, like it is in psycho-analysis, self-examination must, in some form and at some point, inform any attempt to understand aspects of the human predicament. This may, beyond a point, lapse into solipsism. But, then, the risk of solipsism is endemic to any enquiry of which the human consciousness constitutes both the subject and the object. Why, then, am I, an academic speaking among fellow academics, invoking Gandhi's injunction? The reason lies in the centrality of morality in Gandhi's injunction. Unlike academic self-understanding, which may or may not consider morality important, the Gandhian call for self-examination necessarily implicates the examining self morally. Faced with surging inhumanity, and desperate to restore peace, he could have blamed the others. Instead he asked everyone to examine themselves, and felt no less bound to do the same himself. Each self needed to know where it had erred.

Let me, in this introspective spirit, recapitulate an actual incident which may well be a parable about the paradox of our multicultural selves in today's world.

It was a beautiful summer evening in Melbourne. We were assembled for a dinner in honour of a distinguished academic. The first woman from the Philippines to have graduated from the Melbourne University, she was on a brief visit to her alma mater. The President of the College, where she was staying, had invited to the dinner two fellow Australians, two Americans, one Japanese and one Indian.

Once we were settled around the table, the President asked everyone to introduce themselves briefly. This done, the guest of honour was requested to talk about her life and work. A gracious woman in her seventies, she began with her life as a girl in the jungles where her father, a forest officer, had summoned the whole family from Manila following the Japanese occupation. In terms hauntingly restrained, she recounted the horrors of Japanese occupation, including a reference – so veiled and fleeting that you could almost miss it – to her own elder sister falling, not atypically, into Japanese hands.

Then followed an enthusiastic account of the American 'liberators' who, ending her country's thraldom, set it on the path of development. Also remembered gratefully were the Australians for contributing to the Philippines' reconstruction. Among the first beneficiaries of Australian aid, she was awarded a scholarship at the Melbourne University. Finishing her M.A. in Melbourne, she returned home for a while, and then got a fellowship to do her Ph.D. in the USA.

This is a skeletal summary of a long, unhurried, almost elemental recall. It was the recall of a remembrance irrevocably traumatised by the Japanese occupation. Speaking through the venerable scholar was the young runaway from Manila into the Philippine jungles, detailing the story of her life and country. The unself-critical innocence of her account was untouched by considerations of civility. It mattered little if the lone Japanese at the table was hurt, or the five Americans and Australians felt flattered and proud.

It was difficult not to be moved by the Filipino's narrative. It was equally difficult, at least for me, not to be struck by the fallacy of its stereotyping of the Japanese, Americans and Australians as distinct peoples. Sympathising with the Japanese, who suffered the narrative in silence, I imagined how easily the Filipino's stereotyping would give way to an alternative, equally fallacious, stereotyping if the narrative were focused on Hiroshima and Nagasaki. Also, its poignancy notwithstanding, the Filipino's narrative sounded eerily unreal in the aftermath of Iraq. More so in John Howard's Australia. For, besides proudly lackeying the Bush administration, this dog-whistling Conservative Australian Prime Minister, violating his country's much trumpeted multiculturalism, had returned to power on the strength of an inhuman policy towards asylum seekers and 'natives'.

None of this, though, would have dented the Filipino's faith in the veracity of her account. Nothing is easier than to objectively expose the fallacy of stereotypes. Nothing more difficult than to render the expose acceptable to those rooted to a vantage point producing a different [view of] reality.

Everyone assembled that evening was, in their separate ways, multicultural. But they were multicultural in the context of a putative 'core self' which, at that moment, was framed in terms of the nation. Even I, with all my suspicion of nationalism, could not but be conscious of my Indian identity. And, for once, feel relieved to be an Indian and be answerable neither, unlike the Japanese, for the atrocities described by the Filipino scholar, nor, unlike the Americans and Australians, for the horrors of New Imperialism.

That relief was transient. As if unveiling a pattern that bound together these representative horrors of our times, my mind hopped from Hiroshima, Nagasaki and Iraq on to Gujarat. Gujarat which is a metaphor for the manichean intolerance, violence and inhumanity that seeks to destroy the country's multicultural fabric. Hindutva is its most organised, and ideologically the most explicit, form. But the phenomenon of intolerance, violence and inhumanity is wider spread than formal Hindutva. Recall the sudden eruption of violence against the Sikhs in 1984. Bizarre graffiti appeared out of nowhere to screech brazenly: *'Hindu Muslim bhai bhai, Sikhon ki ab karo safai.'* The very Sikhs whom the Republic's Constitution had subsumed among the Hindus, were pronounced to be alien and targeted for liquidation. That was not an achievement of formal Hindutva.

Gathering strength slowly, Hindutva registered its first major triumph with the gleeful demolition of the Babri Masjid and the attendant violence against the Muslims. I was during that seismic occurrence working at the Centre for Social Studies in Surat. I vividly remember how, meeting for the usual afternoon tea on the fateful 6 December 1992, the Centre's faculty was able to talk about nothing except what could/would happen in Ayodhya. We even imagined the worst, and shuddered to speculate as to what that would imply and unleash. On one thing, however, we were all agreed. Whatever might happen elsewhere, Surat would remain peaceful, given its history of communal amity and the intricate nexus of economic interdependence across the communal divide. Less than twenty-four hours later, the city's Muslims were being looted, maimed, killed, raped, and hunted out of their homes. What dark Hindu depths – not confined to formal Hindutva – had harboured that unsuspected hatred and violence?

These are unfathomable depths as is evident from the quintessential savagery of Gujarat 2002. Terrifying as that savagery was, immeasurably more terrifying is the electoral verdict that followed. In what by all accounts was a fair election, when that savagery in all its harrowing details had become known to the whole world, the 'civil' society in Gujarat chose to repose its confidence among the perpetrators of that savagery. Revealing something of those depths, even the supposedly secular opposition to those barbarians was informed by what has come to be known as soft Hindutva.

Best exemplified by the 1984 alienation of the Sikhs, the pervasive readiness to imagine and demonise an 'other' is illustrated also by the ease with which, for the first time in the two millennia of their existence in India, Christians have been reduced to a marked, besieged community. The intrinsic enormity of the antagonism against Christians apart, it negates the naturalisation of Christianity in India as also the fact that in no way have Christian Indians been any less integral a part of India than any other Indian community.

This is an inadequate account, retrospectively structured here, of what hit me in the form of Gujarat as I listened to the Filipino scholar that December evening. Surely there must have been something more compelling than masochism that, interrupting what seemed a justified relief at not being implicated, brought Gujarat to impinge upon my consciousness. And made me feel guilty.

Guilty as a Hindu. There was inside me, I can now see, a shift of the 'core' self. The relieved Indian core self had given way to a guilty Hindu core self.

I have had a fraught relationship with my Hindu self. Ranging over a wide spectrum, the relationship has included an unselfconscious immersion, during early boyhood, in an orthodox Brahman Hindu ethos, an ideologically motivated conscious rejection of it, and now a reassertion of Hindu identity. The reassertion – and it is not a tactical move – is in response to a conviction that Hindutva is an unwarranted degradation of Hindu culture. I am a true Hindu, not the likes of Advani from whom Hindu culture urgently needs to be saved. This Hindu self, needless to say in the context of multiculturalism, exists within me as part of an ever fluid constellation of many selves.

Gandhi once again comes to mind. He had the perspicacity and the vision to define a good Hindu as one who was also a good Muslim, a good Christian, a good Zoroastrian, and so on. Not one to let a shadow fall between precept and practice, he sought to become such a Hindu, and believed that he had succeeded. Gandhi was blessed with true audacity. He could dream impossible dreams and demonstrate their translatability in real life. However, I say this with trepidation, in the matter of realising his own ideal of being a good Hindu, he overestimated his success.

Gandhi's failure in this respect, combined with his unawareness of the failure, is related to something I have learnt in the course of writing *The Oppressive Present: Literature and Social Consciousness in Colonial India*. This, to my mind, bears a genealogical connection with the fast developing threat that, in its various hues, Hindutva poses to multiculturalism – to civilised existence – in our society. From the very early stage of its emergence in the 19th century, Indian nationalism was marked by a synonymisation of Hindu and Indian. Even the pioneers of what is described as secular, as opposed to cultural, nationalism – such as Romesh Chandra Dutt, Surendranath Banerji, Mahadev Govind Ranade and Gopal Krishna Gokhale – tended to take Hindu to mean Indian, and vice versa, without consciously doing so. Gandhi, too, despite his exceptional self-reflexivity, betrayed at least in one respect the subtle hold on him of this unconscious equation of Hindu and Indian. He did this while extending the idea of swadeshi to the realm of religion. Defining swadeshi as 'the use and service of our immediate surroundings to the exclusion of the more remote', he identified Hinduism as the locus of religious swadeshi for the multireligious Indian population. Given that swadeshi presupposes a small scale, Gandhi's privileging of a homogenised pan-Indian Hinduism is fundamentally violative of the basic spirit of swadeshi. He could not have missed this crucial point, I hazard the guess, save for his predisposition to equate Hindu and Indian. Save for this, again, he could not have kept Islam and Christianity and other faiths, along with their various local permutations, out of the Indian religious swadeshi. If not held back by that equation, he would have realised that the immediate and the remote in matters spiritual may not always converge with the physically immediate and remote.

For long much of the power exercised by the equation of Hindu and Indian was at the unconscious level. Proud Hindus though they were, the Dutts and the Ranades, let alone Gandhi, were not tinged with what in Indian public parlance is called communalism. There was nothing compromising or dishonest in their consciously stated ideological positions.

The Hindu-Indian equation, that was once implicit and unconscious, has increasingly become a matter of unabashed ideological assertion. Hindutva is its most aggressive assertion. Ideologically it is a very far cry from the plural ethos nurtured by our nationalist forebears. In terms of consciousness, however, a resemblance and a continuity is discernible. Growing ideological aggression notwithstanding, most Hindus still believe themselves to be feeling and acting as Indians without quite realising how the belief rests on the assumption of a non-duality between Hindu and Indian.

I am not suggesting that this is the only thing that is happening in contemporary India. Nor am I assuming the Hindus to be an undifferentiated collectivity. Yet, there are occasions when, for whatever length of time and vis-à-vis whichever 'other', more and more Hindus feel bound together in spite of all their differences. Recent display of antagonism against Muslims and Christians by Dalits and Adivasis, and their participation in acts of communal violence constitute an ominous shift in social consciousness that it will not do to explain away as mere manipulation by vested interests.

It is this coming together, in the midst of myriad other cleavages, that makes possible a metaphor like Gujarat.

Better equipped and more optimistically inclined minds have faith in their mediational efficacy. I am not so privileged. To go back to the dinner with which I began, I am convinced that, whatever my own thoughts in the matter, I could have managed nothing by way of unsettling the Filipino scholar's views. Nearer home, I have, like most of us, seen my near and dear ones slide away from a liberal, humane position towards monocultural insolence. It does not matter that they still chant *vasudhaiva kutumbakam*, that wonderful venerable mantra of multiculturalism, and believe themselves to be its exemplars. It helps little that I can see this, for I can do little to help them see this.

What I can do is to attempt to see myself. To the best of my ability. The insight that *The Oppressive Present* made available to me, I can see, was the result of a slow, often imperceptible, causal interaction between my life around and the formal research I was engaged in. The insight was that the understanding of a social reality is best sought in terms of ambivalence rather than through neat binary categories. The constant interplay of multiple identities, e.g., Hindu/Indian or communal/secular/national, was but part of the unfolding of that ambivalence. Such has been the dialectic of my life and work that today it is difficult to separately evaluate their role. It is difficult, for example, to precisely analyse how *The Oppressive Present* was influenced by what I saw of the sudden eruption of the 1984 anti-Sikh violence in Delhi; or, conversely, how my study of the interplay of nationalism/regionalism in the 19th century affects my attitudes to contemporary Indian politics. Be that as it may, I have come to respect multiple selves without hierarchising them (as is often done in order to valorise the national identity).

I am, consequently, not embarrassed about the Hindu I have rediscovered within me. I am not among those who counter the Hindutva call to take pride in being Hindu with the exhortation to feel ashamed about it. The Hindu in me can't get over a burning impotent rage against the barbarity that has been unleashed by those who call themselves Hindu. That Hindu is ashamed, and puzzled, that such barbarity should for so long fail to inspire any contrition among so many human beings, Hindu or whatever.

Have I then exorcised from within me the kind of Hindu of whom I am ashamed? Have I become the kind of human being that, through constant reading and reflection and progressive exposure to a cosmopolitan ambience, I have wished and tried to be? How I wish I could say 'yes'. But a traumatising encounter with a vestige of that which until then I believed I had overcome, rules out that categorical 'yes'. Painful as it is, and for some years I could not even talk about it, I must end with that encounter.

It happened when Surat was gripped by anti-Muslim violence in the wake of the Babri Masjid demolition. I was with a friend when a middle-aged Gujarati woman came in to say that a train had been forcibly stopped at the outskirts of the city and some women passengers had been raped. Even as the friend insisted that it was one of those rumours, I caught myself wondering if the rape victims were Hindu women. Before the thought could occur in its fullness, I was seized with shame.

It is not easy to go over it again. May I reproduce here my reaction to this encounter as I recorded it a couple of years ago:

Neither the fleetingness of the thought nor the quickness of the shame can mitigate the enormity of the occurrence. It happened – that monstrous realisation of difference between Hindu and Muslim – years after I had trained myself against such perversities. And it happened in the most unlikely of moments, against the grain, as I trembled over the consequences of 6 December and witnessed the savagery in Surat. Who within me had leapt out to possess me? Though the better purged by this humbling experience, I can no longer vouch for my dark interior. It can shame me again, in this or in any other respect.

It is important to intellectually grasp the monocultural implications of 'Hindu nationalism' which is fundamentally irreconcilable with the country's multi-religious, multi-linguistic reality. Whatever semantic manipulation may be attempted to stretch the term 'Hindu' so as to make it mean 'Indian', 'Hindu nationalism' is bound in practice to destroy what it prizes most, i.e., Indian unity. (I am not arguing that the unity of India is an intrinsically desirable end; much less that multiculturalism is desirable only as a means to that end.) We should also realise that this monoculturalism will soon seek to replicate within India the New World Order, the lords of which believe themselves to be capable of no wrong and must possess the prerogative of pre-emptive strike? (Cf. George W. Bush: '... when we see a threat, we deal with these threats before they become imminent. It's too late if they become imminent.') It may be necessary to organize offensives against this more than imminent threat. Meanwhile it will help to examine our own complicity, if any, in it.

2
Multiculturalism and Self
Issues of Comparison Between Canada and India

Kushal Deb

In this paper an attempt has been made to get a comparative perspective between Canada and India on the various conceptualizations of the self that emerge in a multicultural setting due to the multiplex relationships between the state, the communities and individual citizens. But before undertaking that task, we would need to briefly analyze the two crucial concepts i.e. multiculturalism and self.

I
Multiculturalism and Self

Multiculturalism is a term, which can be used both in a descriptive as well as in a normative sense (Joseph: 2002). As a descriptive category it usually has no analytical value, as it simply points towards the presence of different culturally defined groups within a nation-state.[1] It doesn't help us therefore to distinguish one nation-state from the other because presently all nation-states have various cultural groups existing within their territory. In the normative sense it refers to a desired end-state, as a way of referring to a society in which different cultural groups are respected, provisions made for the reproduction of their respective cultures and social diversity is celebrated as a value.[2] One needs to further point out that multiculturalism in the normative sense is a modern concept, having emerged out of the Enlightenment project and the French Revolution. It can be labelled as *liberal* multiculturalism as equal recognition of cultural groups must be compatible with requirements of basic individual liberties and also with individual autonomy. It is different from Ashis Nandy's conceptualization on religious pluralism and toleration, purported to be present in traditional India (Nandy: 1990) or the kind of *authoritarian* multiculturalism, which was prevalent in the Millet system practiced in the Ottoman Empire (Bhargava: 2002). In these systems, multiple communities co-existed but within an acknowledged framework of hierarchy with the ruler's religion and culture occupying the highest position. Whenever the implicit structure of dominance was challenged even indirectly, tolerance swiftly vanished (Mahajan: 2002). This distinction is very crucial because in India, critics of minority rights and secularism from both within the academia and from the Hindu right, often attempt to provide an alternate vision of religious tolerance based on conceptualizations on religious pluralism prevalent in ancient or medieval India.

We also need to distinguish between state sponsored multiculturalism, which is also known as *multiculturalism from the top* from the radicalized version of identity politics, which is called *multiculturalism from below*. As pointed out by Bannerji (2000) in the case of Canada, multiculturalism can be used as a diffusing agent, as a tool used by the state for internal *diversity management*. Efforts may range from usage of the policy of multiculturalism for maintaining the hegemony of the ruling race/class/caste/gender and shaping the so-called *national identity* or national character to innocuous efforts at placating the immigrant ethnic groups through ethnic food, costume and dance festivals, often termed as *boutique* multiculturalism (Fish: 1998). The *Iftaar* party and Christmas celebrations, which take place annually at Rashtrapati Bhavan in India, also fall into this category. On the other side, we have the radical/oppositional politics of *women of colour* in Canada (Bannerji: 2000) who are increasingly questioning the racialized/ethnicized and patriarchal policies of the Canadian state or the challenge posed by Dalit scholars and activists in India (Rege: 1998, Nigam: 2000, Ilaiah: 2001 and Pandian: 2002), to the taken for granted conceptualizations around the binary of nationalism/colonialism and secularism/communalism, thereby interrogating the very foundations of Indian modernity. This kind of identity politics is labelled as multiculturalism from below as these are the struggles waged by the oppressed groups for equality, dignity and freedom.

The concept of 'self' can also be similarly problematized. According to Mead's cognitive view, every human being develops a 'self' initially in childhood through his/her interaction with *significant* others (i.e., concrete individuals directly involved in his/her life like parents, siblings, relatives) and later in life through interaction with *generalized* others (i.e., abstract statuses and roles in society). Crucial for the development of self is also the ability to *'look at oneself as an object'* for which as pointed out by Charles Cooley, we often use others as a "looking glass"(Mead: 1934). Mead's formulations give us certain interesting insights, some of which have also been used by Charles Taylor (1994) in his famous article – 'The Politics of Recognition'. First, as significant others are very crucial for the initial formation of the self, one can generalize and claim that one's community starting from one's primary group i.e. family, kin-relationships, and reaching out to one's caste, ethnic group, religious community, race, etc., plays an important role in shaping one's concept of self. This provides moral justification for the protection and nurturance of groups/communities defining themselves in terms of cultural categories especially when these are minority groups under the threat of assimilation from the dominant community. Secondly, as we use 'others' as a looking glass, recognition or non-recognition by others becomes crucial for one's own self-definition. As Taylor points out, mis/non-recognition can lead to depreciatory image of oneself and this can become a form of oppression especially for the minority communities. Interestingly, even for the dominant community there seems a need for a stereotyped conception of the "*other*" in order to define its own identity positively. This becomes clear in Himani Bannerji's assertion that the Canadian state's official policy of multiculturalism plays a very crucial role in defining the "Canadian" (read 'White European North American') identity because by racializing and ethnicizing the immigrant groups and creating negative stereotypes of them as traditional and conservative, it can define the "Canadian" identity in terms of positive characteristics (Bannerji: 2000).

The crucial insight that one gains from the above discussion is that while one's community (not necessarily primordial) is necessary for one's formulation of self, the presence of an "other" often plays an equally important role in shaping that conception of self. The need for an "other" seems more acute for the dominant group, for by defining the other negatively, it derives its own positive self-conception. But ironically most dominant groups (white European North Americans in Canada and upper-caste communities or supporters of Hindutva in India) seem insensitive to this fact. The subjugated communities (aboriginals, immigrants, dalits and minority communities) on the other hand show much more reflexivity or critical awareness as only by challenging and subverting such negative stereotyping can they really regain their dignity and equal status.

We can develop this insight further, by using the two conceptualizations on 'Self' worked out by Lemert (1994) in order to classify the scholars who have written about 'Self'.[3] Lemert's first category consists of those who consider the Self as a moral or natural thing, out there in real history. He labels this as the *strong-we* group. The *strong-we* is strong because it enforces the illusion that humanity itself constitutes the final and sufficient identifying group. The other category, which he calls as the *weak-we* group is constituted by those who practically locate their sense of self in concrete historical relation with local groups unlike those of the first category who do not hesitate to identify local experience, unreflexively with universal human condition.

Lemert states that the temptation is great to deride the strong-we position as "essentialist" and the weak-we as "tribalist". But then we would miss what is principally the issue. Each of the strong-we theorists struggles seriously, not with essential Truth, but with moral dilemmas. What characterizes even the very best of the strong-we thinkers is that the Self is among those moral entities that entail a final moral dilemma. The only way around it, from within the strong-we culture, is the crude assertion of the abstract Truth of the Human. In other words, as an alternative to essentialism, scholars like Taylor and other left-liberal strong-we thinkers are left with a dilemma for which the only answer is *liberal hope*.

By contrast, those who identify themselves with a weak-we culture are very much less inclined to view mutilation and destruction as a moral "dilemma". They usually have an explicit theory of the moral and political origins of the mutilations, which they experience, which theories, in turn, are very often the historical bases upon which they define their weak-we culture. For example, in the Indian context, Rege (1998) while explicating the dalit feminist standpoint states that this standpoint "emphasizes individual experience within socially constructed groups and focuses on the hierarchical, multiple, changing structural power relations of caste, class and ethnicity, which construct such groups. It is obvious that the subject/agent is multiple, heterogeneous and even contradictory, i.e., the category 'dalit woman' is not homogenous." Lemert makes a similar point when he states that the power of the weak-we group arises less from the cogency of its attack on principles than from the authority of its complexly fractured historical experiences which, poses questions the first group (strong-we group) cannot answer from within.

We will workout the implications of holding either a strong-we or a weak-we position, when we elaborate on the different ways in which the self get conceptualized in a multicultural scenario, where the state, the different communities and individual citizens (who also happen to be members of the various communities) are the major players. But before undertaking that task we need to first make a quick review of the ground realities in both the countries as it brings out interesting similarities and differences.

II
Canada and India: A Comparison of the Issues Involved

The ongoing debates in Canada on minority rights and multiculturalism can be analyzed at three levels. The issues at the three levels are intertwined and together provide the context for the debate. At the first level is the issue of status of Quebec (a province with a dominant French speaking population) as a 'distinct society' with accompanying self-governing rights. At the second level are questions concerning the Aboriginal groups, who can be further categorized as Indians (the 'First Nations'), Inuit (Eskimos) and the Metis (descendents of European trappers and aboriginal women). The issue of the ethnic immigrants from the various Asian and European nations constitutes the third level of analysis.

In India the debates on minority rights and multiculturalism have mostly revolved within political theory around the relationship between the various religious communities particularly the Hindus and the Muslims. The Punjab crises of the 1980s and the resultant tensions between the Hindus and the Sikhs have been analyzed using the analytical category of 'ethnicity' and as a development issue (green revolution) involving Centre-State relationship. The spurt of attacks on Christian missionary organizations and the revival of debates concerning conversions by right wing Hindu organizations have also brought into focus the relation between the Hindu and the Christian communities. The recent ethnic cleansing and destruction of properties of members of the Muslim community, which took place in Gujarat after the reprehensible burning alive of *kar sevaks* at Godhra, the triumphant return of Narendra Modi as the chief minister in the elections held after the riots, have opened up a new chapter in deteriorating Hindu-Muslim relations and members of the minority communities have never felt so alienated since the demolition of the Babri Masjid in the last decade.

Let us look at the comparative issue in a little more details:

(A) The case of Quebec is unique because historically the French colonizers had ruled over Canada before the Britishers defeated them. Canada had emerged as a nation-state out of the Confederation treaty signed between the French and English speaking population and therefore the idea of the 'two founding nations' is put forward so strongly by the French Canadians. Canada has a policy of bilingualism and was also bicultural before the policy of multiculturalism was adopted due to the strong resentment from the already entrenched ethnic immigrant groups. The demands of the Quebeckers for a 'distinct society' status with special minority rights not applicable for other parts of Canada has to be therefore seen keeping these historical situations in mind. Furthermore, the demographic concentration of French speaking population at Quebec strengthens the demand for self-governing rights and has lead to the spread of the nationalist ideology of – '*la nation Quebecois*'.

In contrast the phenomenon is different in India as far as relation between the majority community – the Hindus and the largest minority community – the Muslims are concerned.[4] The minority Muslim community is dispersed all over the country and has not indulged in any territorial claims.[5] In fact the creation of India and Pakistan as separate nation-states was an outcome of the partition of the subcontinent on religious lines, an event marked by crossing of borders by a few million people and the brutal killing of about half a million in the accompanying communal holocaust. Although Pakistan was created on religious lines, India has a large Muslim population (about eleven percent of its population), even larger than the population of Pakistan. The partition of the subcontinent, the accompanying communal holocaust, the presence of Muslim majority Pakistan in its immediate neighbourhood, are all important symbolic markers in the relation between the Hindu and Muslim communities in India. The Muslim community demands are therefore different from the demands of the Quebeckers. There are no nationalist claims over any region. Their demands evolve around their right to maintain their specific cultural and religious distinctiveness and heritage, which has been granted to them under the Indian Constitution. The leaders of the Hindu majoritarian groups or the so-called Hindu Right on the other hand point to some illiberal ideas and practice within the Muslim community (not that they are in any way lacking within the Hindu religious tradition) specially those concerning the personal laws. They decry what they feel as the pampering of the minority community, accuse the secular-democratic forces of pseudo-secularism and insist on the implementation of the Uniform Civil Code (U.C.C.) for the sake of uniformity of civil law within the nation and the removal of discriminatory practices against women.

(B) At the second level of analysis, are the issues concerning the Aboriginal groups of Canada. The Aboriginal peoples were the original inhabitants of Canada before the coming in of the French and the British colonizers. The Indians therefore call themselves the 'First Nations' to draw attention to the chronological priority of inhabitance and thus implicitly challenging the myth of the 'two founding nations'. The aboriginal groups have also historically had a very intimate relationship with land, it being their source of sustenance and livelihood. They have over centuries developed intricate cultural systems, philosophies and life-worlds based on their relationship with land. While the land rights of the Aboriginal people have never been treated uniformly, there did develop in the pre-Confederation period in British North America a consistent body of procedures and tradition in the form of treaties. Under these treaties the Aboriginal people surrendered most of their territorial rights and gained various forms of compensation. After the Confederation, all the terms of the pre-Confederation treaties were turned over to the Canadian Government. Treaty Indians have a number of claims that relate to the cessation of their lands through treaties. Their grouses range from specific terms of treaties being unfulfilled to the complaint that the government has not assumed the broader spirit of the treaties. Most status Indians belong to bands that have rights to reserve lands held in common. Management of band funds and reserve resources and the administration of band affairs is also a central feature of many band claims. Land claims and self-government rights are therefore some of the central demands of the Aboriginal groups.

India too has a large tribal/adivasi population and there is considerable disparity among them in terms of their induction into the so-called modernization or development process. For instance, tribal groups from the northeastern states are on an average far ahead of the groups settled in rest of the country in terms of indicators like education and employment. Right from colonial times, tribal groups have suffered considerable land alienation, displacement and exploitation. After Independence, every large development projects like dams, factories and missile ranges have lead to their displacement from their land. Along with struggles for compensation and rehabilitation, the tribal groups with active support from NGOs and peoples' movements (like the Narmada Bachao Andolan) are increasingly questioning the whole development paradigm, which seemed axiomatic since independence. As the nexus in large development projects between large industrial corporations, big capitalist farmers, bureaucrats, contractors and the political elite is getting increasingly exposed, the question "whose development?" is being poignantly asked. But the issues of the tribal communities/adivasis have hardly been discussed in recent debates concerning multiculturalism and minority rights except for a debate in *Economic and Political Weekly* in 1994 {see K. Subramaniam (1994), N. Chandoke (1994) and N.G. Jayal (1994)}. In addition, a discussion on the displacement caused by Narmada project and the rights of displaced (especially tribal groups) is there in Jayal (1998, 2001).[6] In fact many of the issues raised by Jayal (1998) bring out the similarities between the struggles launched by the Aboriginal groups in Canada and the struggle of the displaced tribal communities in India.[7]

(C) At the third level of analysis is the question of rights of the immigrant groups in Canada. It is stated that multiculturalism was adopted as the official policy of the Canadian government mainly due to the demands from the various immigrant ethnic communities. The Germans, Italians, Ukrainians, Chinese and the South Asians constitute the predominant immigrant communities. The entrenched immigrant communities like the Ukrainians resented the adoption of the policy of Bilingualism and Biculturalism by the Canadian government. They insisted that the government should also take care of their cultural inspirations and interests. Reacting to these pressures, in the early 1970s the federal government and some of the provincial ones officially adopted the policy of multiculturalism.

This view has been challenged by anti-racist feminist scholars like Himani Bannerji (2000) who states that Pierre Trudeau's gift of an official policy of multiculturalism appeared in a period of a rapid influx of third world immigrants into Canada, as well as in a moment of growing intensity of the old English-French rivalry. Quebec displayed tendencies of armed separatist struggles during the late 1960s and the early '70s. In this context the proclamation of multiculturalism could be seen as a diffusing or a muting device for franco-phone national aspirations, as much as way of coping with the non-European immigrants' arrival. It also sidelined the claims of Canada's aboriginal population, which had displayed a propensity towards armed struggles for land claims, as exemplified by the American Indian Movement (AIM). The reduction of these groups' demands into cultural demands was obviously helpful to the nationhood of Canada with its hegemonic Anglo-Canadian national culture. A political discourse relying on a language of culture and ideological constructions of ethnicized and racialized communities quickly gained ground. Bannerji points out that there were no strong multicultural demands on the part of third world immigrant themselves to force such a policy. The issues raised by them were about racism, legal discrimination involving immigration and family reunification, about job discrimination on the basis of Canadian experience, and various adjustment difficulties, mainly of childcare and language. In short, they were difficulties that are endemic to migration, and especially of people coming in to low-income jobs or with few assets. Immigrant demands were not then, or even now, primarily cultural. It began as a state or an official/institutional discourse, and it involved the translation of issues of social and economic injustice into issues of culture. Thus immigrants were ethnicized, culturalized and mapped into traditional/ethnic communities.

In India the issue of immigration is not relevant, it being a developing country. In fact out-migration from India to the developed nations like Canada, USA and UK is the prevalent trend. Hindu rightist groups have tried now and then to whip up passion on the issue of the illegal immigration of poor Bangladeshi Muslims into India but their propaganda has fortunately not had any serious effect so far.

III
Conceptions of Self in a Multicultural Setting: A Comparison between India and Canada

After having described the issues, which concern India and Canada, let us try and delineate the various ways in which the 'self' gets conceptualized in a multicultural setting, where the state, the various communities and the individual citizens (who are simultaneously members of communities) are the major players.

State and its impact on self

The state has a very crucial role to play in the way the self (both at the level of the community and at the level of the individual) gets defined in a multicultural scenario. The constitution of a nation-state has various provisions, which guarantees not only fundamental rights to all its citizens and also protects the rights of the minority communities. The state also formulates various policies and rules, which directly affect the functioning of various communities and its members. Let us look at some of ways in which the state impinges on the development of the self in more details:

Rigidifies community boundaries

Various scholars have pointed out the role, which both colonial and postcolonial states have played in homogenizing community boundaries, thereby restricting the development of the self. Shail Mayaram (1999), for instance states that premodern Indian identities were both fluid and complex. Community, she states is defined not by religion alone and caste, kinship, language, geographic location, shared history and class are as much determinants of the large number of Muslim communities. Policies based on multiculturalism she feels, construct groups in homogenous molds thereby negating the very principles that it upholds, namely, the protection of plural identities. Kumkum Sangari (1995: 3289-93), not only points to the fluid nature of community formation in India but also points out the role played by the state since colonial times in homogenizing religious communities. The British had homogenized personal laws through codification and further codified custom through the accumulation of case law. The reformed Hindu law and the Shariat application act helped to create newly unified versions of Hindus and Muslims.

In another article Sangari (1999) shows that the reform of Hindu personal law undertaken after independence as a first stage towards a more progressive, and possibly uniform civil code in fact produced a legal description of a 'Hindu' by purposively including the Buddhists, Jains and Sikhs despite protests. The bill thus attacked most principles of religious plurality and choice. It recognized the existence and claims of in-between and unclassified areas, discrete belief systems, overlapping religions, non-believers, regional specificity, and then proceeded to deny them. The negative description of a Hindu, as one who was not a member of the four excluded religions (Muslims, Christians, Parsis and Jews) produced a Hindu so highly chained to his/her birth that even non-belief could not provide an exit.

In Canada, as pointed out by Bannerji (2000), state sponsored policy of multiculturalism has not only diffused and muted the sub-national aspirations of the Franco-phones and the aboriginal groups but has also racialized/ethnicized the non-European immigrants. Simultaneously, it has promoted the cultural aspirations of the dominant Anglo-Canadian community by projecting it as the national identity.

By projecting to the world at large that what the incoming third world population of Canada primarily wanted was the same religious, linguistic and cultural life they had in their countries of origin, the immigrant groups were frozen into being seen as traditional cultures and thus socially conservative in entirety. As a result, the political consciousness of the third world immigrants has also got multiculturalized. Wearing or not wearing of turbans, publicly funded heritage language classes, state supported Islamic schools modeled on the existence and patterns of Catholic schools, for example provide the profile of their politics. They themselves often forget how much less important these are than their full citizenship rights.

More importantly, this new cultural politics, which leaves out problems of class and patriarchy, appeals to the conservative elements in the immigrant population, since religion could be made to over determine their uncomfortable actualities. Official multiculturalism therefore empowers the same male leaders as patriarchs and enhanced their sexism and masculinism. In the name of culture and god, within the high walls of community and ethnicity, women and children could be dominated and acted against violently.

State's role in protecting identity/self

Notwithstanding its role in racializing or ethnicizing minority communities or its role in strengthening the hegemony of the majority community; minority communities do in crunch situations need the support of the state for protecting itself and perpetuating its culture. Both in India and in Canada, there are special constitutional provisions to protect the rights of minorities. But there are even more crucial situations where the state plays a very important role especially from the liberal point of view, i.e., when reforms are to be initiated or individuals, especially dissenters or women, are to be protected from conservative forces within communities.

Many scholars are skeptical on the issue of minority communities initiating reforms from within and bringing about these reforms through debate and a democratic process. This is because self-governing democratic institutions do not emerge spontaneously from within minority communities and conservative elements often take charge, especially if there are perceived threats to the community. Bhargava (1999) and Bilgrami (1999) therefore stress on internal reforms emerging from within the community but with the liberal and democratic state providing the conditions that make possible a full and free deliberation over the entire issue, a precondition for any reforms. Many feminist scholars on the other hand are skeptical about the operations of the state especially the judiciary and are not very optimistic of obtaining gender justice through state legislations or judgments by courts (see Cossman and Kapur: 1999, Kapur and Cossman: 1996, Agnes: 1999, Parasher: 1992). Sangari (1995) for instance, points out that it is wrong to draw a sharp line between the community and state on either the question of religions or of patriarchies since there are structural, ideological, political and administrative linkages between the two. However, she makes a very insightful point, which brings out the continuing relevance of the state. Women's relation with their community and the personal laws is essentially as wives, mothers or daughters and from within this relationship they have a schizophrenic relation with citizenship, upholding a harmful opposition between private and public, i.e., between being members of a community and having full rights as citizens. On the other hand the state is theoretically committed to ensuring the rights of citizens as citizens. Therefore, only as citizens can women potentially challenge divisions based on denomination, on public and private, and seek, if they wish, secular collectivities.

Impact of gender relations on self

As is evident from the above discussion, in the tussle between the state and different communities, the women are the worst affected but unfortunately the women's issue never gets highlighted. In India, the whole debate on the reform of Muslim personal laws, which was sparked off by the Supreme Court judgment on the Shah Bano case of 1985, the public as well as the parliamentary debate tended to focus on the conflict between the right of the religious minority to cultural autonomy and to a separate civil code as an important guarantee of its identity on the one hand, and the claims of the state legitimized through representative institutions to articulate the common good on the other (Jayal 1998). The critics ignored the important question of women's rights, which remained confined to feminists and the Left parties. The Muslim leadership focused on the legal issues that linked women and family life to Islamic legal identity and defended the definition of the Muslim community as a legal entity. The Government defended the legislation on the ground that it confirmed to the wishes of the Muslim community and should therefore be conceded irrespective of the opinion of other communities or society at large. In the absence of a reformed divorce law, Muslim women who were unequal vis-à-vis men were now rendered unequal vis-à-vis women from other communities. These issues raise important questions that are not easily reconciled: the claims of rights of women and of individuals as against those of cultures and groups (Hasan 2000: 291). The issue of reform of personal laws is deeply enmeshed with the question of gender justice. But it becomes a sensitive issue because it is perceived as interference by the conservative sections of the minority community. This is because personal laws are unfortunately utilized for marking out group boundaries and any move for reforms are perceived as threats to a community's identity. Women become the unfortunate victims of the process as personal laws of most religions discriminate against women.

In the case of Canada, Himani Bannerji (2000) shows that the politics of multiculturalism leaves out problems of class and patriarchy, and this appeals to the conservative elements in the immigrant population. Official multiculturalism therefore empowers the same male leaders as patriarchs and enhances their masculinism. In the name of culture and god, within the high walls of community and ethnicity, women and children could be dominated and acted against violently because the religions or culture or tradition of others supposedly sanctioned this oppression and brutality. The position of 'women of colour' who are victims of domestic violence is rather awkward because of ethnicization of violence. They are forced to maintain a *public silence*. This silence is highly telling for it can mean anything from complicity to resistance. One of the reasons for this paradoxical silence may be that public utterances put them in a situation of responsibility – it makes them accountable to others and to themselves. The doors of the community open as they speak "out". So obviously they are wary of not only what they say in public, but also where and how they saw it. In India, a similar predicament had forced Shah Bano to give up the right she had fought for so many years, by asking the Supreme Court to record that she now repudiated the petition that they had upheld, and renouncing the maintenance the Court had ordered. Upon this, she was welcomed back to the fold by Muslim fundamentalists, and hailed for having become a *true* Muslim woman.

Group identity and self-definition

Here it would be worthwhile to see how both the majority and the minority communities define their identity vis-à-vis one another and the impact it has on the definition of self of its respective members. In the case of both India and Canada, the majority group's culture is often projected as the national culture and therefore the aspirations of the majority community get portrayed as national aspiration. In all this, often slippages occur and the majority group's religion becomes synonymous with culture and this in turn gets equated with the nation. This can lead to racist tendencies and stereotyping/ethnicization of other groups and cultures. Interestingly, the conservative leaders of these majority communities portray a picture of the group's identity being under constant threat and the notion of *'fighting for survival'* comes to the fore. This is evident both in Canada and in India.

In Canada, there is an attempt from within the conservative sections of the Anglo-Canadians to portray their white-European

Protestant identity as the Canadian national identity. This identity is seen as under constant threat from the French-Canadians with their emphasis on the 'distinct society' status for Quebec; from the aboriginal communities who call themselves the "First Nations" to draw attention to the chronological priority of inhabitance and to implicitly challenge the myth of the "two founding nations"; from the immigrant ethnic population who with their distinct and so called 'traditional and conservative' cultures are seen as a drag to the process of modernity; and finally from the looming presence of 'big brother' USA on whom Canada is not only economically dependent but whose companies control most of its culture industry.

Similarly, in India, the proponents of Hindu nationalism want the national identity to be woven around their version of Hindu culture. They continuously lambast the Muslims in India for having their loyalties 'elsewhere' and even define a code of conduct for the Indian Muslims.[8] They are paranoid of being outnumbered by the Muslims and create myths about their fecundity and about illegal Muslim migrants from Bangladesh. Recently they are also showing increasing hostility towards Indian Christians, especially on the issue of conversion. As pointed out by Aijaz Ahmad (2002:76-77), conversions disturb them, as they think of religion as race and religious conversions as a kind of racial inter-mixing, contrary to the purity and primordiality of belief and belonging. The paranoia about the Hindu identity was starkly evident in the speeches of Narendra Modi, in the aftermath of the massacre of a few thousand Muslims (with state connivance) in the Gujarat. Instead of showing remorse, he kept harping about "Gujarati *Asmita*".

Among the minority groups also, one often finds a hardening of stance, postures of non-negotiability and rigidity in the definition of the self. This usually happens as a *'defensive measure'* especially in an atmosphere of hostility and lack of trust. In such circumstances, the conservative leadership comes to the forefront and the liberal leadership is marginalized. In Canada, during the heights of the *Quebecois* movement, the Bill 101, under which Francophone children must send their children only to French language schools became a *non-negotiable* demand. In India similarly, whenever the issue of Uniform Civil Code arises and is particularly championed by the Hindu nationalist groups, the Muslim community becomes defensive and the conservative leadership claims that the Muslim personal laws are non-negotiable as they are crucial for the Muslim identity.

Naming and its impact on the constitution of the self

What a group calls itself has important implications on how the members of that group perceive themselves and how others perceive the members of that group or community. Naming therefore has important implications for the constitution of the self. We have already seen that the aboriginal groups fighting for their land rights and for self-governing rights over the tracts of land under their control calls themselves the "First Nations" in order to challenge the claims of both the Anglo-Canadians and the French-Canadians of being the "Two Founding Nations".

Himani Bannerji (2000) also brings out the implications of *naming* by taking up and deconstructing the whole notion of *women of colour*. She states that although the term 'women of colour' is of US origin, it has provided the political culture for accepting, using and naturalizing a colour-based notion of subjectivity and agency in Canada. She states that the term women of colour blended with the Canadian state's official terminology of "visible minority" which stresses both the features of being non-white and therefore visible in a way whites are not, and therefore of being politically minor player. This status of visible minority was not felt by a large number of women to be problematic or compromising, since they shared political values with the mainstream. Minor as their part was, set apart by their visibility, which was also the only ground of their political eligibility, they were content.

For those in the alternate feminist politics in Canada the term 'women of colour' blending well with the official terminology of 'visible minority' therefore became the chosen name and solved the problem of finding a name for building coalition among all women. It vaguely and pleasantly gestured to race as colour and, of course, to gender/patriarchy by evoking woman. But the concept of race lost its hard edges of criticality, class disappeared entirely, and colour gave a feeling of brightness, brilliance or vividness, of a celebration of a difference, which was disconnected from social relations of power, but instead perceived as diversity, as existing socio-cultural ontologies or facts. A colour-coded self-perception, an identity declared on the semiological basis of one's colour, was rendered palatable through this ideology of diversity. Moreover, the word "colour" became an associational and connotative path to diverse histories and cultures of the nations of other women. They themselves summoned it to convey their colourfulness through it, thereby quickly slipping into the cultural discourse of tradition versus modernity. Their colour signaled traditional cultures, in a constellation of invented traditions.

Bannerji feels that she may be accused of making a mountain out of a molehill by focusing so much on a single political and cultural term. After all, would not a rose by any other name smell as sweet? She disagrees for she feels that the language with which we build or express our political agency has to be taken very seriously. If, the term *"non-white women"* was used for anti-racist feminist politics, then they would have been able to gesture towards white privilege as the use of a negative prefix automatically raises issues and questions. But a substitution through the language of diversity and colour distracted one from the racialized and gendered class existence and culturalizes ones politics.

Similarly, in India the members of the Scheduled Castes, who were known by derogatory terms such as "outcastes" or "untouchables", later classified as "Depressed Classes" by the British administration and euphemistically called as "Harijans" (people of God) by Gandhi, a term rejected by Ambedkar, presently call themselves by a much more radical term "Dalits" which means oppressed. The term dalit directly points to the centuries of oppression and exploitation suffered by members of the lower castes in the hands of the Brahmins and the other upper castes and has therefore become a radical symbol of hope, identity and struggle.

Implications of a secular concept of self

The secular self emerges because of the individual rights of freedom, equality and justice granted to every individual citizen of a nation-state, and has very important implications in a multicultural society. If we look at some of the positive implications, we find that:

(a) In a liberal society, the rights offered to individual citizens can be extended to demand certain group rights for minority communities, under the rationale that individual members of those communities would be able to enjoy some of their rights, develop a sense of identity, only if their communities were protected from being assimilated by the major communities.

(b) More importantly, the secular self protects individual members of communities from prosecution by community leaders. The right to dissent and the right to exit are very crucial in any liberal society so that internal democracy is practiced within communities, reforms made possible and dissenters, especially women, are not punished by community leaders. These rights are possible due to the protection given to the secular self by the constitution of nation-states.

(c) Finally, the secular self goes a long way in creating an atmosphere of equality and democracy in a country because irrespective of our race/religion/caste/class/gender, we are guaranteed equal rights as citizens of a nation-state.

On the other hand, if we look at some of the negative implications, we find that the values flowing from the ideas of a secular self, especially the rights of equality and non-discrimination can be misused by the majority communities who in the name of difference blindness can choose to ignore the specific needs and demands of the minority communities. In India the issue of Uniform Civil Code, which was essentially a feminist demand, was hijacked by the Hindutva forces so as to embarrass the conservative leadership among the Muslims who were against reform of Muslim personal laws. Similarly in Canada, the Charter of Rights and Freedom is often used by conservative leadership from within the Anglo-Canadian community to oppose the demand for special status for Quebec.

In India recently, certain Dalit intellectuals and scholars while providing a critique of Indian modernity and secularism have challenged the concept of secular self. Aditya Nigam (2000) points out that Dalit politics embodies a dogged resistance to the two binaries set up by modern politics in the era of nationalist struggle and subsequently in the contemporary moment. It refuses to get incorporated into either term of the binary of nationalism/colonialism and secularism/communalism. It represents in its very existence, the problematic 'third term' that continuously challenges the common sense of the secular modern. This resistance to these categories of modern politics is, at its core, a resistance to the very universalisms that characterize the emancipatory discourses of modernity which placed at their very centre, the abstract, unmarked citizen – Universal Man – or the equally abstract 'working class', as the subject of history.

Nigam feels that it was probably not the kinship between Gandhian traditionalism and Nehruvian modernity, as Kancha Ilaiah (2001) suggests, but the very form of articulation of the modern with the traditional that laid the foundation of the Nehruvian state's slide into a domination of the brahmanical upper castes over the modern state institutions. Nigam states that the modern self is not simply a traditional castiest in disguise. It is modern and in its self-perception, thoroughly purged of its traditional, caste socialization. Often it sincerely believes that the best way to be modern is to erase all thoughts of caste and religion from its mind. It is in this way that the modern self appears upper caste just as the way the modern self in the West appears routinely as white, upper class, male.

He also tries to explain the apparent insensitivity of Marxism to dalit oppression and the suspicion that dalit activists harbour towards Marxian explanations. He states that during the first burst of dalit/bahujan assertion in the early years of the twentieth century, there was probably the need for a radical definition of the self, an assertion of dalit subjectivity. This self had to be, of necessity, defined in radical alterity to its brahmanical other. For the dalit to be able to speak its lived experience, it had to speak in terms of Brahmanism. Marxism on the other hand, in its reduction of all oppressions to class, tended to do violence to that enterprise of self-definition. The absolute prioritization of 'class' made caste oppression unspeakable. Further, the dalit enterprise of self definition was predicated on another, quintessentially modern project, a search for dalit history. Marxism's rendering of history, its claim to be the sole agent of that history and its privileging of the anti-imperialist struggle over all others was likely to be much more irksome, given the fact that it, in effect proposed what the 'brahmanical' Hinduism wanted, although in a language that was irritatingly close to that of the dalit-bahujan leaders.

Nigam concludes that the very existence of dalit politics both during the anti-colonial struggle as well as in the present continuously disturbs and challenges the binaries of nationalism/imperialism and secularism/communalism, refusing incorporation in either of the binaries. What continuously pits the dalit against these categories framing thought and political action is the experience of subaltern location, which experiences modernity as simultaneously liberating and as denial of voice and agency. This is what gives centrality to the category of experience in dalit scholarship and lies at the root of the widespread distrust of non-dalit accounts of dalit history. What appears here, as the essentialisation of dalit identity in this insistence of dalit accounts of their own history, seems to be in fact, an attempt to reclaim dalit voice from the hegemonic practices of historiography.

The 'strong-we' versus the 'weak-we' conceptions of self

We find that both in Canada and in India, there is this apparent tension between the two concepts of self, which Lemert calls as the strong-we position, i.e., those who hold an abstract, universal concept of truth and selfhood and those who hold the weak-we position, i.e., those who locate the self in concrete historical relations of subjugation and domination. It would be unfair to look at this debate on 'self' as one between the 'essentialist' position and the 'non-essentialist position' which emerged out of post-modernism. Those upholding the strong-we position are not all essentialist as many of them are grappling with existential moral dilemmas in which there is a clash between the highest ideals and factual life. Similarly many of the proponents of the weak-we position indulge in politics, which involve essentialising identities such as dalit women's stand point or Afrocentric positions. The main difference is that proponents of strong-we position refuse to look at the concrete historical differences between human beings (in terms of their social, economic and political positions), and at the hegemonic power structures, which create 'selves' while simultaneously ethnicizing/racializing 'others'. Instead they fall back into arguments about human progress, rationality, etc. Liberal 'hope' is the only way out for them. But then we should also not overlook the fact that this 'hope' can play a very crucial role even in the politics of identity practiced by the upholders of weak-we position. Decades and sometimes centuries of subordination, exploitation and deception make the upholders of weak-we position highly suspicious of positions, which talk in terms of humanity, modernity and secular-self. But many a times movements against subjugation and exploitation have to be launched in the name of 'truth', freedom and other such abstract universal principles. However if one is asked to take a position between these two positions on the self, one would have to accept that the politics of identity of the weak-we position provides much richer theoretical promise for a social scientist because by subverting the taken for granted aspects of life, by challenging hegemonic ideologies, by radicalizing politics they ultimately serve better the aspirations of Enlightenment and the ideals of the French revolution from which the strong-we position ultimately draws its inspiration. But this politics of identity would require a certain kind of sensitivity and moral integrity. This is because relations of domination-subjugation run like a chain through out the world and those who are subjugated at one level may be exploiters for the level below. For example, the women's movement may have empowered white middle class women in the West and upper caste women in India at certain period of time. But this same identity politics in course of time would reveal their implicit complicity in exploitation of black and dalit women respectively. Similarly, the anti-colonial movement had empowered third world upper class/caste elite and given them certain privileges and moral capital. These privileges and moral capital, these elites should be ready to give up when the dalit movement shows that the anti-colonial nationalist struggle had elided the issue of 'caste' thereby marginalizing the lower caste groups. Will the subjugated at one point of time or one level accept their complicity in relations of further subjugation remains the crucial question?

Endnotes

1. A caveat needs to be added as often an attempt is made by the state to rob multiculturalism of its political connotation and present is simply as a descriptive category representing 'diversity'. As pointed out by Bannerji (2000), such descriptive notions of diversity obscure any understanding of difference as a construction of power. One cannot then make a distinction between racist stereotypes and ordinary cultural differences of everyday life.

2. We need to add a caveat here too as often provisions made by the state for the reproduction of cultures of different ethnic groups can as pointed out by feminist scholars lead to the empowerment of conservative leadership within ethnic communities resulting in increased violence towards women and children.

3. Lemert categorizes those writing about Self into two groups. In the first category he puts all those writers who believe strongly in the idea of a Self. This group of writers includes William James (1981[1890]), Charles Taylor (1989), Craig Calhoun (1991) and Anthony Giddens (1991). For Lemert it is no coincidence that the authors classified in the first group are by and large white, male, and of less complicated blood histories and

superficially more familiar sexual orientation. By and large, they consider the Self a moral or natural thing, out there in real history and thus susceptible to analysis. He labels this as the *strong-we group*. The strong –we is strong because it enforces the illusion that humanity itself constitutes the final and sufficient identifying group. In the second category he includes writers such as Patricia Hill Collins (1990), Donna Haraway (1991), Trinh T. Minh-ha (1989), Gayatri Chakravorty Spivak (1988) and Seidman (1992). Members of this group often use the word "identity" instead of "Self". Lemert points out that in the second group are individuals whose ancestors were not European or, if they were, only by descent through complicated blood lines; and are less inclined to present themselves as sexually straight. He labels this as the *weak-we group*.

4. It should be noted that neither the Hindus nor the Muslims form a homogenous community in India being divided in terms of sects, denominations, region, language and castes. The terms Hindu and Muslim communities are being used only to facilitate certain theoretical propositions. The author recognizes the fact there are differing opinions within each community and the considerable amount of overlap between the two communities in many regions of the country in term of life-styles, beliefs and values. But the author feels that in spite of these overlaps and heterogeneity, there is considerable amount of prejudice, perceptions of threat, differing interests which during times of crises or violent conflicts tend to shape the political stance adopted by large sections within each community. Guaranteeing basic minimum needs and security of life to all its citizens is mandatory on any state, and for this endeavor it helps to accept the spiralling estrangement between the majority and the minority communities. The author therefore feels that acceptance of a Majority-Minority framework [see Rajeev Bhargava (1999)] may help the state to deal with communalized situations in a far more adept fashion than has been done till now.

5. Certain scholars may feel that the issue of Kashmir contradicts my statement. But the fight for autonomy/independence in Kashmir is based more on its distinct socio-cultural and historical identity and very marginally on its religious character despite the fact that the Kashmiri Pandits have been forced to migrate from that region.

6. In the *EPW* debate between Subramaniam (1994), Jayal (1994) and Chandoke (1994), Subramaniam tries to defend the rights of the tribal groups to common property resources using Nozickean ideas on rights. But both Jayal and Chandoke point out that Nozick's liberal philosophy is highly individualistic and his conceptions on right to property cannot be used for common property resources of the tribal groups. Chandoke follows Alan Gewirth (1982) who adds wellbeing to autonomy as the

necessary pre-condition for the pursuit of any moral good. She seeks to ground rights in the human capacity for agency. She says that if welfare includes every aspect of human wellbeing, then the capacity for agency is a concept, which is not independent of but linked up with the kind of support structures, which the society can provide. If an individual's life-plan involves the existence in a community, then the claims of that community to their own cultural practices and to the common property resources as the minimal pre-conditions of these practices must be respected. Therefore if a tribal's notion of agency is connected deeply to the way he/she feels about his/her land, access to that land ought to be secured.

Jayal (2001) looks at the displacement of tribal communities caused by the Narmada Valley Projects, especially the Sardar Sarovar Dam and the resultant questioning of the whole development/modernization project of the Indian State. She shows how issues such as citizenship, democracy, and rights get undermined in the resulting confrontation with the state. But she has not looked at the issue within a multicultural framework but rather as an issue where the Nehruvian framework for development is being questioned.

7. In this article Jayal (1998) discusses the issue of displacement and the rights of the displaced persons. She states that a paradoxical situation arising from the fact that on the one hand rights are presently being branded as illusory and without any emancipatory potential, while on the other they are still looked at as devices providing protection to individuals from state oppression. She feels that the conflict between statist and meta-statist claims to conflict evolve around two kinds of issues: first, the conflict between a right to development vs the right not to be displaced; second, the apparent inconsistency of appealing to universal codified conventions disregarding state sovereignty, even while opposing ecological and human rights conditionalities on development assistance from a national perspective. She shows how both the state and the affected tribal population marshal democratic arguments. The three ostensibly democratic arguments given in the defense of large development projects like dams are: (1) The political argument of majoritarianism which chooses as a test of democracy the number of people affected both positively and negatively and weighs their numbers. (2) The developmentalist argument of 'public purpose', which enables the state to ask sections of society to make sacrifices so that society as a whole may benefit. (3) The cultural argument where there is an appeal to the notion of the 'national mainstream' culture, claiming that tribals should be brought into the development process and people opposing are conspiring to keep them out. She states that opposed to the official discourse of democracy, the rights discourse of NBA is appealing to

broader concepts of democracy such as participatory democracy say in the development process which is affecting their lives), right of association, etc. The central rights of the movement however relate to the rights of minority culture. The other rights invoked include right to primary resources such as forests, pastures and water, the right to traditional institutions of self-government, the right to life and existence; and the right to the preservation of their particular cultures and way of life.

8. A student at IIT Bombay, who was a hardcore supporter of Hindu nationalism, defined the following code of behaviour for Indian Muslims in a web based discussion group under the title *"Indianization of Muslims"*:

   (1) Indian Muslims should go easy on the mandatory Islamic Muslim/Kafir divide and accept that there exist other legitimate belief systems. They should formally distance themselves from irrelevant and dangerous verses from the Koran like 9:5, which calls for the slaughter of Kafirs.

   (2) Indian Muslims should make a formal break with the painful past of Islamic Rule by working with the Hindus to arrive at a method to return their holiest Hindu sites – Kashi, Mathura, and Ayodhya.

   (3) Indian Muslims should reduce the importance given to Arabic. They should be encouraged to adopt Sanskrit-based Indian languages.

   (4) Transnational connections like the pilgrimage to Mecca should be downplayed and perhaps discouraged.

References

Agnes, F. *Law and Gender Inequality: The Politics of Women's Rights in India*. Delhi: Oxford University Press, 1999.

Ahmad, Aijaz. *On Communalism and Globalization: Offensives of the Far Right*. New Delhi: Three Essays, 2002.

Bannerji, Himani. *The Dark Side of the Nation: Essays on Multiculturalism, Nationalism and Gender*. Toronto: Canadian Scholars' Press Inc., 2000.

Bhargava, R. 'Should We Abandon the Majority-Minority Framework?' in *Minority Identities and the Nation-State*. Eds. D.L. Sheth and G. Mahajan. New Delhi: Oxford University Press, 1999.

Bhargava, Rajeev. 'The Multicultural Framework' in *Mapping Multiculturalism*. Ed. Kushal Deb. Jaipur: Rawat Publications, 2002.

Bilgrami, A. 'The Moral Psychology of Identity' in *Multiculturalism, Liberalism and Democracy*. Eds. R. Bhargava, A.K. Bagchi and N. Sudershan. Delhi: Oxford University Press, 1999.

Calhoun, Craig. "Morality, Identity, and Historical Explanation: Charles Taylor on the Sources of the Self," *Sociological Theory*, 10 (2). 1991.

Chandoke, N. 'Why People Should have Rights', *Economic and Political Weekly*, vol. XXIX, no 41, October 8. 1994.

Collins, Patricia Hill. *Black Feminist Thought: Knowledge, Consciousness, and the Politics of Empowerment*. Boston: Unwin Hyman, 1990.

Cossman, B., and Kapur, R. *Secularism's Last Sigh?: Hindutva and the (Mis) Rule of Law*. Delhi: Oxford University Press, 1999.

Fish, Stanley. 'Boutique Multiculturalism' in *Multiculturalism and American Democracy*. Eds. A. Melzers et al., Lawrence: University of Kansas Press, 1998.

Gewirth, A. *Human Rights*. Chicago: University of Chicago Press, 1982.

Giddens, Anthony. *Modernity and Identity: Self and Society in the Late Modern Age*. Stanford CA: Stanford University Press, 1991.

Haraway, Donna. "Manifesto of Cyborgs," in *Simians, Cyborgs, and Woman*. Routledge, (1989) 1991.

Hasan, Z. 'Uniform Civil Code and Gender Justice in India' in *Contemporary India—transitions*. Ed. P.R. deSouza. New Delhi: Sage Publications, 2000.

Ilaiah, Kancha. "Dalitism vs Brahmanism: The Epistemological Conflict in History" in *Dalit Identity and Politics*. Ed. Ghanshyam Shah, New Delhi: Sage Publications, 2001.

James, William. *Principles of Psychology*, vol.1. Cambridge, MA: Harvard University Press, (1890) 1980.

Jayal, N.G. 'Rights, Justice and Common Property Resources', *Economic and Political Weekly*, July 9, 1994.

Jayal, N.G. 'Displaced Persons and Discourses of Rights', *Economic and Political Weekly*, vol. XXXIII no.5, Jan 31-Feb 6,PE-30 to 36, 1998.

Jayal, N.G. *Democracy and the State: Welfare, Secularism and Development in Contemporary India*. New Delhi: Oxford University Press, 2001.

Joseph, Sarah. 'Do Multicultural Individuals Require a Multicultural State?' in *Mapping Multiculturalism*. Ed. Kushal Deb. Jaipur: Rawat Publications, 2002.

Kapur, R. and Cossman, B. *Subversive Sites: Feminist Engagements with Law in India*. New Delhi: Sage Publications, 1996.

Lemert, Charles. 'Dark Thoughts about the Self' in *Social Theory and the Politics of Identity*. Ed. Craig Calhoun. Oxford: Blackwell, 1994.

Mahajan, Gurpreet. *The Multicultural Path: Issues of Diversity and Discrimination in Democracy*. New Delhi: Sage Publications, 2002.

Mayaram, S. 'Recognizing Whom?: Multiculturalism, Muslim Minority Identity and the Mers' in *Multiculturalism, Liberalism and Democracy*. Eds. R. Bhargava, A.K. Bagchi, and N. Sudershan. Delhi: Oxford University Press, 1999.

Mead, George Herbert. *Mind, Self and Society*. Chicago: University of Chicago Press, 1934.

Nandy, Ashis. 'The Politics of Secularism and the Recovery of Religious Tolerance' in *Mirrors of Violence: Communities, Riots and Survivors in South Asia*. Ed. Veena Das, Delhi: Oxford University Press, 1990.

Nigam, Aditya. 'Secularism, Modernity, Nation: Epistemology of the Dalit Critique', *Economic and Political Weekly*, November 25, 2000.

Pandian, M.S.S. 'One Step Outside Modernity: Caste, Identity Politics and Public Sphere', *Economic and Political Weekly*, May 4, 2002.

Parasher, A., *Women and Family Law Reforms in India: Uniform Civil Code and Gender Equality*. New Delhi: Sage Publications, 1992.

Rege, Sharmila. "A Dalit Woman's Standpoint" in *Seminar* 471-November, 1998.

Sangari, K. 'Politics of Diversity: Religious Communities and Multiple Patriarchies' in *Economic and Political Weekly*, Vol. XXX, No. 51 and 52, Dec 23 and 30, 1995.

Sangari, K., 'Gender lines: Personal Laws, Uniform Laws, Conversion', *Social Scientist*, vol. 27, nos. 5-6, May-June also reprinted in *Pluralism and Equality: Values in Indian Society and Politics*. Eds. I. Ahmad, P.S. Ghosh and H. Reifeld, New Delhi: Sage Publications, 1999.

Seidman, Steve. "Race, Sexuality and the Politics of Difference", Unpublished, 1992.

Smith, D. *India as a Secular State*. Bombay, London: Oxford University Press, 1963.

Spivak, Gayatri Chakravorty. "Can the Subaltern Speak?" in *Marxism and the Interpretation of Culture*. Eds. Cary Nelson and Lawrence Grossberg. Urbana: University of Illinois Press, 1988.

Subramaniam, K. 'Science and Ethics in Public Decision-Making: Case of Big dams', *Economic and Political Weekly*, April 2, 1994.

Taylor, Charles. *Sources of the Self*. Cambridge, MA: Harvard University Press, 1989.

Taylor, Charles. 'The Politics of Recognition' in *Multiculturalism: Examining the Politics of Recognition*. Ed. A. Gutmann, Princeton, New Jersey: Princeton University Press, 1994.

Trinh T. Minh-Ha. *Woman, Native, Other*. Bloomington: Indiana University Press, 1989.

3

Aesthetics of Dislocation and the Dislocation of Aesthetics

Santosh Gupta

Large scale migrations of Africans, Asians and Europeans, due to varied political and economic reasons, have taken place throughout the last three centuries. Imposed shifts of territories have been targeted at different class levels. The masses that were transported as indentured labour became the silenced, invisible ground beneath the feet of the empire builders in their large scale, capitalistic agricultural and other economic enterprises, people who inhabited more than one culture, yet belonged nowhere.

Since the late 19th century and most of the 20th century, voluntary migrants to the metropolitan cities along with the second and third generations of the early migrants have formed a part of the existing diaspora. The move to the west, towards the centre, may be due to "uneven development", as Gurubhagat Singh notes, "within capitalism" (21). This global movement has led to the emergence of a new narration of travel, dislocation, displacement and uprooting. The loss of the originary homeland has inspired visions of imaginary homelands, which in themselves constitute a longed-for utopia. In these narratives, new themes, new anxieties and searches have been expressed that reflect the traumas and tensions of the displaced as they strive to recover a sense of self or construct a new selfhood. The literatures of the diaspora have taken a position beside the mainstreams, calling for recognition for their acute agony, contingency and subversion of the established literary principles of genera and use of language.

The relation between location and literary aesthetics and creativity has been emphasized by several critics. The sense of being rooted in a particular milieu governs the creative surges. Malcolm Bradbury, in his discussion of modernist literature, reflects upon the close impact of the metropolitan cities where the movement shaped up, its peculiar kind of stimuli and the freedom and environment they provided to the travelling writers who rebelled against the prevalent literary aesthetic norms and destabilized the earlier aesthetic values.

The diasporic writers from the Asia and Africa to the west have now begun to express their discontent against the hegemonic aesthetics that they have learnt all through their lives – in their reading of literature, in the literary histories, through canonical texts and the principles of aesthetic evaluation they have been taught. Subsequently, a dislocation of aesthetics has emerged which is accompanied by a formulation of an aesthetics of dislocation, redefining practices/principles of reading, teaching and critical evaluation of literature, old and new.

The Nobel prize award to V.S. Naipaul is a recognition of the hitherto unacknowledged value of the writings from exiles, indentured/migrant people. The enigma of arrival, of (not) belonging, of never arriving at a destination that is final, is a permanent diasporic experience, which is persistently and poignantly expressed in various fictional and non-fictional works of Naipaul. Satendra Nandan reflects upon this aspect of Naipaul's work in these words: "it is my reading of Naipaul that made me aware of my personal history" (302). The travails of forced movements in his own life time, as Fiji faced two coups in quick succession, brought afresh to Nandan the sense of loss, uncertainty and anguish. Naipaul's work, made him aware of the global phenomena of these movements, "Few writers give you those perceptions of yourself, your past and your present pains as does Naipaul if your consciousness is part of the indenture system, an offshoot of slavery, through which the Indian diaspora spread to many obscure corners of our now nuclear desecrated earth ... to the islands of slavery, genocide and cannibalism" (Nandan 302). Naipaul's works revealed "the terrible layers of history of these hidden, unfinished journeys and made fragments of it comprehensible and credible" to people of similar experiences.

These lines of Satendra Nandan indicate the poignant themes of the unfinished nature of diasporic journeys, and the importance of history to these people. These are some of aspects of the diasporic experience that become crucial to their writing, which are in dissonance with the prevalent aesthetic norms that are being questioned. Time, space, history and identity are sites which are visited through the concerns of a past that has experienced suppression, atrocities, inhuman oppression and a silencing that has transformed all perceptions of their world. These experiences are now being articulated and the writers from such groups ask for a reflection of their histories in the literary world.

Writing from expatriate, diasporic writers – from South Asia, Africa and other former colonies – find their present inevitably bound up with the history, politics and geographical factors whereas the literary aesthetics that most of them have learnt at school (mostly through English medium education) have guided them to consider purely literary merits of the texts. Literary aesthetics have become a site of contestation as several of the writers belonging to minority sub-cultural, diasporic groups in Canada, USA and England question the values they were taught and their own readings of literature. The theory of literary appreciation is seen to be narrow and prejudiced, refusing to perceive some very obvious and noticeable truths. A need for a new aesthetics is repeatedly being felt as these readers, writers, critics (sometimes all these in one person), begin to question the existing aesthetics and attempt to destabilize it through their own endeavours.

The most important of the diasporic theorists presently of course are Edward Said, Homi Bhabha and Gayatri Chakravorty Spivak. Through their conceptualisations of the 'hybridity' of the exile/ expatriate/diasporic person and the significant politics of the margin, in reinventing a diasporic self that negotiates the centre while maintaining its hybrid nature, these three have created a theoretical base for developing further the aesthetics of dislocation. Their works have voiced the need to subvert the metanarratives of the west, to let the repressed cultures of minority subcultural groups emerge into their own hybrid modes of self articulation.

Moving beyond the larger issues of identity, and location, there are other writers like Arun P. Mukherjee, Toni Morrison, Kumkum Sangari, who specifically question the reading and interpretative processes of the west. They take up the details of interpretation of the texts they have read, and question the literary values that they have learnt. This intensive examination opens up wider issues – of the politics of pedagogy, of criticism and canon formation.

The questioning of the mainstream aesthetics is done from several viewpoints. As a feminist African American situated in the US, Toni Morrison raises serious issues about the literary critical practices in the United States. In her essays *Playing in the Dark: Whiteness and Literary Imagination,* Morrison exposes the complete silence of the white critics in the US about the presence of the transported black people in America and their contribution to the making of the American culture. The entire literary history and criticism talk of only one colour – the white. She says "As a reader (before becoming a writer) I read as I had been taught to do. But books revealed themselves rather differently to me as a writer" (3). While she understands that the African presence in the US has shaped its culture and the making of its literature, it is not acknowledged anywhere in the critical interpretations. She questions the existing canon, for this silence seemed to be a deliberate conspiracy, to maintain an image of the American country, culture and history that is very different from its bicoloured reality (4). The gendered, racialized nature formats that govern the reality, that dictate the cognition of this reality, bring about, Morrison says, a whole different process of "becoming" than what is publicly, ostensibly acknowledged. She questions then the "validity or vulnerability of a certain set of assumptions" conventionally accepted among literary historians and critics and circulated as "knowledge" (4). Her own readings of Henry James's short stories and Hemingway's novels support her argument.

Toni Morrison argues with the aesthetics of the white racist historians of American literature, and demands the inclusion of the minorities and marginalized sections. She says "I want to draw a map, so to speak, of critical geography and use that map to open as much space for discovery, intellectual adventure and close exploration as did the original charting of the New World – without the mandate for conquest" (3).

The mapping out of a new territory becomes possible through opening up of the borders set by the older approaches. The literary principles that have been taken to colonies where English literature was introduced as an important prestigious subject have carefully, but quietly, nurtured imperialistic, colonialist mental approaches.

The critical and historical research done on this politics of pedagogy has been influential in creating an awareness for the decolonizing of education in the Third World countries.

The generations that grew up in the 1940s and 50s, in the colonized countries were taught English literature and aesthetics of the western tradition, from the classical to the modern. Arun Mukherjee reflects upon this political role of education in completely blinding young minds to large areas of the world's geography and history. She realized how one's educational system can insensitize one to the really important issues in the literary texts through an over valorisation of verbal complexity and plot construction. Her own learning process matched, to a large extent, with those of her students in the Canadian University where she took up a teaching assignment (1998: 10-15).

In *Oppositional Aesthetics* (1994), she recounts her experiences at teaching the short story of Margaret Laurence "The Sea of Perfume" which she considered to have clear political ideas. She discussed the story with her students from her point of view, but in the term papers submitted by them, found these aspects ignored. They had focused instead on characterisation and plot. She realized that "their education had allowed them to neutralize the subversive meanings implicit in a piece of good literature, such as the Laurence Story" (1994: 30). Emphasis on analysing metaphors and symbols reduce the text's embedded important socio-political and cultural comments and realities. Such readings narrow down the force of literature (1).

Arun Mukherjee's oppositional aesthetics builds up her criticism of a historical reading of literature encouraged by western criticism. She also objects to the canon construction by a group of Canadian critics who build up a history of only purely white writers. 'Canadian' she says has become code for 'white' refusing recognition to immigrants of other colour, race and ethnicities. Even when mentioned, they are placed 'down the ladder' and named as a hyphenated group 'South Asian-Canadian' for example. Here Mukherjee points out the complicity of the white western feminists in the racism of their culture. In a text like Charlotte Perkins Gilman's *Herland* the vision of a purely white women's utopia commits blatant "textual genocide" as it "wiped out all the non-white women in order to create the racially pure utopia of Herland." (1994, x) The implicit racism in white women's feminist writing has also become a discursive site as postcolonial feminists draw attention to the differences of culture and history creating different groups within women.

In the histories of Canadian literature that are considered standard histories there is a complete silence about Aboriginal and Native writers. Minority writers are put into slots of 'minority', 'migrants' and never called 'Canadian'. This critical practice is in itself a form of 'cultural imperialism'. In her essay 'The Vocabulary of the "Universal": The Cultural Imperialism of the Universalist Criteria of Western literary Criticism', Mukherjee examines the claims to universality of approach, the truth of their interpretations, and shows up their narrow racist underpinnings. The 'Afro-Asian' group of writers among the Commonwealth family is compelled to point out to the West European critics that they have "imposed the traditional western categories on the works from the new Commonwealth" (1994: 17). She quotes Chinua Achebe's comment upon this 'dogma of universality' and the western presence of speaking in the universal mode when they have a specific location in space, history and politics. She says "Achebe is denying another sacred liberal humanist assumption which believes that good literature concerns itself with universals" (1994: 18). It is considered to be a great praise for a Commonwealth writer when his work is said to have universal appeal. But as Mukherjee points out Achebe and "several other Afro-Asian writers and critics", voice their objections against this form of "cultural imperialism".

These groups feel humiliated by the western imposition. Arun Mukherjee expressly rejects this "condescending and ignorant approach of the white critics towards literature from the Third World." She wrote her essay 'The Vocabulary of the "Universal": The Cultural Imperialism of the Universalist Criteria of Western Literary Criticism' in "the white heat of anger" on reading a quotation from Northrop Frye which implied the "assumption that Third World literary works could be read as derivative and inter-textually linked with the works of Western European tradition" (7). Shame, anger and desperation at the western critics' attitude of ignoring the presence and the responses to the western literature of the immigrant writers are reflected in all the essays written by Mukherjee, Morrison, Vijay Mishra, Satendra Nandan and several other diasporic critics.

Mukherjee's two books *Oppositional Aesthetics* (1994) and *Postcolonialism: My Living* (1998) have become part of the diasporic exploration of the prevalent canon, literary principles and norms of aesthetics. Emphasis is laid on the specific historical contexts of the writer, and, the reader's attention is called to the multifaceted cultural sources rather than to the experience of one dominating hegemonic power wielding group. As a result one perceives several shades of coloured people, their versions of the historical cultural developments, and hears dialogic, heteroglossic polyphony. Narrative innovations are related to the traditions of narratives other than the mainstream, western tradition, for a multiplicity of such traditions have existed and have had their deep impact on the aesthetic sense of the diverse people who have come to the metropolitan centres and tried to assimilate.

This paper has tried to discuss the ideas of some of the recent, critically more articulate writers who have shown concern with cultural imperialism, colonialism and racism. Several other diasporic writers from different backgrounds are now contesting these ideas as they also significantly control readership and critical opinions.

Endnote

1. Kumkum Sangari's essay 'The Politics of the Possible' comments upon the American critics' readings of narrative features in the novels of Salman Rushdie and Gabriel Garcia Marquez. She tends to view the writings of the Latin American, Indian and many recent writers in their specificity of history and culture, pp. 143-145 in *The Postcolonial Studies Reader*, Eds. Bill Ashcroft, Gareth Griffiths and Helen Tiffin. New York: Routledge, 1995.

References

Bradbury, Malcolm and James McFarlane. eds. *Modernism*, Pelican Guide to European Literature. Harmondsworth: Penguin, 1976.

Morrison, Toni. *Playing in the Dark: Whiteness and the Literary Imagination.* Harvard: Picador, Harvard Univ. Press, 1992.

Mukherjee, Arun. *Oppositional Aesthetics: Reading From a Hyphenated Space.* Toronto: TSAR, 1994.

Mukherjee, Arun. *Postcolonialism: My Living.* Toronto: TSAR, 1998.

Nandan, Satendra. "The Feudal Post-colonial: The Fiji Crisis", *In Diaspora, Theories, Histories, Texts.* Ed. Makarand Paranjpe. New Delhi: Indialog Publications Pvt. Ltd., 2001.

Singh, Gurubhagat. "Expatriate Writing and the Problematic of Centre: Edward Said and Homi Bhabha", *Writers of the Indian Diaspora.* Ed. Jasbir Jain. Jaipur: Rawat Publication, 2000.

4

Refugee Problem in South Asia
An Overview

B.C. Upreti

The refugee problem is a world wide one and, over the years, it has reached unprecedented proportions. Some scholars have even called the present century as the century of uprooted people. The total number of refugees all over the world is believed to be 20 million. In every corner and everywhere refugees are victims of various political, socio-economic, ethno-cultural and environmental circumstances. The problem of refugees also involve the violation of human rights which is a setback to human civilisation.[1] They are victims of human rights violation.[2] This problem is a complex and involves many countries and multiple issues. Their repatriation and peaceful resettlement is a serious issue. They are indeed deprived people and to meet their expectations and necessities is a big economic liability for the host country. They are also an issue for disputes between nation states. According to UN, a refugee is "any person who owing to well founded fear of being persecuted for reasons of race, religion, nationality, membership of a particular social group or political opinions is outside the country of his nationality and is unable, owing to such fear, unwilling to avail of the protection of that country".[3]

Thus it can be said that a refugee is a person who is compelled to leave his native place due to some reason to seek refuge in an unknown place.

Nature and Dimensions of Refugee Problem

The South Asian region has the fourth largest concentration of refugees in the world. It has rightly been pointed out that:

> The history of these post-partition states of South Asia has been one of consolidating majoritarian elites producing persecuted minorities, of citizenships giving rise to statelessness, of borders resulting in illegal but not *unnatural cross-border* movements and of development policies uprooting millions.[4]

Table 1
Estimated Refugees in South Asia

Host Country	Origin	Number	Total
Bangladesh	Myanmar	24,000	24,000
India	Afghanistan	19,800	
	Myanmar	50,000	
	Bhutan	40,000	
	Chakma	43,000	
	Sri Lanka	96,000	
	Tibet	1,19,000	
	Others	700	36,85,000
Pakistan	Afghanistan	13,00,000	
	Iraq	1,200	
	Iran	300	
	Somalia	1,000	13,02,600
Nepal	Bhutan	93,000	
	Tibet	18,000	1,21,000
Total			18,16,000

Source: Bose and Manchanda, n.2

The flow of refugees across the national boundaries began immediately after the withdrawal of the British colonial rule from the subcontinent resulting in the partition of India and the creation of a new state of Pakistan having a distinct religious identity. The partition of India gave rise to a serious problem of refugees. However, there have been many other problems in South Asia which have given rise to this problem. The estimated number of refugees in different countries of the region is given in the Table 1. These figures do not include stateless migrants and internally displaced people.

In South Asia almost all the countries have produced refugees at one time or the other. Most of the countries are refugee-receiving as well as refugee-producing ones. The primary direction of these refugees has been towards other countries of the region. Only those who have been involved in terrorist activities against the state have sought asylum outside the region. It may also be pointed out here that the refugees have strong ethno-religious affiliations with the country of their asylum. Hence, they find it easier to stay over there. In most of the countries there is good number of internally displaced people.

Streams of Refugees

In the South Asian region refugee flow is a complex problem as there are various streams of refugees. These streams of refugees flow in to the region from outside, within the region and within the country.

External Refugees in South Asia

South Asia is a refugee receiving region. People have been taking refuge in the South Asian countries from outside the region. In this category there are the following streams.
1. *Arkanese*: from the Arkan hills of Myanmer who have taken refuge in India. These Arkanese people trace their ancestral linkages with the Magadh empire in India. It is estimated that 75,000 Arkanese are living in the north-eastern region of India. There are nearly 700 Arkanese in New Delhi. Many of them have been living here for the last 30 years. In the United States the Arkanese refugees have also formed a government in exile. The Arkanese refugees are opposed to the Military Junta of Myanmar. They are supporters of democratic forces. They cannot go back to Myanmar and also cannot talk to their

relatives living in Myanmar. The Arkanese are followers of Buddhism.

2. *Chins*: are small in number. They are also refugees from Myanmar and living mostly in Nagaland. They are tribal people and mostly Christians. Chins also faced persecution by the military rulers of Myanmar.

3. *Rohingyas:* Rohingyas are also refugees from Myanmar living in the Chittagong Hill Tracts of Bangladesh. Their number has been estimated at 1.16 lac. There is a controversy about Rohingyas. The Myanmar Military Junta believes that Rohingyas belong to Bangladesh by origin who had migrated to Myanmar. Now they have remigrated to Bangladesh. But Bangladesh believes that they are illegal migrants. In 1978 an agreement was concluded regarding their repatriation. But the problem is that they cannot go back to their country as long as military rule continues in Myanmar. Hence, even if they are repatriated they come back. The Myanmar government has alleged that they are involved in terrorist activities.[5]

4. *Afghans:* Since 1978, Pakistan has hosted one of the largest refugee populations from Afghanistan. Their total number was said to be 12 lac. In 2000 alone, during the American war against Taliban, 1.72 lac Afghanis took shelter in Pakistan. Pakistan had to close its border with Afghanistan due to the large scale refugee influx. They were largely placed in the North West Frontier Province, particularly at Peshawar, Saripul, Jalozai, Shamshatoo, Nasir Bagh, etc. Many of these refugees have returned back to Afghanistan after the normalisation of situation there. But it is reported that many of them do not want to go back.[6]

5. *Tibetans*: The Tibetans began to take refuge in India, Nepal and Bhutan after the Chinese occupation of Tibet in 1950. There are nearly 1.10 lac Tibetan refugees in India and 20,000 in Nepal. Their number is not large in Bhutan. In India, Tibetan refugees are placed in Himachal Pradesh, Jammu and Kashmir, Sikkim, Uttaranchal, Arunachal Pradesh and West Bengal. They also have a government in exile at Maclodgunj in Himachal Pradesh. Tibetans are peaceful refugees engaged in small scale business, trading, agriculture, horticulture, etc. Thus they are not dependent refugees and are almost resettled.[7] These refugees

are still trying to influence the world opinion for the independence of Tibet.
6. *Others:* Apart from these major groups of external refugees in South Asia, there are some small groups of refugees such as Somalians (1,000), Iraqis (1,200), and Iranians (nearly 300-500). These refugee groups are in Pakistan.

Intra-Regional Refugees

Following are the major streams of intra-regional refugees in South Asia, originating in one country of the region and taking refuge in another:

(i) *Indo-Pakistan Refugees:* The partition of India in 1947 witnessed one of the largest flow of refugees in the world history. Nearly 8 million Hindus and Sikhs left Pakistan immediately after partition, while 6-7 million Muslims from India went to Pakistan. It was indeed a painful human tragedy. These refugees became victims of communal riots and resulted in loss of life and property. The pangs of partition are still felt by these people as it divided the families, relatives and so on.

(ii) *Bangladeshis:* At the time of 1971 liberation war nearly 10 million people left East Pakistan to take refuge in India. Most of them returned voluntarily after the formation of Bangladesh. But a small number of them stayed back in India.

(iii) *Bihari Muslims in Bangladesh:* Bihari Muslims are those people who went to East Pakistan at the time of India's partition. They are not accepted by Bangladesh. Moreover, they are not acceptable to Pakistan as well.

(iv) *Tamil Refugees from Sri Lanka:* The ethnic conflict between Tamils and Sinhalese in Sri Lanka resulted in large scale Tamil refugees in India. There are 150 Tamil refugee camps in Tamil Nadu and one camp in Orissa. Around 50,000 refugees are living in these camps. It is believed that nearly 40,000 Tamil refugees have been staying outside these camps. They are not prepared to go back unless a separate Tamil land is given to them.[8]

(v) *Chakma Refugees*: The Chakma refugees from the Chittagong Hill Tracts (CHT) in Bangladesh have taken shelter in the north-eastern region of India for a long time. They are living in camps mostly in Tripura and Arunachal Pradesh as well as outside the camps. In Tripura alone there are about 50,000 Chakma refugees. These refugees keep coming in and going out. Actually whenever the Chakma leaders and the Bangladesh government reach an understanding their repatriation begins. But as they are again persecuted, they are compelled to flee back to India. These Chakma refugees are Buddhist tribals. They have been fighting for autonomy. They want that the outside settlers in CHT be sent back. The problem is still unresolved.[9]

(vi) *Bhutani Nepali Refugees in Nepal*: Towards the end of the decade of 1980s nearly 1 lakh people of Nepali origin who had migrated to Bhutan as economic migrants and had settled there over the years had to take refuge in Nepal. These people of Nepali origin were considered to be a threat to Bhutanese culture and society. The Bhutanese rulers wanted to impose a cultural code on them which they resented and demanded cultural freedom and a democratic governance in the country. As a result of their assertion they were declared illegal migrants and driven out of the country. They have been staying since then in camps in Jhapa and Illam in Nepal. The two countries have negotiated many times on the issue of their repatriation but nothing has happened as yet.[10]

South Asian Refugees Outside the Region

(i) Many people from different countries of South Asia have taken refuge in the countries outside the region in different time period and for different reasons. The Tamils of Sri Lanka have taken refuge in many countries of the world. According to one estimation they are 21,000 in Germany, 2,600 in Switzerland, 2,000 in Britain, 1,500 in France.

(ii) The Mizo and Naga rebels from Mizoram and Nagaland in India have taken asylum in Myanmar and some other countries of South East Asia. They also have their militant organisations there.

Some of the Sikh militants had also taken refuge in USA and Britain during the days of Khalistan movement.

(iii) A large number of Muhazirs of Pakistan who have been involved in Muhazir Quami movement have been living in Britain.

Internally Displaced People

In most of the South Asian countries there is a good number of people who had to move to other parts of the country as it became difficult for them to stay back at the place of their origin. Generally there have been two types of internally displaced people:

(i) *The Ethno-regional Movements*: Movements based on sons of the soil, insurgency of various types have resulted in the internal displacement of people. In India such incidents have largely taken place due to movements/insurgencies in Jammu and Kashmir, Assam and other north-eastern states, Gurkhaland movement, Punjab, Telangana, etc. In Pakistan, the Pashtoon, Baluch, Sind and Ahmadia movements have lead to internal displacement of people. In Sri Lanka the Tamils living in non-Tamil dominant areas have been compelled to move to Tamil dominated areas due to the ongoing conflict between Tamils and Sinhalese.

(ii) *Environmental Refugees*: There are development induced internally displaced people. The construction of high dams has been a major source of internal displacement of people. For example the Tehari and Narmada in India, Kaptai and Mangla dams in Bangladesh, Tarbalu and Ghazi Barotha dams in Pakistan and Mohabelly project in Sri Lanka gave rise to the problem of displacement of people. Their rehabilitation has been a big problem.

The floods, famine, droughts and landslides also cause temporary or long term displacement of people. This problem has been particularly faced in India, Bangladesh, Nepal and Pakistan.

It may be clarified here that although we have discussed here the internally displaced people but we have not included this category in further discussion and analysis for the reason that it is controversial whether they should be treated as refugees or not.

Following general observations can be made here:

(i) The refugee is a continuous and complex problem in South Asia.
(ii) Total repatriation or resettlement of refugees based on negotiations has not been possible.
(iii) A regional initiative for the resolution of refugee problem is yet to take place.
(iv) The refugee issue has often been politicised by the host country.

Factors Behind Refugee Problem

The creation of refugees cannot be associated with any one particular cause. Instead, different factors may be held responsible for the recurrence of the refugee problem in different contexts and at different points of time. This problem may be the result of a particular process in a historico-political context or there might be a sudden exposure of events causing displacement of people within or beyond national boundaries. The following factors may be identified behind refugee problem in South Asia:

Decolonization and Restructuring of State Boundaries

The independence from the British colonial rule caused refugee flows in two ways. Firstly, India was divided and a separate independent state of Pakistan based on religious identity was created. As a result a large number of Muslims from North India migrated to Pakistan and similarly Hindus from Pakistan fled away leaving behind their property, etc. However, the refugee problem caused by the partition was resolved through negotiations and through rehabilitation policies.[11] Another dimension of this problem was the refugee influx from Burma and Sri Lanka which was aggravated in the post independence era. Under the patronage of colonial rule, a lot of migration took place from India to Burma and Sri Lanka. Soon after Independence, Burma adopted the policy of nationalization and the people of Indian origin were pushed out of the country.[12]

Similarly in Sri Lanka the deprivation of rights to the Indian Tamil estate workers led to their displacement. They consequently remigrated to India. It created a category of stateless Indian Tamils because neither India nor Sri Lanka was willing to accept them for their own reasons.[13]

Self-Determination

Assertion of the right of self-determination and seeking the status of an independent statehood by Bangladesh caused refugee problem. While during the struggle for Bangladesh nearly 10 million refugees took asylum in India, the emergence of Bangladesh created a new category of refugees called stranded Pakistanis consisting of Bihari

Muslims who wanted to go to Pakistan as they did not accept the emergence of Bangladesh. Under an agreement concluded in 1974 Pakistan accepted nearly 1.7 lac Bihari Muslims but nearly 3.00 lac were left behind and Pakistan was not prepared to accept them.[14]

Ethno-Religious and Communal Conflicts

It is well known that South Asian societies are multi-ethnic and the large scale interstate migration has resulted in crosscountry linkages of various ethnic groups. The socio-political conflicts based on ethnicity, religion, and culture, are deep rooted in these societies.[15] The ethno-religious conflicts based on majority-minority lines have generated internal as well as external refugees. The Tamils from Sri Lanka, Hindus from Bangladesh, Nepalis from Bhutan are examples of refugees who have ethno-religious connections with their host country.

Authoritarian Political Order

The authoritarian nature of the political systems which have been reluctant to accept the status and rights of the minority communities, have also created the refugee problem. The undemocratic political structures, identification of the state power with dominant social groups and the coercive nature of the state policies have led to the marginalization of minority communities.[16] Consequently, they are compelled to move out and take asylum in other countries. Tamils from Sri Lanka, Nepali migrants from Bhutan, Chakmas from Bangladesh and Rohingyas from Myanmar refugees from Afghanistan and the like are examples of this category of refugees.

External Aggression

The political assertion over a sovereign country by another has also resulted in the eviction of people. China's occupation over Tibet and the subsequent coercive policies of the Chinese government vis-á-vis Tibetans had resulted in large scale eviction of Tibetans to India, Nepal and Bhutan.

Economic and Environmental Refugees

Most of the South Asian countries are poor and they have not been able to face the challenges of development and fulfil basic needs of the people. This incapacity on the one hand and discriminatory developmental policies on the other hand have generated economic and environmental migration in South Asia. Bangladesh and Nepal are the main countries sending refugees under this category.

Factors Encouraging Refugees

A number of factors have been helpful in encouraging refugees:

Geographical Compactness and Easy Physical Accessibility

Due to geographical integrity of the region, easily accessible borders, similar geographical conditions, etc., it is easy for the refugees to move from one to another country such as for Chakmas to North East India, Tamils to Tamil Nadu, Afghans to Baluchistan and Pakhtoonistan in Pakistan, and Tibetans to the hills of Nepal, Bhutan and India and Bhutani Nepalese to Nepal.

Socio-cultural Compactness

The religious, cultural and linguistic identity also encourages refugees to move across the national boundaries. The presence of similar ethnic groups in the host country provides them an inbuilt support base.

Political Encouragement

The political support provided by the host country also attracts refugees. They feel that their purpose of fighting against the home state government may be fulfilled by obtaining a refugee status. At times a country may encourage refugees from a particular country keeping in view the nature of its relationship and her interest in the internal political dynamics of that country.[17]

Problems, Issues and Future of Refugees

In South Asia there have been two types of situations arising due to the presence of refugees. On the one hand there are refugees whose peaceful accommodation and assimilation has been possible to some extent such as Tibetans in India and Nepal and Afghans in Pakistan. But there are refugees whose presence in the host country has generated a hostile situation despite tolerating them such as Sri Lankan Tamils in India, Rohingyas in Bangladesh, Chakmas in North-East India and Bhutani Nepalese in Nepal. But on the whole refugees are subject to various types of problems, conflicts and contradictions. It can be said that:

> refugees are a product of conflict and insecurity situations and their presence in a given country, in turn creates, contributes to or exacerbates conflict, tension and insecurity situation.[18]

The problem faced by the host countries due to the presence of refugees over a long period may be stated as following:

(1) The refugees are a persistent threat to internal security.[19] The intensity of security may depend upon the number, demands, etc. of refugees.
(2) Refugees invite involvement of external countries and agencies which also tends to affect the host country.
(3) Refugees strain law and order situation.
(4) The different ethno-cultural religious and ideological background of refugees creates social tensions.
(5) Large scale refugees in smaller countries may be perceived as a cultural threat to them.
(6) Refugees are an economic burden on the host country in various ways.
(7) Presence of refugees may generate various types of social abuses thereby disturbing the social fabric.
(8) The tensions and fights among refugees themselves like groupism and leadership conflicts also create problems for the host country such as in the case of Tamil and Afghan refugees.
(9) The involvement of refugees in arms supply trafficking in drugs, women, etc., is a matter of serious concern.
(10) Conflicts may arise between refugees and local people due to their larger concentration in a particular area. The reasons of such conflicts could be property resources, employment opportunities, etc.
(11) Refugees may get themselves involved in local politics.
(12) The presence of refugees may cause internal destabilisation in the host country.
(13) The ethnic identity of the refugees with the local people may lead to solidarity among refugees and local people and the latter may turn against the state for the cause of refugees.
(14) Refugees are a potential source of tensions between the host and the home state. Such tensions may arise due to encouragement

and support to refugees, involvement of refugees in cross boundary illegal activities, question of repatriation, etc.
(15) The demographic pressure due to refugee inflow may create ethno-demographic imbalances in a particular region. The pressure on local resources thus generated may give way to more problems.
(16) The host country may have to face strong protest movements against the refugees from local people thereby facing more problems of instability, conflict and tensions.

Refugees are also a potential source of tensions and threat to the home state. They are subject to constant criticism from other countries and international agencies. They are subject to external pressures to repatriate refugees. Such states may also face economic hardships from international community of nations and organisations. The refugees may also be a source of threat to the security of the home state as these refugees may be involved in antinational activities from across the border.

Conclusion

It is clear that refugees are a potential threat to the host and the home state. Since the problems are more for the host country, it becomes an issue of greater concern for her. Refugees are displaced persons, struggling for their rights and basic needs against an uncertain future. They have to live under the constant threat of eviction or forced repatriation.

Refugees are victims of human rights violation. It may be said that they are not only victims of human rights violation but they also constitute a distinct group of people which does not have protection of a state.

With the adoption of the convention relating to the status of refugees in 1951 a number of international organisations have come into operation to protect human rights. These include Universal Declaration on Human Rights (1948), the International Convention on Civil and Political Rights (1966), International Bill of Rights (1966), the Convention Relating to the Status of Stateless Persons (1954), Convention on Elimination of Racial Discrimination (1965), Convention on the Elimination of Discrimination Against Women (1979), Convention Against Torture and Other Cruel Inhuman or Degrading Treatment or Punishment (1984), Convention on the

Rights of the Child (1989), American Convention on Human Rights and the African Charter on Human and People's Rights (1981).

In South Asia some countries have framed national laws relating to human rights but none has ratified international laws and conventions. No efforts have been made towards evolving a regional human rights framework. Three countries of the region – India, Bangladesh and Pakistan are members of UNHCR executive committee but none is committed to protect rights of refugees within the framework of international laws. This is indeed a challenge for the countries of the region to evolve a framework for the protection of rights of refugees. Thus, the main issue in the context of a refugee is how to protect the individual who is unable to defend himself when his individual interests are in danger and which are not defended by the state to which he belongs. Therefore, there is a need to adopt a structural approach for the protection of rights of refugees.

The individual home states have taken measures to repatriate refugees such as Tamils, Afghan and Chakmas and Biharis in Sri Lanka, Afghanistan and Bangladesh respectively but they still persist. There are political, social and economic reasons behind their complete repatriation. Nepal and Bhutan have negotiated over the issue of repatriation of refugees but without success. There is no hope for the repatriation of Tibetan refugees.

In such circumstances, until the problem of repatriation and resettlement of refugees takes place, certain steps can be taken to resolve refugee problems.

The need for the institutionalisation of the rights of refugees has been expressed. UNHCR has been taking interest and in this regard it has been suggested to frame National Law on Refugees. It will prescribe rights and duties of the refugees and will ensure justice to refugees beyond national boundaries. In this regard it has been suggested that the South Asian states need to evolve a regional mechanism to resolve this problem both in terms of sharing costs and repatriation of refugees.[20] It may again be stressed here that the refugee problem is a transnational problem and it cannot be resolved individually and in an uncoordinated manner. Therefore, a proper coordination among states of South Asia is essential.[21] In this regard, SAARC can play a vital role in coordinating attempts towards rehabilitation and repatriation of refugees.

It may be pointed out here that the violation of human rights today gives rise to refugee problem tomorrow. Hence a greater attention by the state machinery, social organisations and institution towards protection and promotion of human rights can prevent refugee problems to some extent.

It may also be stressed here that there is a need to adopt a holistic attitude towards the refugee problem. It has to be understood that there are interlinkages between population movement and social, economic and political order in a given context. Hence, while dealing with this issue the whole context has to be taken into consideration. In this regard one may also state that the large opportunities for cheap labour and availability of easy employment and business opportunities and lack of employment opportunities in the home state has led to large scale inter-state migration. These migrants have played a vital role in the economic development of the concerned countries.[22] But once the local educated and entreprenural class emerged these migrants were being opposed in the name of rights of 'sons of the soil' resulting in eviction of these migrants in the form of refugees.[23] Hence these countries need to activise their developmental activities so that more employment opportunities are available at home and people are not compelled to move out of national boundaries as economic migrants. Lastly, one may suggest formation of South Asian Commission on Migration and Refugees which may be entrusted with the task of looking on the issues related to refugee problem. There is also a need to properly recognise the status and role of international refugee agencies and ensure their access to all types of refugee problems in the region.

Endnotes

1. Naorem Sanajooba, *Human Rights, Practices and Abuses*. Cosmos Publications, New Delhi, 1994: 1.
2. Brain Gorlick, "Refugees and Human Rights", *Seminar,* 463 March, 1998: 23.
3. "The 1951 UN Convention Relating to the Status of Refugees", UN Treaty, vol. 189, no. 2545: 137.
4. Tapan K. Bose and Rita Manchanda, *State, Citizens and Outsiders: The Uprooted People of South Asia,* South Asia Forum for Human Rights, Kathmandu, 1997: 1.

5. See Ganganath Jha, "Rohingya. The Implications, for Bangladesh", in S.R. Chakravarty (ed.), *Foreign Policy of Bangladesh*. HarAnand, New Delhi, 1994: 293-297.
6. Parvez Iqbal Cheema, "The Afghan Refugees and Pakistan's Internal Security Problem", in S.D. Muni & Lok Raj Baral (eds), *Refugees and Regional Security in South Asia*. Konark, New Delhi, 1996: 178-190.
7. Girija Saklani, *The Uprooted Tibetans in India: A Sociological Study of Continuity and Change*, Cosmo Publications, New Delhi, 1984.
8. Refer Rohini Hensman, *Journey without a Destination: Is there a Solution of Sri Lankan Refugees?* Colombo, 1993; J. Spencer & E. Nossan (eds.), *Sri Lanka: History and the Roots of Conflict*. Oxford, 1990; A. Zolberg, *Escape from Violence: Conflict and the Refugee Crisis in the Developing World*, Oxford, 1989.
9. For more details S.P. Talukdar, *The Chakmas: Life and Struggle*. Gyan Publishing House, New Delhi, 1988, Nothan A. Limpert, "People without a Country", *Seminar*, 463, March, 1998; 41-49.
10. For details of the problem see, DNS Dhakal, Chitophar Straun, *Bhutan: A Movement in Exile*. Nirala, New Delhi, 1994.
11. For an indepth analysis of the refugee problems due to partition see, Ramakant et.al. (eds.), *Prelude and Legacies of Partition*. Rawat, Jaipur, 1996.
12. See N.R. Chakravarti, *The Indian Minority in Burma*. Oxford University Press, 1971.
13. For details see P. Sahadevan, *India and Overseas Indians: The Case of Sri Lanka*, Kalinga Publishers, New Delhi, 1995.
14. Bin Whitaker, *The Bhari in Bangladesh*, Minority Rights Group, London, 1982.
15. B.C. Upreti, "Ethnic Mobilisation, Patterns of Demand Politics and Response of State in South Asia", paper presented at a seminar on *Political Elite and Crisis of Governance in South Asia*, SASC, UOR, Jaipur, 22-23 December, 1997; Urmila Phadnis, *Ethnicity and Nation Building in South Asia*, Sage, New Delhi, 1990; Sumit Ganguly, "Ethno-Religious Conflicts in South Asia", *Survival*, vol. 35, no.2, Summer, 1993; Krishan Gopal, Ethnic Crisis and Nation-Building Process in Sri Lanka, *Journal of International Relations*, (Dhaka), vol. 5, nos. 1&2, July-December 1997-98.
16. Kathleen Newland, "Ethnic Conflict and Refugees", *Survival* vol. 35, no.1, Spring, 1993.
17. Loecher Gill and Laila Mohan (eds), *Refugees and International Relations*, Oxford, 1990.

18. Lok Raj Baral & S.D. Muni, "Introduction: Refugees, South Asia and Security" in Muni & Baral, 24.
19. See, Lok Raj Baral, *Regional Migrations, Ethnicity and Security: The South Asian Case,* Sterling, New Delhi, 1990.
20. Tapan K. Bose, "The Changing Nature of Refugee Crisis", in *n.4: 64-66.*
21. Ranbir Samaddar, "Understanding Migratory Flows in South Asia", *n. 4: 71.*
22. See for detailed illustrations, B.C. Upreti, *Poverty, Unemployment and Migration from Far Western Nepal, A Case study of Nepali Migrants in Pithoragarh,* Kalinga, Delhi, 2002.
23. Myron Weiner, "Rejected Peoples and Unwanted Migrants in South Asia", *Economic and Political Weekly,* August 21, 1993.

5

False Consciousness and the Postcolonial Subject

Dorothy M. Figueira

Postcolonial theory champions the inclusion within the Western literary canon of works by groups with historical grievances against Western power structures. As a field of inquiry, postcolonial theory has been made possible by a radicalization of theory and a paradigm shift from the aesthetic to the political that has occurred over the last two decades. Literature, once a central mode of aesthetic expression, has come to be viewed as an outmoded form of cultural capital belonging to the bourgeoisie. The paradigm shift from the literary to the cultural studies model presumably sought to install a more immediate and less conservative hierarchical format. In reality, however, it addressed certain political and psychopathological needs, first and foremost of which being the abstract identification of critics with victims of repression. Although postcolonial theory celebrates diversity, it does so without compromising American tendencies toward cultural provincialism, triumphalism or indifference to the world. Like those popular ethnic fairs one finds throughout the United States, postcolonial theory allows students to taste other cultures without having to travel or learn hard languages. In the Internet age, when the globalization of English has contributed to a diminishing need to learn other languages, the 'Other' can now be consumed "on the cheap." One can grasp the world, for example, by reading selections from representative women of colour writing in the English language. Thus, postcolonial criticism as practiced in institutions of higher learning in the States feeds both the intellectual's need for engagement and the pretense that academic criticism can and should function as a political act. It presumes to transform textual culture into activist culture.

Like most poststructuralist theories, postcolonial criticism relies on the notion that some heritage of systems limits the reader. It supposes that our present condition, although seemingly benign, imposes an existential limit, and theory alone can liberate us from systemic constraints (Fluck 1996:216). Curiously missing from the discussion is any serious questioning of how the text's appearance as a network of hegemonic or subversive gestures tend to suit the state of literary theoretical professionalization. Unexamined also is the manner in which theory has allowed individuals cut-off from any effective social action and buoyed by their security as academic professionals to claim solidarity with the disenfranchised. The alienation from real powerlessness (such as the academic Marxist's guilt vis à vis the worker) can then be replaced and absolved by a posture of powerlessness vis à vis representation.

This strategy, however, often backfires. Rhetorical engagement cannot really serve as a blueprint for social change, just as critics cannot presume access to positional knowledge. The critic's self-fashioning through imaginary marginalization only results in the wide-ranging identification of an academic privileged class with the marginalized other. The historically oppressed has become the new role model for the critic, giving political authority to the search for cultural difference. The postcolonial critic then positions her/himself, in a quasimessianic manner, to speak for the Other. This masquerade poses a significant problem of representation. Critics assume roles as spokespersons for minority communities, regardless of their own socio-economic status and privileges. They claim to speak as/for minorities and as representatives for a minority community and its victimization. They function, to quote Deepika Bahri, as "victims by proxy" (Bahri 1995:73). Critical discourse, moreover, has made this shift in positionality possible.

The postcolonial theorizes always from the impregnable position of "the margin," invoking "ambiguity," "binarism," and splitting," as constitutive of the centre and those that inhabit it. This concept of the margin versus the centre, derives from Derrida's critique of logocentrism. Postcolonial critics invoke Foucault to establish the disequilibrium of the modern state and Bhabha to establish the conception of the marginality of the people. According to Bhabha, the postcolonial theorist is not constrained to "stand" on particular ground or take up a position, but instead can "slide ceaselessly" along the moveable margin (Bhabha 1990:300). Edward Said and Bhabha accept Foucault's dubious claim that the most individualized group in modern society are the marginals, yet to be integrated into the political reality. They attempt to validate interpretation from the margin, where the exiled Third-World metropolitan intellectuals are the most authoritative voices. Critics such as Said, Bhabha and Spivak can then be located at a place where theorists are necessary to interpret across cultures without the inconvenience of having to pinpoint cultural particularities. The theorist can say whatever he or she likes, the only constraint, or test of validity, being that the proper cultural space is occupied and that the writing validates and promotes the ambiguity and contradictoriness of that position.

Postcolonialism thus reflects postmodernism's concern with hybridity and sites of ambivalence. It discovers those subversions that compromise meaning and effectiveness. It seeks to link dispersed groups across ruptures of space, time, nation or language. Since the appearance of Benedict Anderson's *Imagined Communities* (1983), nationalism (previously seen as an ideology of oneness), is studied for its plural roots and dependence on others for the construction of the national self. In the quest for an alternative beyond identity, a post-identitarian model, the critical trope of postcolonial subject functions as an identity free from the constraints of identitarianism. Moreover, like the postcolonial critic who moves along the unfixed margin, the postcolonial subject is believed to incarnate notions of intellectual freedom of movement and escape from ideology and bourgeois values. Critics embrace the grandiose identity and exorbitant role that theory has assigned them. They then seek to identify with an idealized persona that theory has ascribed to the postcolonial subject. This entire process exhibits false consciousness, that reified perception with identificatory, antidialectical, and egocentric structure defined by existential psychoanalysis (Gabel 1975:253ff). It is my belief that the critic's quest for reification through gestures of false consciousness betrays an intellectual and institutional refusal to deal honestly with the Other. In the remainder of this paper, I wish to address this concern. In many American universities, the Third World appears almost exclusively under the rubric of postcolonial literatures. As such, it is largely circumscribed by a theoretical politics of opposition and struggle. The work of generations of linguists, historians and anthropologists who might have made genuine efforts to bring nonfirst-world cultures into the Euro-American continuum, is often dismissed as serving a decrepit ideology (Clark 1996:23). The emphasis placed on Eurocentric cultural theory also overshadows the testimony of native voices. Multitudinous cultures are thus marked and marketed with their chronologies collapsed, particulars essentialized and geopolitical distinctions telescoped into invisibility. Indiscriminately embracing the Other levels out the various competing Others. They tend to look the same, since their actuality is never taken seriously.

Critics foster acontextual and fragmentary analyses out of a deep cynicism regarding the Other as a fossilized object of "clinical" experimentation. If one is disengaged from reality and has retreated into a rarefied zone of postmodern abstraction, one can ignore significant issues of neocolonialism, especially since what is ultimately important is that the Other always be perceived as correct, regardless of differences and histories. The other must be correct in order to fulfil the postcolonial critic's desire for a pure otherness in all its pristine luminosity (Chow 1995:45). Postcolonial criticism exhibits and relies upon an uncritical primitivism that privileges non-western culture and glories in its presumptive, eventual and always revolutionary resurgence.

The identitarian politics at work are blatent. The Amero-European critic theorizing the postcolonial subject extols life in smooth spaces with non-ideological consciousness and exemplary freedoms. Here, we are in the realm of pure exoticism, where an identity is being established not of the Other, but of the hypertrophied Amero-European subject. As I have suggested, it is the properties metaphorically accorded to this subject that are of particular interest. The critic can taste the romance of exile and can play at being diasporic, nomadic or disenfranchised without having to dirty his/her hands. The critic can claim to talk for the margin and, in doing so, pretend to speak from the margin, while actually inhabiting a space that is quite close to the centre.

Theoretical notions of the margin, periphery, and exilic space allow critics to create a metaphorical space in which to dwell that is separate from the real space they inhabit. In this metaphorical space, critics can voice ideologies of subversion and rebellion that would be too unsettling, if voiced from their own actual space. Critics' delicate balancing acts stem from the paradox of inhabiting a space of bourgeois comfort, while needing at the same time to distance themselves from global capitalism. When critics appropriate the metaphorical space of the postcolonial, nomad, exile, and marginal, they hope to exonerate themselves for all the benefits they receive from this same capitalism. Criticism thus functions as an act of penance or, to give it a clinical diagnosis, criticism becomes an expression of false consciousness.

In a seminal work in the field of social psychology, Joseph Gabel defined false consciousness as a dissociation produced by a reification of the past. False consciousness is primarily a distortion of the perception and experience of time. When the natural flow of time is "dissociated" by ideology, utopianism or schizophrenia, it produces a perception which is out of touch with reality and at odds with historical fact; it becomes false consciousness (Gable 1975: xiv). In postcolonial criticism, ideology that is uninformed by historical and linguistic facts distorts a vision of the past. This past, dissociated from reality is further circumscribed by the critic's strategies of self-representation.

The postcolonial critic's personal search serves as a mask for a lack of calling or significance. The stakes are considerable: the critic seeks personal validation within a community of theorists in an incestuously boundaried field. The Third World is totally eclipsed by the critic's emplotment of it. The authoritative critic who has carefully picked through shards of information provided by individuals writing in these postcolonial places provides the dominant voice. Postcolonial critics claim acuity vis-à-vis the intricacies of their readings, although an ignorance of key aspects in the narrative they seek to deconstruct often leads to gross distortions. However, these mistakes are neither given significance or, for that matter, even acknowledged because of the overriding importance assigned to the idealized image of the critic's own theory or of theory itself. This aestheticization of the critical project is truly "criticism for criticism's sake.". Postcolonial criticism places desire on the level of the critic's own need for validation. Knowing the other was never really at issue.

Third-World reality is thus bracketed before the argument begins. The critic's primary interest lies in structuring the Third World thematically for a milieu that consumes these structures. In this process, we find the meeting of incommensurables – a deep-seated need for the experience of political engagement coming out of the 1960s meeting a 1990's need to be media savvy, to package and market intellectual capital. There is no small irony here, in how easily these two conceptual frameworks have welded. If the belief in criticism as a viable intervention is a relic of the 60's that has proven itself bankrupt, then the whole critical project functions as nothing but an investigation of socio-political impotence. Potency, when it exists, resides in the critic's relationship to colleagues, through the coining and usage of jargon. The dexterity of language manipulation becomes an exercise in pyrotechnics garnering the critic points in a rarefied professional game. Theory, understood as symbolic capital and combined with spokespersonship, becomes even more a form of professional empowerment. Postcolonial criticism has allowed critics to appear relevant on a global level.

Like ideologues, schizophrenics and utopian idealists, postcolonial critics seek to reify historical existence and understand their visions as an organized system of meaning produced to balance and disguise the disorder of their being-in-the-world (Gabel 1975: 22). By reifying the history of colonialism, making it the sole source of all socio-cultural evils, postcolonial critics foreclose the possibility of interrogating and transcending the endemic social and cultural dysfunction that predates colonialism and lives on after the colonial masters have left. it is with the repercussions of this systemic failure that I wish to conclude my discussion today.

Colonial discourse analysis developed in the last twenty-five years, following the publication of Edward Said's *Orientalism*. Said defined "Orientalism" as the systematic stereotyping and degradation of the Easterner that enabled Western colonial powers to victimize their subjects and consolidate hegemonic control. For the last two decades, practitioners of the Orientalist critique have catalogued the myriad and grave sins of the West to such a degree that one might say that they have trivialized the discussion. Orientalist criticism has engendered a form of fetishism wherein all current Third World ills are traced to colonial oppression. In certain respects, Orientalist criticism has rewritten history. However, it has done so only partially. It provided a one-sided apologia regarding Western sins and sinners without addressing its flip side. Examining the East to see if it too might be cluttered with stereotypes or misconceptions has never been a sustained part of this critique. Moreover, there has not been an inquiry into the dehumanizing trends in the East toward itself and its Other, the West. Precolonial society is presented as sanitized, the Third-World equivalent of an Arcadian idyll. This revisionist history has allowed Third-World elites to avoid scrutiny of time-honoured corrupt practices and nativist racism and sexism. It has allowed customary indigenous exploitation to continue. In short, for postcolonial elites, thanks to Orientalist readings of the past, colonialism has become an opportunity, not a burden. Because of the evil of colonialism in the past, the West has lost all rights in the present to address any subject having to do with the East. With regard to the East, the West is permanently guilty.

Postcolonial criticism has inherited these limitations of the Orientalist critique and developed some of its own, first and foremost, the exorbitant role that it has assigned to the critic. Imperial consumer fantasies formed the subject matter of Orientalist criticism. Postcolonial criticism has replaced the colonizer and the subject has become the practitioners of the critique itself. Postcolonial criticism no longer examines the culture's original Orientalist consumers, but postcolonial culture's contemporary interpreters. We have come a long way from discussing nineteenth-century paintings of odalisques and harems and now discuss the contemporary critics themselves and what they see in such paintings. It is no longer a question of revealing how a text codifies Eurocentric sexual or political superiority, but rather an examination of the contemporary critic's intellectual insecurity and alienation. It is no longer a question of describing how the West has managed the East, but an investigation of how critics manage their relationship with the West. The critique of Orientalism has shifted from a discussion of imperial fantasies to an examination of academic fantasies. The twenty-five years spent analyzing the numerous and real sins of the West have not resulted in a clarification or improvement of relations.

During that same period, Eastern nations, relying on Western epistemes to construct their arguments,, have not confronted their own history in any critical fashion. In fact, many Third-World scholars have become Orientalists themselves. Some critics of postcolonial theory have questioned the degree to which the whole endeavor has become less a critique of Western power and more an apologia for Eastern failure and a leftist intellectual adventure in rationalization. In the West, it has been enough to embrace guilt and complicity. In the East, it has been enough to condemn and feel victimized. This is the great legacy that this criticism has handed down to us. This heritage was put into grand relief in the rhetoric that surfaced after September 11.

As Edward Rothstein noted in the *New York Times* (Sept. 22, 2001), the general response to September 11 was not particularly novel. In numerous accounts, we were presented with what might be described as the flip side of Orientalism. The same reductionist misrepresentation that the West had applied to the Arab world was now being applied to America. For the monolithic portrayal of America presented in both Eastern and Western media, Rothstein resuscitated the term "Occidentalism." However, the stage for this critique was set much earlier by postmodernism's effort to relativize the fundamental philosophical and political premises of the West. In literary circles, quidities such as truth, morality, objectivity and universality have for some time been understood as culturally constructed. Literary theory teaches us that we must reject universal values. Orientalism has taught us that Western claims to objectivity and universality are nothing but strategies of imperial control. In arguments common to the protests against globalization and echoed by Said in *The Nation* (September 17, 2001), universals are false and serve merely to "legitimize corporate profit-taking and political power." Postcolonialism adds to the critique based on Orientalist criticism its own universal: Western imperialism, appearing as the Original Sin, is to blame. Any act against the West by a postcolonial power cannot be viewed as anything but a reaction to a previous imperial act by the West. We cannot then condemn the World Trade Centre attack, since Western hegemonic behaviour is the fundamental cause of terrorism and the United States, against which this act was directed, is the most powerful Western hegemonic power. Rothstein opined that some may well view such logic and relativism as ethically perverse. What disturbs me, however, is that we, as readers of recent literary criticism, will find this logic commonplace and conventional.

References

Bahri, Deepika. "Once More with Feeling: What is Postcoloniality?" *Ariel* 26 (1995):51-82.

Bhabha, Homi K. "Dissemination: Time, Narrative and the Margins of the Modern Nation." *Nation and Narration*. Ed. Homi K. Bhabha. London: Routledge, 1990: 291-322.

Chow, Rey. "The Fascist Longings in Our Midst." *Ariel* 26 (1995):23-50.

Clark, John. "On Two Books by Edward Said." *Jurnal Bicara Seni. Universiti Sains Malaysia* (June 1996):20-47.

Fluck, Winfried. "Literature, Liberalism, and the Current Radicalism." *Why Literature Matters: Themes and Functions of Literature*. Eds. R. Ahrens and L. Volkmann. Heidelberg: Winter, 1996.

Gabel, Joseph. *False Consciousness: An Essay in Reification*. New York: Harper and Row, 1975.

6

Reconstructing Time and Experience
Variations on the Theme of Dislocation

Tej N. Dhar

I

The main title of this essay is a variation on Edward Said's characterization of his memoir, *Out of Place,* an intense and moving account of how a person dislocated in time and place retrieves his past for himself and for others.[1] The number of such dislocated beings has been constantly on the increase in our times because widespread social and political changes and massive upheavals have produced "more refugees, migrants, displaced persons, and exiles than ever before in history" (Said 1994: 402). This is also reflected in writings from all over the world, in a substantial body of so-called literature of exile, embracing various genres, which admit of large variations, for the writings vary in their scope, range, depth, and style, a fact that has been widely noticed (See, for example, David Bevan 1990; Andrew Gurr 1981; Said 2001). That is why discriminations become necessary, and hence the subtitle in the essay, which looks closely at three distinct variations: in the work of Said, Salman Rushdie and Nurrudin Farah. Though all of them share the common condition of being out of their home and place, yet their situation and its effect on their work has been different.

At one extreme end of the spectrum of displaced persons are the ones who move out to the metropolis, the big city, because they find the cribbed and confined environs of their small close-knit communities limiting and inhibiting, and want to take advantage of the freedom and openness of their new location. James Joyce, for example, "went into exile to get the artistic freedom which Dublin refused him" (Gurr 8), and, in fact, invented excuses to stay away from there for as long as he could. Though it proved conducive for fulfilling his creative and aesthetic ambitions, because being "alone and friendless" gave "force to his artistic vocation" (Said 2001:182), Joyce's exile is a voluntary escape from the society of his birth, and, therefore, quite different from that of a refugee or a migrant. Since it does not lead to permanent severance from where a person belongs, and keeps open the possibility of going back to it, it is hardly painful.

It is also true that some writers leave their homes for economic gains, and for making reputations that transcend national boundaries, but justify their move by valorizing the condition of exile. A large number of writers from erstwhile colonies have often succumbed to such a temptation. We have, for example, an interesting account of several young Caribbean writers who left their homes for the gains of London. The move not only forced a change in their thematic concerns, to meet different literary standards, but also affected their "sense of community" (See Amon Saakana 107-110). Because of this, Chinua Achebe writes somewhat guardedly about the creative value of such a self-imposed condition, for "it may take the form of an excessive eagerness to demonstrate flair and worldliness, a facility to tag on to whatever the metropolis says is the latest movement..." (81-82). Whether writers go into exile for aesthetic or economic considerations, or just for fanciful reasons, their narratives of reconstruction of their home and country are generally less painful and more playful, less emotional and more intellectual. Invariably, they are also characterized by a high degree of artifice and cleverness, which may add to their readability and appeal but not necessarily to their value, because there is always a danger that writers may lose sight of the very place and home that they had initially decided to write about, prompting even a writer of Rushdie's eminence to remark that "Literature has little or nothing to do with a writer's home address" (Quoted in Achebe 105).

In some situations, however, a self-imposed exile can provide positive gains; this too is proved by the experience of Third World writers. It is the condition of a colonial exile. Though a writer leaves his home for the metropolis, almost like an aesthetic exile, it is not for savouring its freedom but to escape what Gurr calls the "culturally subservient status of his home" (8). Away from the pernicious gaze of the imperial control, the country of exile provides him a congenial and healthy location for recreating a vision of his home and country, and of his identity, too. Such a reconstruction proves a source of understanding and awareness, even empowerment. The work of several African writers exemplifies this in ample measure.

It is only the people who are pushed out of their homes against their will, for one or the other reason, who constitute the bulk of the exiles of this world. They are forced to experience what Said calls the "unhealable rift forced between a human being and a native place, between the self and its true home," because of which "its essential sadness can never be surmounted" (Said 2001:173). This kind of dislocation is painful because it leads to a denial of what one has grown up with, of being rooted in a definite place and clime, within a network of social and cultural relationships, which are crucial for defining one's self. In course of time, a person so displaced may learn the art of surviving in a strange place, get used to it, and even do well there, but his memory often takes him back to what he has been distanced from. Even though it is famed to play tricks, memory can and does have its moments of strength and power, which stimulate people to visit and revisit their past, their place, their home, their country, to create narratives of dislocation.

Thus we see that because there are different kinds of exile, there are different kinds of narratives of dislocation as well, which differ in their nature, range, and density. This essay focuses on three significant variations. Some accounts are intensely personal and *familial*, and can be created only in one's own voice, as Said does in *Out of Place*. Some take the shape of fictional narratives, which are somewhat faded and playful, and marked by a high degree of artifice and cleverness, such as Rushdie's *Midnight's Children* and *Shame*. Many others are informed with an acute awareness of pain and brutality, of vicious exercise of power, and are, therefore, trenchantly critical. *Sweet and Sour Milk, Sardines* and *Close Sesame* – the first major trilogy of Nurrudin Farah – are powerful examples of this kind. Since the three writers have also written on their state of exile and its effect on their writing, the essay makes a brief mention of their views for a better understanding of the nature of narratives of dislocation.

II

Edward Said is known primarily as an influential critic of our times who has radically changed our understanding of postcolonial writings. Throughout his illustrious career, in which he busied himself, almost compulsively, with intellectual labours of a high order, he could not get over the acutely painful consciousness of being a displaced person, who suffered not just one but a series of displacements: "To me, nothing more painful and paradoxically sought after characterizes my life than the many displacements from countries, cities, abodes, languages, environments that have kept in motion all these years" (2000: 217). Though he wrote about them in his own voice, in the shape of an autobiographical memoir, "to articulate a history of loss and dispossession," and to make things "visible despite occlusions, misrepresentations, and denials" (2001: 563) – when he realized that his life was about to end, he lived with its constant pain, which impinged heavily on whatever he did in his life.

A careful reading of his critical work – his pioneering studies on Orientalism and cultural imperialism, his political activism, reflected in books like *The Question of Palestine* and *The Politics of Dispossession* and the central role he accorded to the intellectual in a world vitiated by political adventurism and pompous bluster, and articulated with vigour and forceful brilliance – almost in the spirit of Gramsci, in *The Representations of an Intellectual* – reveals that its trajectory and direction was determined by his acute awareness of his displacement, which also dictated his choice of writers on whom he spent his critical energy. In "Between Worlds" he affirms that his interest in the fiction of Joseph Conrad, the subject of his first major work, and references to whose writings are scattered in his other essays too, was because he shared with him his "loss of home and language." In fact, it worked as a kind of substitute mechanism for the work that he would have liked to do on his own: "For years I seemed to be going over the same kind of thing in the work I did, but always through the writings of other people" (2001:555).

Said's consciousness of being in exile, of being forcibly displaced, is reflected in several of his critical essays, of which "Reflections on Exile" has proved the most influential. Acutely aware of the scale of exile in our times because of the spread of Western culture, which has brought with it warfare, imperialism, totalitarianism, and even fundamentalism, he also shows his awareness of the very obvious and subtle forms of exilic consciousness. If on the one end stand émigrés and expatriates, who believe in the beneficial effect of exile on one's creative powers, on the other extreme end are those who think that homelessness is a part of human condition. Quoting Adorno, Said writes that, at some point, the very notion of a home gets dissolved, and a writer's writing becomes his place for living. At the end of it, though, even this is denied to a writer, for "the writer is not even allowed to live in his writing" (2001:568).

Between these extremes of wilful homelessness and a kind of existential homelessness fall those unfortunate beings who have to reckon with actual homelessness, a condition in which they are cut off from "their roots, their land, their past" (Said 2001:177), and of their identity, too. This painful awareness is at the root of creating, recreating, and reconstructing what one has lost, and the cause of the narratives of dislocation. Though this condition is distressing, even traumatizing, Said believes that it has its compensations, too. By crossing borders of several kinds, as he himself did, a person breaks the "barriers of thought and experience" (2001:185), which open up new ways of understanding people and situations. The gains that aesthetic exiles seek wilfully become available even to those who are pushed out of places against their will. It helps them to have a clearer perspective on what they had in the past, which is the main subject of these narratives. In Said's words: "Most people are principally aware of one culture, one setting, one home; exiles are aware of at least two, and this plurality of vision gives rise to an awareness of simultaneous dimensions, an awareness [that is] contrapuntal" (2001:186).

Out of Place is Said's narrative about his life, a recreation of the world of his past – individual, familial, and communal – which bears the clear imprint of a carefully conceived and organized effort at imposing "a narrative on a life that I had left more or less to itself, disorganized, scattered, uncentred" (2001:556). Since actual life is in a continuous state of flux, in many ways unknown, unseen, and unpredictable, it is this ordering that gives it a shape, a pattern, in which the advantages of distancing, of being away from one's place, come into full play. These provide Said with new insights into his past, and his self, compelling him to provide a cautionary clarification in the preface: "Much as I have no wish to hurt anyone's feelings my first obligation has not been to be nice but to be true to my perhaps peculiar memories, experiences, and feelings. I and only I, am responsible for what I recall and see, not individuals in the past who could not have known what effect they might have on me" (2000: xii-xiii).

In Said's case the level of disorganization in his past was more than ordinary. He had a complicated ancestry, with too many names – inherited and assumed – and had to do a thorough sifting job to make a proper account. The title clarifies that the primary reason behind this effort is his awareness of being a person who always felt out of place. Even though he spent the most vital and productive part of his life in the US, where he achieved well-deserved fame for his work, it still remained for him "a place of exile, removal, unwilling dislocation," (2000:218) with "a sense of provisionality about it," where he strove to find his lost territory "not socially but intellectually" (2000:231). Being not in Palestine, having gone through dislocations, and tasting torment and despair, his final words are quite revealing. Almost in the vein of Adorno, he writes: "Better to wander out of place, not to own a house, and not ever to feel too much at home anywhere, especially in a city like New York, where I shall be until I die" (2000:294).

Said looks back on his childhood, his parents, and their role in his life, and the various places where he had to stay, with exceptional clarity and objectivity, but the underlying tone is one of pain and sadness. His father's career was a compilation of numerous invented versions – of jobs taken and places visited – many of which Said learnt only after his death. His mother was exasperatingly enigmatic, and he had to put up with her unpredictably alternating moods of love and indifference. Said sees his own being as a land of creation, which was "made necessary by the fact that his parents were themselves self-creations" (2000:19). Feeling somewhat stuffed and alienated, he looks upon himself as a collage, and with no possibility except to be "out of place" (2000:19).

He had to live with several difficulties during his early years: a "parentally controlled life at home," which included a strictly regulated relationship even with his sisters; the colonial attitude of the British in his school; and a restricted access to the world outside. Because of this, he went through a series of identity crises. In trying to overcome them, he developed the habit of "fantasizing about other lives and especially other people's houses" (2000:37), and also an acute consciousness of his body with a sense of shame. His only moments of joy are associated with his stay in Palestine, the only place where he felt "totally at home" (2000:108). When he lost it for good, he could not fully grasp the magnitude of its loss. Writing from the vantage point of his present, he comments:

> What overcomes me now is the scale of dislocation our family and friends experienced and of which I was scarcely conscious, essentially unknowing witness in 1948. As a boy of twelve and a half in Cairo, I often saw the sadness and destitution in the faces and lives of people I had formerly known as ordinary middle-class people in Palestine but I couldn't really comprehend the tragedy that had befallen them nor could I piece together all the different narrative fragments to understand what had really happened in Palestine. (2000:114)

Only later could Said understand that it was because his father consistently strove to shelter him and, in fact, all his children, from political events, so that they could be left free to make their own lives. That is why his short comment that the "repression of Palestine in our lives occurred as a part of a larger depoliticization" (2000:117). The only bit of it that he experienced then was during his aunt Nabiha's charity work, who devoted her later life to ameliorating the hapless lot of the refugees, in whom he saw "the raw, almost brutal core of Palestinian suffering" (2000:121).

Said's recreation also records with care and gratitude the role of several people in the early years of Palestinian struggle, especially because he understood only much later how, in spite of suffering "dispossession and effacement," the Palestinians had been rendered "outside history, and certainly outside discussion" (Said 1980: xv-xvi). He also understood how after being pushed into the US by his father, he looked upon himself as an insecure alien, quite far from the "Palestine of remote memory, unresolved sorrow, and uncomprehending anger" (2000:147). But it was not for long. His early acts of revolt against colonial control, when, for example, he defied the school regulation of speaking with his classmates only in English by secret use of Arabic language as "a criminalized discourse where we took refuge from the world of masters" (2000:184), acquired a new purposeful focus in the US Palestinian identity became his passion, and the dispossession of Palestinians a cause to fight for. He directed his energies towards carving out a new mode of intellectual discourse, in which critics take centre stage in the public domain, resistance to injustice informs their thinking and practice, and critical activity acquires a plasticity that ensures new hope for human freedom: "Criticism must think of itself as life-enhancing and constitutively opposed to every form of tyranny, domination, and abuse: its social goals are non-coercive knowledge produced in the interests of human freedom" (Said 1983:29). The words that he used for his friend Eqbal Ahmad could as well be applicable to him: "One of the most remarkable things about him was that even though he crossed more borders and traversed more boundaries than most people, Eqbal was reassuringly himself in each new place, new situation, new context" (2000a: xix). Said's memoir amply confirms that being out of place helps people to be in all those places where one sees and feels the pain of dislocation.

III

Salman Rushdie's displacement is quite different from that of Said. For Said it was not merely a physical condition; his parents used it to foist a new identity on him. So he not only mourned the loss of his home but also struggled to find his true self. In contrast to this, Rushdie's early childhood in Bombay was reasonably happy. When his parents migrated to Pakistan, a country that he did not particularly like, he stayed on in England even after completing his education, because it was a part of his cherished dream (1991:18).

After publishing his first novel, which was hardly noticed, he chose to write about his past in India, which he explains thus: "...I wanted to restore the past to myself not in the faded grays of old family-album snapshots but whole in Cinemascope and Glorious Technicolour" (1991: 9-10). He saw himself as a part of the large community of "exiles or emigrants or expatriates" who "are haunted by some sense of loss, some urge to reclaim, to look back," and this is quite different from the painful and anguished desire of Said. That is why his sub-continental connection, which he invokes more to defend than to explain his involvement with India and Pakistan, is more of an elastic bond than an emotional bond. This gives Rushdie's fictional recreations a different tone and texture, with a pronounced tilt that stems from his realization that he cannot reclaim "precisely the thing that was lost," and the consequent fear that he would only create "fictions, not actual cities or villages, but invisible ones, imaginary homelands, Indias of the mind" (10). This awareness is at the core of both *Midnight's Children* and *Shame*. Whatever little bit of the past figures in them is in colours that are far from real: it is draped in a cloak of fantasy.

A crucial consequence of this is Rushdie's concentrated focus on the act of retrieval itself. With a faltering memory and a fragmented vision, past can be retrieved only in bits and parts. Through "broken mirrors" and in "fragmented sheets," it comes through a unique process of filtration, which admits of opportunities for fun and colour. Rushdie is so overwhelmingly fascinated by the process of recreation that the past itself becomes a secondary consideration. Because of this, both novels build into them a very strong element of self-reflexivity in which the reader's attention is continuously drawn to the process of retrieval and recovery. We have a seminal statement on this in one of his essays, when he writes that while he was trying to imagine India through a filter that he could use for recollecting and recounting India's past, he realized that "what interested me was the filtration process itself. So my subject changed, was no longer a search for lost time, had become the way in which we remake the past to suit our present purposes, using memory as our tool" (1984:24). This admission defines the distinctive as well as the problematic quality of Rushdie's mode of creating narratives of dislocation, with several attendant complexities. For it is not simply a clarificatory statement that he shares with his readers for their better understanding of the nature and quality of his narrative, but a realization that is woven into the narrative fabric of the two novels. I use *Midnight's Children* for illustrating this because in this novel it is worked out in its fullness, and there is evidence of this in *Shame*, as well.

The narrator, Saleem Sinai, constantly speaks to his interlocutress, Padma, about the nature of his narrative, characterizing the novel with a high degree of self-consciousness. Rushdie uses this as a strategy to achieve two things simultaneously. It ruptures the narrative much too often, breaking in the process the novelistic convention of seducing the reader into believing that his/her narrative is "real," and thus bringing into the mainstream the lesser known and little appreciated variety of fiction that self-consciously, as Robert Alter puts it, "expresses its seriousness through playfulness [and] systematically flaunts its own condition of artifice and that by so doing probes into the problematic relationship between real-seeming artifice and reality" (ix, x). Some critics believe that

Rushdie had precedents here, such as Marquez and other practitioners of "magic realism" and its variants. Nevertheless, Rushdie does it in a manner, especially in his use of language, and on a scale that gives his narrative a distinct colouration.

The second is related to Rushdie's self-avowed concern for retrieving the past, which he could have done with relative ease by choosing the verisimilar mode, because it would have approximated the realistic manner of historical accounts. But he mixes realism with fantasy to make the point that the process of recovering the past is beset with haziness and inaccuracy, making the account far from being a solid and confident narrative of what happened. Inbuilt into this is the assumption that all historical accounts are linked to the perceptions of their creators. Rushdie's narrative, in this way, is simultaneously concerned with the act of writing a fictional narrative and a historical recreation of the past that is largely concerned with methodological problems related both to novel writing and historical writing. Though Linda Hutcheon characterizes this combination "historical metafiction or metafictional historiography," which is the postmodernist fictional frame for the novelist's active intervention into the problematics of history (285-86), Rushdie's engagement with history has other complicated edges as well, which are dramatized within the narrative space of both *Midnight's Children* and *Shame*.

Like traditional historians, Saleem aspires to produce a total account of the past, which provides even continuities and missing links. Elaborating on a metaphor from family histories, which tend to suppress details that are considered unpleasant, unmentionable, or derogatory to persons who figure in them, which makes the account partial, he resolves to eschew the temptation of resorting to such a deliberate, selective representation of events; very soon, however, he realizes that that is not possible. In his understanding and representation of the past, he cannot escape the fate of his mother, who was doomed to learn "to love a man in segments, and which condemned me to see my own life – its meanings, its structures – in fragments also..." (Rushdie 1981:106-7).

Rushdie illustrates this by expounding the idea of history reclaimed through memory, which "selects, eliminates, alters, exaggerates, *minimizes,* glorifies, and vilifies also: but in the end it creates its own reality, its heterogeneous but usually coherent version of events; and no sane human being ever trusts someone else's version more than his own" (1981:207). This he calls chutnification of history. As a suggestive metaphor it draws attention to the mixtures that become inevitable in such a process of preservation. Modestly, Saleem says: "in words and pickles, I have immortalized my memories, although distortions are inevitable in both methods. We must live, I'm afraid, with the shadows of imperfection" (1981: 442). So errors are bound to creep in, and because revisions and redoings are exasperating and time-consuming, these also stay. Saleem's error about the year of Gandhi's death is used by Rushdie to illustrate that our reconstructions are "built on our prejudices, misconceptions and ignorance as well as on our perceptiveness and knowledge. The reading of Saleem's unreliable narration might be, I believed, a useful analogy for the way in which we all, every day, attempt to 'read' the world" (Rushdie 1984: 100).

If the past cannot be created in its wholeness and fullness, does it mean that whatever is retrieved is not truthful? Rushdie's statement that "imaginative truth is simultaneously honourable and suspect" might give the impression that he is not too sure, but when read together with his earlier assertion that howsoever hard we might try, imperfections will still be there, it becomes clear that he upholds the idea of plurality of truths. Implicit in this is also the realization that individual perceptions are of key importance in building a picture of the past. Since these are grounded in beliefs and ideas or ideologies, all accounts of the past are constructed around stated and unstated assumptions. This is where history turns into a discourse, and Rushdie brings into the narrative ambit the ideas of philosophers of history, from Collingwood to Hayden White, without of course invoking them directly, that the picture of the past that one actually creates is an imaginary one, for it is first conceived by the historian and then the 'facts' are used to fill it out. If the writer of fiction chooses his set of details to create his picture of society, the historian chooses his set of facts to create his picture of the past. Thus Rushdie not only works out similarities between fictive and historical imagination but also merges them to create an engaging as well as a highly ideological narrative that has implications for both.

This mixture also creates scope for dealing with the politics of representation. Rushdie posits a frontal clash between politicians and writers as "natural rivals" for both "try to make the world in their own image" (1991:14). This shows that recreating the past is not a disinterested activity, as positivist historians assumed, because it is used as a means for legitimizing structures of power and control, with serious cultural consequences. If history writing, as we all know, was an essential part of colonial engineering, for creating a moral and ethical base for justifying the imperial enterprise, in many other places it has been used for legitimizing policies and practices that would otherwise have been indefensible.

Apart from problematizing the historical discourse in both his novels, Rushdie also builds into them a strong element of historiographic contest, as part of his distinctive filter for understanding the past of both India and Pakistan. Since India is an older country, and Pakistan came apart from it only in 1947, the construction of their past and the nature of its contest in them are also different. In *Midnight's Children* Rushdie assumes that India became a nation only in 1947, which makes it into an invented and imaginary country made possible through a massive collective dream, which is clarified in a passage of remarkable power: "...there was an extra festival on the calendar, a new myth to celebrate, because a nation which had never previously existed was about to win its freedom, catapulting us into a world which, although it has five thousand years of history ... was nevertheless quite imaginary; into a mythical land, a country which would never exist except by the efforts of a phenomenal will... a mass fantasy ... a collective fiction ... (1991:11).

The passage suggests much more than the belief that the British made India into a nation, for Rushdie invests the new country with a character that contrasts sharply with its pre-1947 past, which consists of "everything antiquated and retrogressive in our myth-ridden nation...the bizarre creation of a rambling, diseased mind" (1991:197). Thus Rushdie assumes that India has two kinds of past that are qualitatively polar opposites, in which the movement of events is understood differently because of the alternative notions of time. The one is based on the Western way and also on reason and secular ideal; the other is of the native variety, shaded by myth and legend, and aided by superstition. Rushdie believes that people's tendency to go back to their old mythical ways in the post-independence times is the main reason for a slide in the country's progress, thus neutralizing the advantages that it gained in 1947.

Pakistan's shamelessness too is traced to its birth, for though it got a chance to make a fresh start, it could not get over its shared past with India. All the diseased aspects of its polity were compounded by the sick minds of two of its major leaders. The historiographical contest that is presented so elaborately in *Midnight's Children* is woven into *Shame* through Isky's (Bhutto's) daughter Arjumand, who covers up his shameful past to make him into a mythical figure of gigantic proportions. She virtually deifies him to restore him to history in his new incarnation. Consistently, Rushdie uses the fine ironic mock-epic style to show how the mythical and historical versions of Isky are at variance.

Thus we see that Rushdie uses his position of a dislocated being to create novelistic narratives, and makes a special claim for their value because "the physical act of discontinuity" of being "elsewhere" provides him a new perspective on recreating one's past. [6] Apart from problematizing the historical discourse, he projects a new understanding of the past of India and Pakistan, which is rooted in assumptions that I have tried to uncover. Since his perception of what happened in Pakistan is near to our times and his objects of censure are too obvious, it is somewhat easy to accept what he says, but his interpretation of India's pre-1947 past, in which he writes off five thousand years of its history by a simple stroke of his pen, and which he uses as a basis for understanding and evaluating its post-1947 past, does not inspire the same kind of confidence. However, by admitting that there can be plural versions of the past, he also creates space for the ones that might look eccentric.

IV

We have seen how Said's memoir is suffused with clear signs and traces of a dislocated sensibility, which are fairly visible in Rushdie's fiction, too, but we see very little of them in Farah's novels. We know that he has been in exile for many years; in fact, compared with Said's and Rushdie's, his exile has been the most painful. He has written and talked about it extensively, but his response to this in his novels is only anger against the Somali state and its rulers, the kind of anger that informs satirical writings of conscientious idealists who attack deviations from their cherished ideals. Farah subjects the recent past of Somalia to a severe scrutiny, and brings out its repulsive aspects because it is contrary to what he would have wished it to be.

Farah's writings differ from that of Said and Rushdie in several other respects. There is a strong element of self-consciousness in Said's memoir, because he writes about his life in his own voice. In

Rushdie it is flaunted as a part of his fictional style, which has a functional use as well. In contrast to this, Farah's novels read like that of a traditional novelist who uses fictional space to hit at aspects of social, political, and cultural life that he does not like, though he uses language more like a poet than a writer of prose. Rushdie eventually moved away from his sub-continental connection into new areas of experience where time and space are in a different sphere, but Farah has steadfastly held on to his country, even though he has not been able to go back to it for more than two decades. His passionate attachment for his land is grounded in his belief that one can "never write effective fiction unless it is based on your own country" (Jonas 60). In fact, for keeping himself connected to his country, he has deliberately chosen to live only in Africa. While Rushdie's views on the recreation of past are largely rooted in the fallibility of memory, and the tricks it plays on us, memory holds no terrors for Farah. In fact, quite contrarily, he believes that "Memory is active when you are in exile and it calls at the awkward hour, like a baby waking up its parents at the crack of dawn" (Jonas 60). Unlike Rushdie, he is quite comfortable with writing in a tried-out verisimilar mode. Even though satirical writing necessitates a bit of exaggeration, and even token fantasy, Farah uses them sparingly.

The circumstances of Farah's exile provide a special angle to his fictional creations, for he was not pushed out of Somalia, but prevented from returning home in 1976 because the government had found his novel *A Naked Needle* objectionable. From that time onwards, as he himself says, he "changed from being a homeward bound traveler, in transit, to an exile, and became the proverbial hunchback who must get used to his misfortunes" (Farah 2000:58). The inability to return has been rankling in his heart ever since, for he considers it like losing a part of him. This sense of loss has been his main impetus for writing novels: "I write because a theme has chosen me: the theme of Africa's upheaval and societal disorganization. And I write to recover my missing half" (Farah 1988:159).

This missing half is reflected in his acute consciousness of the state of his country, so much so that even though he is out of it, he does not feel that he is in exile. On the contrary, "it is the leadership, the dictators of Africa that are in exile. I may be absent physically, but I am not absent spiritually, nor am I exiled from my own people who, to the best of my knowledge, have a high respect for the principles by which I stand, and still retain their trust in me" (Jaggi 173). To articulate the principles he shares with his people, to judge the leaders for what they are worth, and to lay bare the pain and suffering inflicted by them on Somali people are the prime concerns of his writing.

Farah's dislocation provides him with distinct advantages. At one level almost in the Joycean manner, it gives him an opportunity to be away from the restraining and inhibiting influences that are a part of living in Somalia, which, quite understandably, are different from what Joyce faced in Dublin. In Somalia, Farah would have been forced either to be the camp follower of some political group or to produce anaemic apolitical writing. Being out of his place enables him to be a "depository of the nation's memory, trustee to the nation's wishes and custodian of the people's views" (1989:187). At another level, as we have already seen in the case of Said and Rushdie, his state of exile provides him a better understanding of the place, by seeing it sharply and clearly than ever before. It is because distance distils: "I think I have learned a lot more about Somalia by questioning myself and my country from afar. One needs to extricate oneself from the daily needs and demands of living at home" (Jonas 60).

There is a strong political edge to Farah's writing, even though he knows that "combining politics and writing is a lonely business" (2000: 59). He cannot get over the feeling of disgust at the rot that has set into the social and political system of his country, and being out of it helps him to write about it without any danger of censorship or reprisal. Knowing that millions of Somalis have been pushed into exile by the barbarity of its rulers, he has followed their lives in other parts of the world. One of his most recent works documents their life in different countries of Europe, and records their horrific tales of ouster, torture, thuggery, and decapitation, and the poignancy of their "damaged memories."

It is quite understandable that while thinking about his home and country, his memory gets focused only on its *inhuman* political system and the deformed social structure that sustains it. Unlike many African writers, he sees no point in digging into the distant past of Somalia, but concentrates on its recent past in which the big blot is the dictatorial system of the country, which is the main theme of what he calls the dictatorship trilogy.

The first of these novels, *Sweet and Sour,* is a variation on a quest narrative, in which Loyaan comes home to untangle the mystery about the sudden and mysterious death of his twin brother Soyaan. He was the economic advisor to the President of the country, but also part of a small clandestine group, working for spreading disaffection against the regime. When found out, he is secretly poisoned, but artfully appropriated by the regime to glorify its programmes and policies.

Loyaan's search takes him to his numerous friends and collaborators, people from the government, and his mistress, who help him to piece together the narrative of Soyaan's life and activities; whatever he learns about his actions and his writings function as a kind of satiric voice, condemning the political system and uncovering its true face. Thus we learn that the General, the head of the government, is like the "Grand Warden of a Gulag" who abuses and humiliates people daily and minutely (10). Ahmed-Wellie, the doctor friend of Soyaan, tells Loyaan how people "executed by a firing squad for their political beliefs [are] buried in unnumbered tombs" (40). By enforcing strict disciplinary codes, the "General had regimented the nation's manpower" (53), and voices of protest and derogatory actions invite severe punishment. When the portrait of the General is disfigured in a village, hundreds of boys and girls are arrested and interrogated, and the ones who are forced to stay back remain "untried: tortured nightly" (111).

Farah's analysis of the political scene focuses on two aspects of the history of Somalia. First, he sees parallels between the colonial and postindependence past of the country. Loyaan observes that the rulers were taking the country back to the era of "European dictatorship, concentration camps. Africa is again a torture chamber. Africa is humiliation" (124). Secondly, like Rushdie, Farah also touches upon the problems related to history writing, though in a slightly different manner. The attempt by the regime to rewrite Soyaan's family history, in which his father turns into an accomplice because of petty economic gain and personal security, clearly illustrates how history is used as a weapon of power. In his new historical reincarnation, slogans are ascribed to Soyaan that lend respectability to the General and his policies, and lies are fabricated to present them as truth. This is compared with the rewriting of history in Russia of "Lenin's, Stalin's or that of any of the heroes their system created to survive subversion from within or without" (106-7). One of the state ministers tells Loyaan that "Hero-worship is a phenomenon as necessary as history itself. Every nation needs heroes in which to invest a past, heroes and legendary figures about whom one tells stories to children and future generations" (185).

The novel brings out two more features of Somalia's repulsive reality: the clan politics, which is exploited by the General to strengthen his hold over power, and his invention of the heady mix of "Marxist-Leninist and Mohammedan" beliefs. The General also uses the oral tradition of the country to invent a new security system – "Dionysius' Ear" – in which spies report on people orally and executions too are ordered orally. The result is that Somalia turns into a place where people "are prisoners: the security, the Green Guards, are the jailers: and the General, the Grand warder of them all" (193), and the novel a "demented, deranged world; an Orwellian nightmare of unpersons and rearranged history in winch terror and unreason have taken up an autonomous existence..." (Derek Wright 45).

Sardines elaborates further the picture of coercion and fear in Somalia. Though some members of the secret group are still alive and active, the narrative foregrounds mainly women who, Farah tells us, function "as a symbol for Somalia. Because, when the women are free, then and only then can we talk about a free Somalia" (Kitchner 61). The protagonist is Medina, whose credo combines the symbolic charge, for she fights for "A room of her own [and] a country of her own" (4). Sacked for defying the editorial policy of the paper she had been working for, she also moves out of the home of her husband Samanter because he is under the unhealthy sway of his mother Idil who, in spite of being a woman, represents everything that is anti-woman.

The actions and thoughts of Medina and her friends provide an insight into the reprehensible nature of the regime. The government of the General is a representation of male power; he reminds her of "her grandfather who was a monstrosity and an unchallengeable patriarch" (17). But such is the low estimation of their place in society that in spite of what they say against his government, the General holds that "women are not worth taking seriously" (48). Even Medina's husband, who is no enemy of the government, holds that "in Somali power-politics there was no room for women and that in a set-up such as the General's there was no hope for them" (76). They are treated like "commodities bought and sold" and "sexually mutilated" (62) and subjugated. Two such major incidents are the unpunished rape of Amina and the brutal circumcision of the visiting American-Somali girl. Medina leaves her home because her mother-in-law insisted upon circumcising her small daughter. The only punishment that the society has for a rapist is that "he marries the victim" and "accepts her hand in marriage in the presence of the elders of the clan" (128).

Besides exposing the deformities of the male-dominated Somali society, Farah dwells on the intellectual activities of women, including those of young girls, and their growing awareness of their inferior status and the general degradation of the country. Two young girls, Cadar and Hindiya, risk their chances of going abroad by writing against the President on the walls of a village, to emerge as "heroines of resistance." Even Samanter changes in the end, but it proves of no avail.

The last novel of the trilogy – *Close Sesame* – in the words of Farah "pulls together some loose threads" (Kitchner 61) from the two earlier novels. Its main protagonist is Deeriye, a kind and sympathetic old man, who stays alternatively with Ins son and daughter, Mursal and Zeinab. He is a strong character, an epitome of courage, who suffered imprisonment during colonial and post-independence times, a man willing to die for the sake of principles, the only man "who staunchly believed in national rather than trivial clannish politicking" (7). The remnants of the old resistance group are also there, and it gets some new members, including the son of Deeriye.

Though the political core of the novel is the same, Farah provides for some variation by putting the oppressive present in a historical perspective that gradually recedes from the near past into the distant past, to the times of Italian colonialism, the war against the British in the earlier part of the twentieth century, and then into the legendary past of King Wiil-Waal and the Islamic Caliphate. Though some critics consider building these parallels like accumulating "too many coincidences" (Bardolph 203), it still remains true that these serve the purpose of reinforcing the element of repression in the existing regime, and also stressing that resisting it is the only way to overcome it. When the resistance group is eventually liquidated, Deeriye makes a bold attempt to finish off the General on his own, but things do not work his way.

Through Mursal, who has a Ph.D. on the relevance of Koran in an Islamic state, Farah exposes the absurd untruth of mixing Koran with Marxism, and shows that it is a perversion perpetrated only for legitimizing oppression and tyranny, and through Deeriya's death he affirms the values of nationalism, idealism, and belief in true Islam. His daughter Zeinab rightly comments that Deeriye had the energy and vision to fight and to hit back.

Thus we see that Farah's dislocation leads him to create narratives of his home that are extremely critical of its rulers because they have turned it into the colony of yesteryears, where there is brutality and repression, and the social system glorifies only patriarchy and decadent clannish politics, both of which tyrannize women.

Endnotes

1. In his preface to *Out of Place* Said uses the expression "reconstructing a remote time and experience" (xii).
2. In *Shame,* the narrator defends his involvement with Pakistan by stating that "It is part of the world to which, whether I like it or not, I am still joined, if only by elastic bands" (28).
3. See, for example, Patricia Merivale (12).
4. For a fuller account on this, see Dhar (1993:93-111 and 1999:159-206).
5. For an elaboration on this, see Dhar (1998:27-43).
6. This probably explains why the critical response to Rushdie has largely picked on theoretical and methodological issues related to retrieval of the past rather than on the nature and quality of his writing. For some interesting responses, see Meenakshi Mukherjee (1999).

References

Achebe, Chinua. *Home and Exile.* 2000. New York: Anchor Books, 2001.

Alter, Robert. *Partial Magic: The Novel as a Self-Conscious Genre.* 1975. Berkeley: Univ. of California Press, 1978.

Bardolph, Jacqueline. "Time and History in Nuruddin Farah's *Close Sesame". Journal of Commonwealth Literature,* 24, 1 (1989): 193-206.

Bevan, David, ed. *Literature and Exile.* Amsterdam: Rodopi, 1990.

Dhar, T. N. *History-Fiction Interface in Indian English Novel.* New Delhi: Prestige Books, 1999.

—. "Historiographic Contest and Post-Colonial Theory". *Literature and Ideology: Essays in Interpretation.* Ed. Veena Singh. Jaipur and Delhi: Rawat Publications, 1998.

—. "Problematizing History with Rushdie in *Midnight's Children*". *Journal of South Asian Literature*, A, 1&2 (Fall-Spring 1993): 93-111.

Farah, Nuruddin. *Close Sesame*. 1983. Minnesota: Graywolf Press, 1992.

—. *Sardines*. 1981. Minnesota: Graywolf Press, 1992.

—. *Sweet and Sour Milk*. 1979. Minnesota: Graywolf Press, 1992.

—. "Why I Write?" *Third World Quarterly* 10, 4 (1988): 1591-99.

—. *Yesterday, Tomorrow: Voices From the Somali Diaspora*. London and New York: Cassell, 2000.

Guff, Andrew. *Writers in Exile: The Identity of Home in Modem Literature*. Sussex: Harvester Press, 1981.

Hutcheon, Linda. "The Pastness of Past Time: Fiction, History, Historiographic Metafiction". *Genre*, 20, 3-4 (Fall-Winter 1987): 285-305.

Jaggi, Maya. "A Combination of Gifts: An Interview with Nuruddin Farah". *Third World Quarterly*, 11, 3 (July 1989): 171-187.

Jonas, Maggie. "Farah – Living in a Country of the Mind?" *New African* (December 1987): 60-6 1.

Kitchner, Julie. "Author in Search of an Identity". *New African* (December 1981):61.

Merivale, Patricia. "Saleem Fathered by Oskar: Intertextual Strategies in *Midnight's Children* and *Tin Drum*". *Ariel* 21, 3 (1974): 455-73.

Mukherjee, Meenakshi. *Midnight's Children: A Book of Reading*. Delhi: Pencraft International, 1999.

Rushdie, Salman. ' "Errata": Unreliable Narration in *Midnight's Children'*. *A Sense of Place: Essays in Post-Colonial Literatures*. Ed. Britta Olinder. Gothenburg: Gothenburg University, 1984.

—. *Imaginary Homelands: Essays and Criticism 1981-1991*. New Delhi: Penguin India, 1991.

—. *Midnight's Children*. London: Jonathan Cape, 1981.

—. *Shame*. London: Jonathan Cape, 1983.

Saakana, Amón Saba. *The Colonial Legacy in Caribbean Literature*. London: Karnak House, 1987.

Said, Edward. "Cherish the Man's Courage". *Eqbal Ahmad: Confronting Empire: Interviews with David Barsamian* (Cambridge, Massachussets: South End Press, 2000a): xix-xxv.

—. *Culture and Imperialism*. 1993. London: Vintage, 1994.

—. *Out of Place: A Memoir*. 1999. New York: Vintage Books, 2000.

—. *Reflections on Exile and Other Literary and Cultural Essays*. New Delhi: Penguin India, 2001.
—. *The Question of Palestine*. London: Routledge and Kegan Paul, 1980.
—. *The World, the Text, and the Critic*. Cambridge, Massachusetts: Harvard Univ. Press, 1983.
Wright, Derek. *The Novels of Nuruddin Farah*. Bayreuth: Bayreuth University, 1994.

7

Of Immigrant Writing...

Vijay Lakshmi

> – Bi-lingual, Bi-cultural,
> able to slip from "How's life?"
> to "Me'stan volviendo loca,"
> able to sit in a paneled office
> drafting memos in smooth English,
> able to order in a fluent Spanish
> at a Mexican restaurant,
> American but hyphenated,
> viewed by Anglos as perhaps exotic,
> perhaps inferior, definitely different,
> perhaps inferior, definitely different,
> (their eyes say, "You may speak
> Spanish but you're not like me")
> an American to Mexicans
> a Mexican to Americans...
>
> Pat Mora, "Legal Alien"

Edmund Wilson, in his famous essay "The Wound and the Bow," reads *Philoctetes* as Sophocles' universal statement on the role of the artist in society. Though suffering from a foul-smelling wound and, thus, an outcast, Philoctetes was nevertheless sought by the Greeks. Ulysses needed his bow to win the Trojan War. Similarly, the society needs the artist, who by the necessity of his/her creativity is forced into some kind of an inner exile, metaphorically speaking.

Today, however, real exiles have taken over the stage who have crossed national boundaries and have exchanged cultural codes. They are, however, different from the Western writers, as Andrei Codrescu, a Romanian poet settled in America, argues. Not having "lost their 'real' countries," he says, "Western writers seem stuck with alienation, which is a kind of psychological exile afflicting the entire society" (93). For the immigrant writers, on the other hand, the gulf physically between the known world to which they can go back only in imagination and their present world is always there and always real. That is why "the creations of exiles have gained central part in contemporary discourse..." (Codrescu 93).

Exchanging one tradition for another, one culture for another, and one home for another, the immigrant writers create and inscribe 'alternative worlds.' Hardly the twin worlds in the words of Shelley – "one dead and the other powerless to be born," these worlds are vibrant, demanding, resisting any notion of annihilation. The opposition between the two may cause anguish to the writers, for the existential dilemma of nothingness or not belonging is not an imaginary state of mind. And going back is not without peril as Chamcha in Rushdie's *The Satanic Verses* says, "When you have stepped through the looking glass, you step back at your own peril. The mirror may cut you to shreds" (58). And yet, this very tension becomes a source of creativity as can be seen in the works of V.S. Naipaul, Salman Rushdie, Julia Alvarez, Hong Kingston, to name a few.

Maxine Hong Kingston, for instance, describes how the writer is born when she remembers the harsh reality of life for the Chinese woman.

> Long ago in China, knot makers tied string into buttons and frogs, and rope into bell pulls. There was one knot so complicated that it blinded the knot maker. Finally the emperor outlawed this cruel knot, and the nobles could not order it any more. If I had lived in China, I would have been an outlaw knot maker. (163)

There is a sense of relief that she has escaped that harshness. One cannot, however, draw the conclusion that she has found reprieve in the new country.

This is a terrible ghost country, where a human being works her life away. . . . I have not stopped working since the day the ship landed. I was on my feet the moment the babies were out. In China I never even had to hang up my own clothes. (*The Woman Warrior* 104)

The tension between what was and what is, between memory and reality, energizes the writer's work. The constant diving into the deep waters of memory helps the writer re-constitute or re-create a remembered past. In the process of re-creation the writer evolves into a new being who *is* and *is not* the person who had started out. Memory, besides language, becomes the most significant factor that sets the diasporic writer's discourse in the 'centre.'

Initially, the immigrant survives by nostalgia for the past. The later years may be richer and more important, as Milan Kundera writes, "but the subconscious, memory, language, all the understructures of creativity, are formed very early" (94). We all cling to a time and place without which as Loren Eiseley says, "man is lost, not only man but life." So nostalgia is the first step, for it sustains memory, even creates memory. And memory is the scaffolding that keeps the self from crumbling, that prevents the present from obliterating the past, prevents the now from annihilating the then. Memory is what stops the writer from being easily consumed by the new culture. It is the only weapon for fighting what Milan Kundera calls the "organized forgetting" forced upon us by the New World. So the writer remembers unabashedly, without any reserve. In the words of the poet Cordescu this is the "ontological remembering, *anamnesis*, the flashback that contains everything in brilliant detail" (103). It is the Proustian memory which transports us into a past we have left behind. It doesn't bring back the presence. It only makes us more aware of the absence. "memories are only confirmations of [...] absence" (Kundera 280).

One may argue that memory may not always be accurate. It doesn't have to be. The imaginative memory of the exile thrives in excess and stalls the forgetting perpetuated by the new impressions. Besides, as Monica Wehner argues,

Memories do not in an obvious and ordinary sense 'exist' until they are remembered until they are brought back into waking life and understood by the individual as memories, separate from the present. This is one reason why they are so slippery and difficult to conceptualise, and why too, of course, they are such a source of fascination. (35)

Memory, invented or real, helps the writer escape the confines of conformity and creates new literature – a hybrid literature – , which does not conform to any one tradition or culture, but creates a new world. The immigrant writer, like Saladin Chamcha in the *Satanic Verses*, becomes a creature "of *selected* discontinuities, a willing re-invention" (47).

The second factor that makes immigrant writing so colourful and vibrant is the writers' ability to write in another language. Writing as they do in a second language Conrad, Naipaul, Ishiguro could achieve the simplicity and grandeur of the English language. In the hands of these writers, English language has become a more powerful tool. They have enriched the language, loading it with fresh expressions and emotions.

It's not relevant what language the immigrant writer thinks in, for the mind does not compartmentalize the two. The mother tongue works at the level of myth, of poetry, while the other, the acquired language, deals at the level of physical reality. Eva Hoffman writes that she chose to write in English, because "If I'm to write about the present, I have to write in the language of the present, even if it's not the language of the self " (121). The immigrant writers' facility in two languages gives them an edge over those who work in but one language. They write with the rhythm of their own language which provides poetry and fuel to their English. "The acquired language is permanently under the watch of the native tongue like a prisoner in a cage" says Codrescu (105). The exuberance of the mother tongue is held in check by the brisk, precise, clear, and pointed quality of the other. When everything falls into place, as finally it does, the English cadence and syntax is clearly enriched. In fact, the diasporic writer coins new words by combining English and Hindi, or English and Urdu, as Rushdie does. They *appropriate* the English language for their own situations. Some like Ngugi or Sandra Estavez plug in words from Kikuyu or Spanish without feeling the need to translate or to provide a glossary. Writers like Naipaul and Ishiguro use the language in a more poetic way. They redefine the boundaries of language, destroying old forms and fashioning new ones. Immigrant writers, well-versed in two languages, may not feel the need to eradicate the old one. They can feel in two languages. T.S. Eliot in

"The Social Functions of Poetry," writes, "The *spiritual* communication between people and people cannot be carried on without the individuals who take the trouble to learn at least one foreign language as well as one can learn any language but one's own, and who consequently are able, to a greater or less degree, To feel in another language as well as in their own" (23). Eliot was, of course, referring to the European languages. Eventually, English becomes the "conduit" to go back and down. Once at ease with the acquired language, the writer begins to see where the different languages meet and then she can move between them without a split. The acquired language can become the language of interiority as well.

Inscribing two literatures, two languages and two traditions, the diasporic writers are no longer "culturally homeless." In their works "the language of reverie," to use Bachelard's phrase merges with "the language of daylight life" (58).

References

Bachelard, Gaston. *The Poetics of Reverie: Childhood, Language and the Cosmos.* Trans. Daniel Russell. Boston: Beacon Press, 1969.

Codrescu, Andrei. *The Disappearance of the Outside: A Manifesto for Escape.* Reading, MA: Addison-Wesley, 1990.

Eliot, T.S. "The Social Function of Poetry." *On Poetry and Poets.* London: Faber and Faber, 1984.

Hoffman, Eva. *Lost in Translation: A Life in a New Language.* New York: Penguin, 1990.

Kingston, Maxine Hong. *The Woman Warrior.* New York: Alford A. Knopf, 1984 (1975).

Kundera, Milan. *Testaments Betrayed.* Trans. Linda Asher. New York: Harper Perennial, 1995.

Rushdie, Salman. *The Satanic Verses.* New York: Viking, 1989.

Wehner, Monica. "Typologies of memory and forgetting among the expatriates of Rabaul." *Journal of Pacific History* June, 2002.

Excerpt from *Pomegranate Dreams**

Whenever I came home with silken cobwebs trembling in my eyes, everyone knew I had seen the girl with her dog. Ma would open the fridge and stare into it as if she were seeing fruit trees growing inside. Bansi would remember some task he had to finish and disappear into his room. I sulked into the glass of milk Ma placed in front of me.

"Drink it! You must be hungry," she would say, holding a cookie jar in front of me. I would down the milk in a gulp, grab a cookie, and slink off to my room without a word.

One day, however, as I was about to leave the room, Papa stopped me. "You want to make friends with that girl, don't you?"

He pushed aside the papers he was always reading and grading, even when he was drinking his tea, or talking over the telephone, or watching the evening news. Sometimes, when he was not preparing for those extra courses he taught, Papa would sit late into the night pounding at the typewriter, working on a book. I had secretly centered all my dreams on that book. I was certain it was going to be a bestseller. The moment it was published, the treasure chests that lay buried under deep seas would float up to the surface. We'd be rich and we'd live in a house on Lincoln Avenue.

Papa repeated his question, tapping the table with his pencil. "You want to be friends with that girl, don't you?"

"Yes, Papa."

"Then why don't you talk to her?"

"How? How can I do that?"

"Very simple!" He leaned back into the chair. "Just say 'Hello!' Introduce yourself. And there you are. You're friends. We never had any problem making friends when we were your age." Papa made everything sound so simple.

"It's not that easy," I mumbled. "You don't understand."

He squinted at me. "What's so complex about it? She's your age. She's Indian," he said. "Like us."

"Like us?" I sprang up, as if I had touched a live wire. My back arched. "How can they be like us? Nobody's like us. They're – we're–" I fumbled for words.

Papa waited for me to finish the sentence.

"Yes?"

---

* *Pomegranate Dreams and Other Stories* by Vijay Lakshmi. New Delhi: Indialog Pvt. Publications, 2002.

I took a deep breath. "She can't be like us, Papa. We don't live in a big house with beautiful trees. We don't have big new cars. We don't even have a dog. We're nobody.
We -"
"Now wait! Wait!"
Before I could complete my list of deprivations, Bansi vaulted in. He always did that, especially if he heard me complaining about what others had and we didn't. He took advantage of being older and in college, but most of all, of being Papa's ambassador. He was cast in Papa's image.
"Don't be ridiculous, Miss Greedy!" He said, looking down at me from his superior height. Bansi was shooting up like a bamboo tree. He was all arms and legs and a big head, too. "What do you mean by a big house and two cars, Ha? Everyone in America has a house and two cars. Don't we?"
Papa returned to his papers, leaving the field to Bansi – his Knight in Armor.
"Papa's car is ancient. And yours? You call that junky-jet a car?"
"It runs, doesn't it? Doesn't it take me wherever I want to go? Didn't all the girls look at me when I picked you up that day?" he asked. "The paint may be chipped and it may have a few dents here and there, so what?"
"So what? Is that all you can say for that scrap?"
He laughed. "It doesn't have to be a limousine, does it?"
I gave up.
I couldn't argue with Bansi, who believed he had resolved all doubts and who thought he possessed everything in the world though he didn't even have a pair of Nike sneakers to his name. Nor a Calvin Klein winter jacket. Not even a CD player. He didn't mind working late in the evening and on weekends while others his age were partying. He didn't have a girl friend. "So what?" He would shrug when I teased him. "I'm happy. I have better things to do than to sit around holding a girl's hand."
Perhaps he was right. College and part-time work in a computer store didn't leave him any time for anything. The only thing for which he could squeeze out some time was his ships. Assembling and collecting miniature boats was Bansi's passion. He had a number of tug boats, sail boats, barges, liners, steamers and battleships lined up on a shelf in his room. I would watch his hands move with the precision of a watchmaker, a jeweler, an artist when he glued tiny

masts, sails, rudders, decks, port windows to a vessel. And when it was completed, he would hold it in the hollow of his hand and look at it with eyes flashing like beacons.

He was content living simply and frugally, satisfied with the minimum, like Papa and his idol, Gandhi. I considered him strange. Wacky. My mother, though, doted on him. She called him her *sadhu*, her monk, her ascetic who demanded nothing, who desired nothing. He was like Baba, the mendicant, who used to come to our house in Jaipur for alms, an ascetic who had renounced the world. He never talked to anyone. No one knew who he was, where he came from, and where he went. We wouldn't see him for months. Then suddenly, one day, he would be standing on the front verandah steps, waiting for my grandmother to bring him whatever she could hurriedly pile up on a tray. Baba wore nothing but a loincloth on his ash-smeared body. Hardly a beggar, he asked for nothing. And he never stood still. Papa said he was one of those mendicants who had taken a vow to keep moving, who never sat down. Motion, he said, was one way of disciplining the mind and body. To stop was to cease. It wasn't for nothing that Papa had chosen to be a professor of philosophy.

In any event, Baba would keep treading the flagstones, as if he were warming up, or marking time to march off. Chanting some strange mantra, beating rhythm with a pair of iron tongs in his hand, he kept his bloodshot eyes fixed upon a point in the ceiling. Hidden behind a door, we would peep at him. Bansi was certain that tiny finches nestled in his tangled and matted hair. With mounting excitement, we would wait for the birds to pop out, chirping and fluttering their tiny wings. They never did.

From the tray piled high with fruit and nuts that my grandmother brought to him, Baba would pick out a banana, or a mango, or a handful of peanuts. Never more. Then he would walk away. Grandmother would beam with joy, for he had accepted a morsel from her home. She would clasp her hands and bow her head to his receding back.

And if my grandmother was late in turning up with the tray, Baba would leave. Without a word. Without a backward glance. Nothing could make him come back for his meager meal. Not his hunger. Not my grandmother's pleas. She would be miserable for days, because a monk had gone away hungry from her door. Not even a stray dog or a cat or a cow went away hungry from her house. How could a monk go away empty-handed? A monk, who had overcome hunger and desire. Who had renounced the world.

Bansi was like Baba. He had overcome desire. He needed no props to be happy. I did. Bansi could be happy not wishing for anything. Not wanting. Not having. But I couldn't. I wanted the whole universe. The sun. The moon. The stars. The wind. The earth. The sky. The rainbow with a pot of gold at the end of it. I wanted to clasp them all in my hands. Isn't that why we had come to America, anyway? I asked myself. Isn't that what everyone came to America for? Rushing in from all the quarters of the world. In boats. In planes. On foot, across the borders. From Africa. From China. From Cuba. From Haiti. From Mexico. From Russia. Ukraine. Yugoslavia. From all points of the compass. We wanted it all.

And if we couldn't have it all, then what was the point in our dreaming America? Wishing America? Craving America? Coming to America?

The first thing that Papa had done as soon as he returned from his year-long stay in America, was to spread out a world map on the table and point out to us the huge land mass sprawling between the Atlantic and the Pacific oceans. "That's where we're all going," he had said, laying his finger on America. We had hung on every word of his as he spun stories about the beauty of the land, its abundance, its opportunities, its prosperity, and its people, especially about a Mr. and Mrs. Miller who had been his host family. Kind, honest, hardworking people, Papa had said. They were a beautiful people who represented the true spirit of a beautiful country. Visions of a distant land with a good people in it began to sprout in our minds. It was the land where pumpkins turned into crystal carriages and mice into white horses and cinder maids into princesses.

So powerful was its lure that, dreaming of America, we dreamed of nothing else.

Wanting America, we wanted nothing else.

"Now to America!" Papa had said, one day, our visas fluttering in his hands like the sails of a ship ready to cross the bar. And we started packing our suitcases. Squealing with delight, at first. Then, squirming with woe, as Papa reduced to a small pile our rising mound of toys, clothes, books, and the childhood treasures that stood for souvenirs. We had to pack our lives into the two suitcases each one was allowed to carry into the new land. Bansi didn't mind leaving everything behind. In fact, he took off with three pairs of pants and the model ship that grandfather had given him upon his tenth birthday. "New country. New life. New Dream." That was his motto.

But I was furious. Leave everything behind? Never.

Going to America couldn't mean dismantling our past and abandoning it like a charred building. The pile of things I couldn't carry with us grew bigger. If I had a genie at my command, I thought, I would transport everything of ours to America in the blink of an eye.

Papa looked at my pile and growled, "No. This is all trash now."

"It's not," I cried, clinging to my treasures.

Papa didn't recant. I wouldn't surrender.

Finally, my grandmother pulled out her trunk and deposited in it all my treasures – my dolls, their tiny china tea service, their bed, table and chairs, my glass beads, crayons, clay animals with chipped noses and bobbed tails, and reams of drawings I had done. "I'll send them by surface mail," she said. They were still there, in the trunk, under her bed when I visited her some years later.

When we set out for America, we left behind so much. Not just my dolls, my glass beads, my plastic jewelry, and the clay menagerie I had collected over the years. Not just Bansi's cricket set, his old Superman and Phantom comic books, and the radio he had assembled for his science class. Not just my mother's brocade and silk saris, her heavy gold jewelry, which she said she would have no use for in America. Not just the koel singing in the mango trees and the peacock dancing on the roof. Not just the friends and cousins we had grown up with. Not just the festivals which popped up every other day and provided us with an excuse to take off from school.

We left behind much more.

We left behind our grandmother with whom I had lived all the years of my life. Despite our pleas and despite her love for us she wouldn't accompany us. She couldn't leave her land behind. She couldn't leave the house with absurdly large rooms filled with wind and the echoes of the fifty-seven years she had spent there. She wanted to die among the familiar.

We left behind the stone house that was cooled in summer by the wind heavy with mango blossom, and warmed in winter by the sun.

We left behind our garden where *champa, chameli,* marigold and bougainvillea jostled to out-bloom each other; the pomegranate trees with slender spiny branches, from which parrots swung, prying the fruit open with their sharp beaks; the *jamun* and guava trees that yielded so much fruit that even the street urchins would stop climbing over the compound wall to steal some.

We left behind the monkeys that leapt from branch to branch, shaking the fruit down so that it lay staining the flagstones purple.

And we left behind something else – a sense of belonging, which seemed to have slipped off like a bundle from the top of a bus climbing a mountain road.

I couldn't believe that we had exchanged that bounty for a tiny house with a grizzly cherry tree whose gnarled roots were splayed like fear unleashed in the dark.

8

Trends in Contemporary Indian Writing in English

Malashri Lal

India celebrated a half-century of Independence in 1997. Many of us noticed, in the condition of English writing in India, an enigma of arrival. India's "tryst with destiny" eloquently formulated by Prime Minister Jawaharlal Nehru for that bewitching midnight hour of August 14-15, 1947, envisaged an ideal of "unity in diversity," but what we see fifty-five years later is divisiveness expressed in terms of caste, class, religion. Within a scene of multilingualism and multiculturalism, which had once been comfortably liberal and secular, a spotlight now picks out scenes of communal rioting, violence against women, dire poverty and child malnutrition. It dwells too upon sites of philanthropy and humanitarian enterprise such as Mother Teresa's "Sisters of Charity", Ela Bhatt's Self-employed Women's Association (SEWA) or Kiran Bedi's Rehabilitation Centre for street children. Elsewhere, almost in contiguity is the rising prestige and power of English, a language not even listed in the original Eighth Schedule, our constitutional dispensation on Indian languages.[1]

Paradoxically, India is best known abroad for its great works of English writing. In the international arena, camera's caught the light on Arundhati Roy's diamond nose pin while she declared, "English is the skin of my thought." According to a report from London about the Booker Prize ceremonial, "The glittering audience focused on her black wavy hair, her maroon saree, the sparkling stud on her nose, the feminine smile, the assortment of gold and glass bangles around her wrists."[2] In March this year, cameras in Delhi recorded Roy's one night stay in jail for defying the Supreme Court of India. Today, Roy is a social activist more than a creative writer but through her extraordinary single novel, ranks along with other favourites: Salman Rushdie, Vikram Seth, Vikram Chandra, Githa Hariharan, Amitav Ghosh, Upamanyu Chatterjee. This is the new generation – midnight's daughters and sons grappling with "a juggernaut of conflicting values" as the *London Magazine* called it.[3] India continues to be a Forsterian muddle, not a mystery. Reflecting the larger reality, Indian English writing is full of energetic contradictions. To quote Aijaz Ahmad, "In the world of literary creativity, Indian writers in English command high visibility and disproportionate power but remain a minority current. All in all, English is the language of a small minority. Among the rest of the literate, however, knowledge of English is reduced to a bare smattering, while knowledge of regional languages has greatly advanced.[4]

I

This paper offers two views on India, one through the diaspora writers, the other through writers who have chosen to reside within the country. In doing so, it opens up the current debates about authenticity and cultural representation even as it seeks to enter the theoretical questions raised by the multi-layered reality of a country of a billion people, 22 official languages, 400 dialects, 3,000 gods and goddesses. By referring to texts in Indian English, I can, today, merely touch a corner of a huge enterprise.

However, literary space is where "word-power" is exerted; it is important for an understanding of nationhood and India is a contested space. Diaspora writers, Salman Rushdie, Gita Mehta, Anita Desai, Sunil Khilnani and Shashi Tharoor offer their insider-outsider perspectives which often contrast sharply with depictions of India's fragmented, chaotic irrationality from home based writers such as Arundhati Roy, Githa Hariharan, Shashi Deshpande. The paper ends with a few remarks about theoretical debate linking Indian-English to representations of India in regional writing, taking the matter into the difficult terrain of translation.

Speaking of the diaspora, I must begin, as so many others have done, with a bout of an affliction that Pankaj Misra amusingly called

"Rushdie-itis." We may remember that Rushdie insisted "Indo-Anglian literature represents perhaps the most valuable contribution India has yet made to the world of books,"[5] at the same time that he admitted to insufficient knowledge of India's vast array of regional output. The debate rolled along in many directions but, as the recent International Festival of Indian Literature held in Delhi in February 2002 showed, there remains a sharp divide on the meaning of the Indian diaspora itself. There seems to be a generational gap. Older writers such as V.S. Naipaul, the Guest of Honour at this Festival, used terms such as "exile" and "homecoming", and showed irritable intolerance with the word "postcolonial." Octogenarian Khushwant Singh called the younger writers "five star exiles" while Vikram Seth, Amitav Ghosh, Farukh Dhondy and Pico Iyer said they are everywhere people and "home" is an unsuitable code of reference in today's fast-paced cyber-world. Rushdie to his credit, had implied the same several years earlier, in his belief that "literature has little or nothing to do with a writer's home address" (*New Yorker* 56).

The most popular Rushdie text in India is still *Midnight's Children* but new approaches can be quite strident. For instance, Rushdie's so called misogynist portrayal of women is drawing considerable criticism from feminists. Passages in the novel make fun of the "omni-competent woman" (*MC* 211); he further tells us how "the twin hearts of her kingdom were the kitchen and the pantry." Rushdie's descriptions of Padma are funny only if one is willing to overlook the patriarchal condescension of many phrases: Padma is forever not just the "lotus", which would be an accurate translation of her name, (and have connections of beauty and spirituality) but also a "dung-lotus." In other derogatory images Padma "beats her heavy breasts" and "wails at the top of her voice." Despite such passages which might upset one's ideological leanings, one cannot deny the literary merit of *Midnight's Children*. The "chutneyfication" of the English language is analogous to the upturning of several cherished assumptions about hierarchy and history. The robust, supple language has spread a gossamer thread of politics over India's complex emergence as a nation, and this one novel has changed the direction for Indian writing in English.

If *The New Yorker,* celebrating 50 years of India's independence, showcased Rushdie in 1997, the *London Magazine's* special issue presented Gita Mehta. A collection, published as *Snakes and Ladders: A View of Modern India,* was advertised in England as "the one book you must read to fully understand independent India at 50." The book is a medley of trite observations. A chapter called "The Voice of the People," reports two quirky events which Mehta reads as emblematic of India's democratic freedom of expression: "Where else would a hundred thousand naked Sadhus with matted hair break off their meditations and descend from their mountain caves to scale the towering gates of the Indian Parliament – Where else would a mass of hermaphrodites and eunuchs, dressed in brilliantly coloured saris and weighted down by jewels, march on the capital to demonstrate against Family Planning." Mehta's reliance upon the visual and sensational impact is all too evident. The Indian exotica is embellished to attract attention to its difference from yet another stereotype, that of an orderly, efficient, rational West.

Elsewhere in *Snakes and Ladders* are phrases disturbingly neo-orientalist in their gaze:

> The smear of colour on a Hindu woman's forehead, the silver ornaments plaited into a Muslim woman's hair, the angular ear-rings in a tribal woman's earlobes, the bright turban on a northern Indian's head, the austere shawl on a southern Indian's shoulders, the muslin mask across a Jain monk's mouth, the saffron robe of the celibate, the matted locks of the ascetic.
> Bread swelling like a cloud on the platter, white rice steaming on the banana leaf, a yard of coffee cooling between steel glasses...
> The stench of the Indian bazaar – flowers, incense, overflowing gutters, petrol, dust, sticky sweets
> The assault of the senses
> The caress of the senses
> Surely God made India at his leisure. (*SL* 119)

To this diaspora guide to the "typical" sights and sounds of India, one may severely object. Surely ornaments and clothing are no longer identity markers in a country tending to large scale internal migration. Must one continue to describe India in terms of the glory and the gutter? Also distressing are Gita Mehta's condescending remarks about India being God's leisure time activity, and "modern India (being) a fiction". Neglecting the evidence of history, she endorses Nirad Chaudhuri's early view: "He chose an apt name for India: her political seductions have truly made swine out of men. And women" (*SL* 97)

It is not pleasant to be called "swine" because one is living in an India seen as Circe-land by an outsider. Moreover, I worry about the ethical implications. Is it "fiction" that sixty percent India lives below poverty line, that only thirty percent women are literate? Keeping to her comfortable notion of "fiction" (the facts would be too hard to bear) Mehta laughingly calls the democratic process of elections, "the greatest show on earth," thus being conveniently distant from a parliamentary process which deals with "half a billion ballot papers in seventeen different languages, each with individual scripts," (*SL* 150).

Let me turn attention to a far more astute diaspora writer, Anita Desai, who in fact makes a transition from being a resident Indian to now living and writing from the US. Her recent novels show an interest in cross-cultural tropes rather than individual psychology which was earlier considered Desai's forte. *Fasting, Feasting* queries ideas of the maternal in both Indian and American contexts. Readers will recall that Mama-Papa constitute a unitary being quite impossible to separate, and the notion of family is brought into discussion. We learn very little of Mama's story in India, and by contrast, we learn very little about Papa's story in Massachusetts! The Indian mother receives and metes out differential treatment to her daughter who must cook, run errands, and drop out of school to baby sit her brother. On the other hand, Arun, who is the favoured male child, is a spoilt brat, a mediocre student but can count on being sent abroad for an expensive university education. Arun in the US gains a surrogate mother in Mrs. Patton, a food fetishist and compulsive shopper who churns out mounds of boiled beans and glutinous spaghettii as a gesture of affection for the vegetarian Indian visitor.

As the title of Desai's novel indicates, food is a cultural measure. Who is fasting and who is feasting? It would be too simplistic to say India is the land of deprivation and America the land of plenty. In a wider sense, the novel is a statement on appetite as desire, inchoate longings expressed through the metaphor of food. One can almost see this as a subversion of Rushdie's phrase about the woman's twin heart beats relying on the kitchen and the pantry. It is worth noting that many women writers in India are using food imagery to talk back to a patriarchal society that insists on situating them in domestic space. A fine outburst of creative retaliation is Bulbul Sharma's *The Anger of the Aubergines* where a series of recipes are used as narrative text.

Theorising about India has been a profitable pastime for some of our talented journalist writers in the diaspora. Sunil Khilnani's *The Idea of India*, locates the problems in the context of history and believes, "It is too simple to see India as pure invention, a complicitous by-product of the opportunities presented by the British Raj" (*Idea* 101). In his celebrated chapter, "Who is an Indian," Khilnani examines the evolution of nation building ideologies and shows how India, "tried to accommodate within the form of a new nation state significant internal diversities; to resist bending to the democratic pressures of religion; and to look outwards." While Khilnani leans towards Nehruvian liberalism, he charts the main trajectory with wisdom: "India's history has shown two broad possibilities of dealing with that diversity: a theoretically untidy, improvising, pluralist approach, or a neatly rationalist and purifying exclusivism" (*Idea* 195). Since such statements of faith only five years ago, secularism in India is today under severe threat from fundamentalists.

Contrast the faith in the survival of democracy with Shashi Tharoor's prophetic observation in his book *India: From Midnight to the Millennium*. There is a bewilderment in his statement, "The only possible idea of India is that of a nation greater that the sum of its parts. An India that denies itself to some Indians could end up being denied to all Indians" (*MM* 5). This is prophetic as we watch Gujarat burning and the troops gathering at the Kashmir border. Tharoor's personalised view of India at half-century criticizes globalisation. Not the word "post-colonial" but his term "Coca-colonial" gives the ironic edge.

Quite evidently, midnight's daughters and sons enjoy jostling in crowded ideological space unlike the father figures of "Indo-Anglian writing" as it was called then, writers who sometimes sought comforting formulas. Even lately Raja Rao's compilation, *The Meaning of India* stresses the philosophical, pacifist heritage of Vedantism and Buddhism. Rao's analogy for India rests in the tale of the tortoise – slow, certain, ageless, accreting the history of the era on faintly marked pigments in its shell. The note to be made then is of the plurality of voice in the diaspora, trying to find broad patterns which suitably package India for a global publishing industry.

The pluralism is made more complex when writers such as Vikram Seth and Amitav Ghosh refuse to be labeled as diaspora or resident, and indeed constantly cross many borders. One might recall that in 2001, Amitav Ghosh refused to accept the Commonwealth Writers Prize for the Eurasia Region as he found the term "Commonwealth" repugnant, and a prize limited to English writing, negligent of history. Ghosh's *The Glass Palace*, which was sought to be awarded, picks for its subject the contentious political relations of Burma, India and colonial Britain. The novel, though in English, successfully alludes to the linguistic and cultural differences which underlie the trauma of defining nations and boundaries. But Ghosh's point was a political one. So many decades into postcolonial experience, should supremacy still be accorded to English, and should the image of a notional Commonwealth dominate official literary institutions?

Vikram Seth eludes labels such as diaspora or any other for a different set of reasons. Residing literally in London and Delhi, Seth's novels display a remarkable range of subject and form. If Indian arranged marriages still raise curiosity, *A Suitable Boy* is a charming compendium to the cultural underpinnings. An elaborate community ritual which will determine the personal lives of two young people, the sequence by which public introductions, discussions and negotiations take place about matrimonial alliance, are presented with humour and sensitivity. Such being his understanding of India, Seth's equal inwardness with British society and classical western music is impressively demonstrated in the novel *An Equal Music* which has no Indian characters. His first literary work *The Golden Gate* was set in California and used a Russian poetic model. If India has produced a truly international writer, I would say it is Vikram Seth.

II

Moving from the international to the national, the second concern of this paper is the literary inventiveness of Indian writers living in India and using local references which have strong cultural codes. I will comment on Arundhati Roy and Githa Hariharan, and briefly refer to a few others. I wish to stress that the Indian reader's knowledge of local customs is evidently privileged.

Let us take *The God of Small Things* as an example. As a resident Indian, one reads of Ayemenem with it's the communist politics around a pickle factory, the layers of caste construction, the silences and taboos about sexuality, the common practice of rituals. Fifty years of a developing country's preoccupations flash upon memory – perhaps embellished by newspaper headlines. Namboodiripad is a familiar person, "The Sound of Music" a childhood remembrance.

Reviewers from abroad, focused on Roy's language not these cultural artifacts. Stuart Proffitt praised Roy for "reinventing our language." *Time* magazine's Anthony Spaeth, attempted a speculation: "Indian readers may be put off by the incessantly brutal depiction of their country. In Roy's India, a land of little hope and unqualified squalor, buildings are in near rot and roads are graced with squashed animals, and at one point, an electrocuted elephant." (*Time* April 15, 1997). Quite the contrary happened in the response in India to *The God of Small Things*. Readers enjoyed and built upon their privileged access to cultural knowledge. They noticed how Roy's novel abounded in amusing examples of linguistic confusion in a postcolonial society. There are shared jokes from our own school days reflected in some marvellous passages about the meaning of meaning:

> Chacko said that the correct word for people like Pappachi was *Anglophile*. He made Rahel and Estha look up *Anglophile* in the *Reader's Digest Great Encyclopaedic Dictionary*. It said *Person well disposed to the English*. Then Estha and Rahel had to look up *disposed*.... (*GOST* 52)

So many of us studied in the shadow of Macaulay's Minutes on Education. We were compelled to speak only English in school and the Oxford English Dictionary (not the *Reader's Digest*) was constantly at hand. The quoted passage shows that a dictionary is of little help in entering the mind of a colonial subject such as Pappachi. Equally Ammu's tendency to dismantle authority begins with questioning language but is ideologically grounded in her rebellion against form. The link with English –both language and political entity – is problematized throughout the text.

From the viewpoint of the novel's subject matter too, the local reader had an advantage. The reception of Roy's novel in India followed a triple track, biography, biology and the body politic. Gender, caste and class has never been more successfully linked in Indian English writing. A 'touchable' woman falls in love with an untouchable man of a lower caste and the smallest of god's creatures tremble with significance (*GOST* 338-339). The caste factor becomes associated with the Communist politics in Kerala. However, Roy's politics also lie elsewhere. The personal is the political in feminist discourse, therefore a few words about this aspect not sufficiently highlighted by critics. Roy exposes the paradoxes in modern India. Despite celebrating economic and political liberalization, the country still places traditional constraints upon female desire and sexuality. As I have elaborated in my book *The Law of the Threshold: Women Writers in Indian English* (1995, rpt.2000), feminism in India is neither anti-male nor anti-family, it is an expression of anger against the patriarchal systems within which women are often complicit. In *The God of Small Things*, Baby Kochamma, Comrade K.N.M. Pillai and Inspector Thomas Mathew are men and woman ranged against Ammu and Velutha's transgression of class, caste, gender "permissions" directed by society. The custodians of justice bring even children into the act of complicity by expecting them to erase visually, orally and spiritually what they have witnessed.

The novel builds towards this climactic tragedy by playing cleverly with other feminist tropes. What, for example, is beauty? The light skinned, light eyed child of mixed blood – Sophie Mol in bell-bottomed trousers clutching a matching bag? What is sexuality? The beautiful Annu at age thirty one. "Not old/Not young/But a viable, die-able age," doomed to remain untimely "pure" because she is divorced? Honour, tradition, duty are invoked as Ammu's motherhood is privileged and her womanhood denied. As in other novels dealing with forbidden love, society ordains the ideal of fulfilled sexuality in marriage and mothering (*GOST* 332).

Is *The God of Small Things* a feminist text? Yes, I would say. The destruction of Velutha the dark man with a name that means "white" (the reader needs Malayalam to understand the implications) by police-power is a sufficient indication of Roy's anti-establishment politics, a strand that has showed up strongly in Roy's polemical essays more recently.

But feminism is only one of many concerns of good novels from India. Roy and other significant women writers are interested in a larger critique of social forms. I offer a few comments on Githa Hariharan's first novel *The Thousand Faces of Night*, a winner of the Commonwealth Writers Prize. The story of a mother and daughter, suggestively named Sita and Devi, it is a choric commentary on the traditions governing a Hindu woman's life. Ancient tales are told and re-told by the family retainer Mayamma (read "Maya" for illusion) so that the impressionable young Devi may grow up to accept her female destiny. But Devi seems born to question all received knowledge, so she asks, always, "Why"? Devi becomes something of a postmodern woman with her intellect honed in New York. As a childless wife, she can no longer bear the accusations of "barrenness" and "unfemininity" from a choric family that defines woman's worth by her mothering of sons. Hariharan delves into the substratum of women's lives in India where there is guilt and shame, sorrow and silence. Marriage is called a "sacrificial knife." (*TFN* 54). Ironical commands are give, "Like Sita you must burn yourself to death" (*TFN* 94). The choice is hardly between an abject submission to tradition and an outright rejection of it. Hariharan's book is about the illusion of continuities in India – myths and legends are the placebos, women's liberation a vague promise.

Linguistically not as inventive as Arundhati Roy, Hariharan nevertheless is among the writers of the 90's decade who use English as an Indian language – not bothering to "write back to the Empire," not seeking a literary umpiring abroad. Several other writers of recent years have unselfconsciously shown the malleability of Indian English. Upamanyu Chatterjee's novel with the title, *English, August* draws attention to the pretentiousness of the brown sahibs thrown up by a Macaulian education. As the hero debunks his inherited colonial structures he remarks "Amazing mix the English we speak – Our accents are Indian but we prefer August to Agastya." Vikram Chandra in *Love and Longing in Bombay* captures the cosmopolitan mood and the linguistic mix of a multi-layered society. An example from a story called "Artha":

> Sandhya's mother was shuffling along. I sang, "*Namaste*, Ma-ji," and she threw a glance over the shoulder and crept on... She didn't like me very much, and I knew that not very behind my back she called me *kalua* and *musalta* and *kattu*.

Thus, standard English is dismantled and tagged to local language variations. Colloquialism and dialect are deliberately left untranslated.

III

Let me attempt a few conclusions at this point. Whether it is the Indian writer in the diaspora or at home, the question no longer is "Who is an Indian" but "What is India". Fifty five years of nation-building has actually taken us further and further away from the possibility of an answer. Old terminology such as hybridity, multiculturalism, secularism, "unity in diversity" are now seen to be untenable comfort phrases. The place of English in the turbulent fragmentations of the nation continues to be debated but its terms of reference are not those of Rao's "Introduction" to *Kanthapura* – that Indian English in encapsulated in phrases such as "quickly-quickly". Language is, no doubt, power. Today, the allegiance of English in India to the regional languages, preferably called *"bhasa"*, is being increasingly asserted at the same time that its commonality with a hypothetical Standard English being parodied and debunked. India's national academy of letters (Sahitya Akademi) is taking a lead role in bringing about a unification package. Awarding translation prizes and *bhasa sammans* in twenty one languages including English, it is ideally positioned to take a pan-Indian view. K. Satchidanandan, eminent Malayalam poet and bilingual critic, who is currently Secretary of the Akademi says Indian writing in English is "a legitimate product of our historical and existential conjecture," but he is troubled by "the politics – the power-knowledge nexus" guiding its publicity. His essay locates the richness of Indian literature in the cross fertilization of many languages and the intersections of many cultures. "Our creativity has thus been dialogic, and our literary discourse marked by the negotiation of a necessary heterogeneity" (Satchidanandan 25).

For me the key term is "necessary heterogeneity." Can this be captured by critical theory in the class room? Authors in India do not bother with theory, academics do! And we are finding it increasingly difficult to teach and accept western theoretical models of postcolonialism but are equally unable to come up with comprehensive theoretical parameters of our own. What we witness is a series of border crossings. The major women writers have declared they don't wish to be identified as primarily "women" – writers are writers, they say. The regional *bhasa* writers of eminence are often bilingual and wish to retain key regional vocabulary in English translations of their works. The diaspora writers are coming home more frequently and for longer durations and the resident writers are touring abroad much of their time. One thing is certain. English is an Indian language, one among the many in constant use in an increasingly divided but multilingual nation. Caste and class are live issues, language and literature vitally linked to them. "What is India?" is a question to which there are many open ended answers.

Endnotes

1. Sadhna Saxena, "Language and Nationality Question." *Economic and Political Weekly*, February 8, 1997, p. 269.
2. *Times of India*, New Delhi, October 16, 1997.
3. *London Magazine*, special issue on India. August/September 1997.
4. Aijaz Ahmad, "Cultures in Conflict." *Frontline*, August 22, 1997.
5. Salman Rushdie, *The New Yorker*, June 23 & 30, 1997, p.50.

References

Ahmad, Aijaz. "Reading Arundhati Roy *Politically*", *Frontline*, August 8, 1997.

—. "Cultures in Conflict", *Frontline*, August 22, 1997.

Chatterjee, Upamanyu. *English August*. London: Faber, 1988.

Desai, Anita. *Fasting, Feasting*. London: Chatto and Windus, 1999.

Ghosh, Amitav. *The Glass Place*. London: Harper Collins, 2001.

Hariharan, Githa. *The Thousand Faces of Night*. New Delhi: Viking, 1992.

Khilanani, Sunil. *The Idea of India*. London: Hamish Hamilton, 1997.

Lal, Malashri. *The Law of the Threshold: Women Writers in Indian English*. IIAS (1995), 2000.

Mehta, Gita. *Snakes and Ladders: A View of Modern India*. London: Minerva, 1997.

Roy, Arundhati. *The God of Small Things*. New Delhi: India Ink, 1997.

Rushdie, Salman. *Midnight's Children*, New York: Knopf, 1981.

Satchidanandan, K. *Indian Literature: Positions and Propositions*. New Delhi: Pencraft International, 1999.

Seth, Vikram. *An Equal Music*. London: Phoenix House, 1996.

—. *A Suitable Boy*. London: Phoenix House, 1993.

—. *The Golden Gate: A Novel in Verse*. London: Faber, 1986

Tharoor, Shashi. *From Midnight to Millennium*. New Delhi: Viking (Penguin) India, 1997.

9

Lost Dreams
Intizar Husain's Search For a Nation

Veena Singh

The partition of India took place on the basis of the two-nation theory (see Kaushik), yet it failed to fulfil the longing for a nation for several of its citizens. Partition, in itself, did not merely dislocate territories, populations and emotional anchorings, it also destroyed dreams and visions and led to a great deal of disillusionment. It divided families, relationships, traditions and languages. But Indians and Pakistanis have had to acknowledge the fact that 'nations' are not constituted merely by geographical boundaries or linguistic or religious identities but also by a shared cultural and historical past. What happens when these are divided?

Intizar Husain, an India born writer migrated to Pakistan at the time of partition. He had hoped that the 'experience of hijrat or emigration, would be a source of creativity and growth in the life of the new nation' (*Basti* xviii). But the longed for dream never materialised. His greatest fear was the loss of collective memory and identity. He also realized that the physical migration was not merely geographical but it was also an emotional upheaval and as a consequence damaged the very texture of life. A historical amnesia was in itself a deterrent to national growth. Husain's writings reflect the anguish of an individual who has lost everything without gaining anything, one who unable to take root in the shallow soil of the new homeland, recollects the past in order to sustain his inner being.

The dominant theme of almost all his work is concerned with the pain of dislocation. Of his stories "The City of Sorrow", "A Letter from India" and "An Unwritten Epic"[1] are ones which are obsessed with the sense of loss brought about by migration. Belonging has an inbuilt polarity of not belonging. In order to 'belong', to look forward there is the need to forget the past. As the past can neither be erased nor resurrected, 'belonging' becomes a process of self-alienation and in some measure self annihilation.

In the story "The City of Sorrow" the three nameless men, metaphorically dead and all three dislocated after partition, through their conversation, bring out the poignant sorrow of migration. One of the men observes that the people who leave their country and go to live in far off places to build homes "like descendents of Israel" just wander in the wilderness. Another remarks "... old man, have you noticed that the earth never accepts those who leave their homeland?" The third man responds, "... I have learnt that from experience, I have seen that with my own eyes, the earth does not forgive" (Bhalla II: 91). The story narrated by the third man and his comment, "Instead of getting lost in the cities of torment, it is better for a man to disappear into some dark and dense forest" (II: 97) attests that for the uprooted there is no coming back. It can never be a homecoming. The feeling of alienation will always be there. The story ends on the dismal note, "Those who have been uprooted can never find a place where they can flourish again" (II: 99) and all that is left for them is to realize this and reconcile to their sense of disillusionment with the new country.

"An Unwritten Epic" also depicts how the dislocated can never strike roots. Pichwa, the protagonist of this story, moves to Pakistan after the partition, in the hope of discovering a new land of joy, happiness and opportunity, beyond the present misery and beyond self-contempt. But ends up becoming "an important political issue" (Bhalla III: 73). Imran Miyan, In "A Letter From India", behaves some what differently from Pichwa. Unable to resist the call of home, he, after migrating to Pakistan, sneaks back to India, to visit his parents. The visit to India disillusions him for he realizes that the familiar has now become unfamiliar. The process of recognition becomes difficult as the visual memories appear deceptive. The father also takes some time to recognize his son. The soil where he was born and was a part of, no longer recognizes him. His desire to visit the ancestors' graves is perhaps what gives him a sense of belonging to the land. The same idea is reiterated in his novel *Basti*. Zakir's Abba Jan is disturbed about the condition of the graves of his ancestors in India. He sadly recollects the arrangements that he had made for his own burial: "The shroud was ready" and he had chosen a place for his grave. Now in Pakistan, the new country, "But here there's no arrangement" (*Basti* 149). Thus the land, graves, place, ancestral houses become a vibrant metaphor and indicate continuity despite change.

Imran ("A Letter...") visits the graves only after the sun has set. He is afraid to move out during the day as he is now an illegal entry in the country of his birth. On one hand if the country of his birth gives him an identity on the other hand it also withholds it. In the annihilation of his identity lies his security. He is left with no choice but to go away for the second time. The sense of non-belonging is almost a permanent state of being for both: Imran is disillusioned by his visit to India and Pichwa is disillusioned by his visit to Pakistan. Naim Miyan scolds Pichwa, "Everyone just marches into Pakistan expecting to get something, as if his father had buried a treasure here. They just don't realize that there isn't that much room in Pakistan" (III: 69). Pichwa fondly continues to believe that if he beseeched any zamindar "Muslim brother" in the name of Allah and the Prophet Muhammad he would give him a small bit of land. Pichwa, a Muslim, is an outcaste amongst the Muslims. It becomes evident that religion or communal identity is not what matters but it is the economic struggle which determines their position. The order that refugees who had come to Pakistan "Can damn well go back to India" infuriates Pichwa and more so the official data that the "Muslims in India are doing fine" (III: 71).

A crestfallen Pichwa returns to India only to die. Pichwa had wished to adopt and rehabilitate himself in the new country but the country does not accept him. In the new country his status is that of an 'outsider', an outcaste, a refugee and there is no place for refugees like Pichwa in the new country. The same idea about the unacceptability in the new country is echoed in 'A Letter from India.' Chacha Karban Ali is told, "Pakistan had declared that the Mirzayis were non-Muslims" (I:81). Both Pichwa and Imran Miyan return to the land of their birth as captives carrying their own corpses. For them and their likes there is the anguish of erasure and separation.[2]

The familiar power struggle between the 'haves' and 'have nots' persists and the narrator with the help of the embedded story illustrates it in "An Unwritten Epic", "how the land shrinks, how food becomes scarce..." thus reiterating how the political system in the new country, with the new power centre and the new heroes is manipulated. A poor man like Pichwa, like a chess piece, is shunted between two squares.

In Pakistan, Pichwa is like an uninvited, unwelcome guest. His sense of 'honour' and 'pride' do not allow him to accept the government's offer to pay for his return to India. Disillusioned Pichwa returns to India only to find that the 'place' where he was hailed as 'Ustad', where he wielded authority and power over his band of followers and where he had hoisted an Islamic flag on the Peepal tree by the Idgah is no more the same.

Subedar's letter from India to the narrator in Pakistan highlights this changed scenario. The letter informs the narrator that Qadirpur is no more Qadirpur. The new residents now call it Jatunagar and they do not appear to understand the old familiar language, Urdu. The writer's deliberate hint that Urdu was projected as the language of Muslims and Hindi was identified with Hindustan strikes at the hollowness of the fact that linguistic divide can be a defining feature of a nation, moreover, can a language be a preserve of a certain religion or community? Or can a language also migrate with the division of a country?

Furthermore, the letter says that there is neither the wrestling arena nor the weaver's mosque, nor that old store owned by Allah Razi. The old group of people like Tidda and others, who flew their own flags on the Peepal tree by the Idgah with Pichwa are all gone. Pichwa returns to this changed and now unfamiliar place. He realizes that his 'place' has been erased from the new map.

Pakistan is "an imagined community" for Pichwa. It is difficult for him to comprehend that "Qadirpur where he lived, could be outside Pakistan". If Pakistan has excluded him he "imagined" he would with his friends "create" his own separate Pakistan for communities existed only in an abstract manner (Anderson 6). The formation of Pakistan is important only as long as it gave him, "a chance to display his skill with the club publicly." The news about the creation of Pakistan chills him because "... it was not his blood that had helped build this empire" (III:66).

Naim Miyam had migrated to Pakistan when he sensed trouble brewing between the two communities in India. Pakistan is his country. It promises safety. His son Azhar Miyan gets a job in the Rehabilitation Department and he is hopeful that his other son Owais Miyan too will find a job soon.

In Pakistan he is amongst the privileged influential people and condescendingly talks to the refugees from India. Like Naim Miyan, Kamaran ("Letter...") too is happily established in Pakistan. He has what he had longed for, and didn't have in India. Contrasted to Kamaran the author of the letter, Kurban Ali, continues to live on in India – the land of his ancestors. But he is faced with acute financial hardships. The old haveli of his ancestors is falling apart for want of funds. Despite several hearings in the court the case regarding the haveli is still pending.

Unlike the author of the letter the narrator of "An Unwritten Epic" is dislocated. He after migrating to Pakistan recounts the pre-partition days and the aftermath of partition. The distancing makes him see the reality. The "life" and people of Qadirpur become "a story." His memories are associated with the old place and now a sense of nostalgia. The eight hundred years' old history of that land is still very fresh in his mind. When in Pakistan, the ideals and beliefs of the idealistic narrator are at clash with the reality around him. The new nation that is born, he feels, is not fully realized and there is a gap between his dreams and hopes and the reality. The narrator sees "the whole nation being disgraced" (III:75). In such a state he feels "... how people can write with their eyes open... I have to write with my eyes closed." He confesses that his head is with him but his "heart is on strike" (III: 69). The newly created country with its political gambit, he is certain is not at all congenial to the creative process. In the narrator's words:

> Politics brings the same doom's day for the writer as the butcher does for the cow. The joke is that politics not only slaughters both literature and the writer, it's the one that eventually sets all the plaudits as well. (III: 73)

Pichwa haplessly looking for a job and a home in Pakistan and his eventual return makes the narrator lament, "People don't care about human emotions here – the mention of human emotions is still an afterthought" (III: 77). Since literature is closely connected with humanity and the narrator's country "doesn't value human beings," he would rather not "debase" his "creative talent and disgrace" his pen. The disruption and uprooting makes the narrator think that a new history has to be written. Of course a rich man's tale cannot be written and therefore it has to be a "Jumhurnama" – a story told about all and not a "Shahnama" (III: 68). Pichwa is the archetypal common man, so only a story like his can be written. He is the symbol of the fractured identity and the desperate experience of homelessness.

The story of the nation's degradation comes full circle, when a flour mill abandoned by its Hindu owners is allotted to the narrator with the help of Naim Miyan. The narrator ultimately reconciles to his situation in Pakistan and identifies with the nation. The allotment of the flour mill makes him feel "a responsible citizen," a dutiful member of a rising nation. Work and a livelihood give him a sense of belonging. He no more feels "cut off" (III: 78). What to him was "this new country" till the diary entry of 20 May 1950 becomes "My nation" by 29 May 1950. The allotment also underlines how material interest wins over ideals. As long as the narrator was just a creative writer with his dreams, hopes and idealism, identification with the new country was difficult. This feeling of alienation ends as the artist in him adjusts to the stark realities around him. "The City of Sorrow", as already pointed out, also ends on a note of acceptance of the nation. If a new nation has to reconstruct itself, acceptance of its birth is essential.

"An Unwritten Epic" is divided into two sections, the first depicts the prowess of Pichwa and the partition of the country and the second section comprises of 21 diary excerpts. The two sections of the story symbolically correspond to the division of the country and the gaps of several days between the jottings in the diary evoke in a sense the story of the nation. Writing a diary is not only a self-confession but it is self-confrontation as well. Also writing a diary helps to stabilize the self and retain sanity. Thus, the narrative form and the story of the nation inform each other in a complex and reflexive way.

Interestingly if one story is in a diary form, the story, "The City of Sorrow" is in the form of the conversation among three men and the third "A Letter from India" is a letter written to a relative in Pakistan by an anxious father. A letter unlike a diary is a way of communicating with others and overtly reaching out to them. But certainly this letter by Kurban Ali is much more than a letter. There is recollection of the past. It has elements of both a dialogue and a debate. The writer, through the letter captures history and also a sense of loss, as the new nation has new tradition and new values. In the "Letter" the concern for history is evident. In fact writing a diary is in itself recording history and time. The story works at multiple levels, it recapitulates Muslim religious history and gender history. Also, in the course of the letter, personal history gets entangled with national history. "The family tree has been lost..." and "A family which has once broken apart can never be united again" (I: 88) writes Kurban Ali. Allegorically the tree is the nation.

Intizar Husain believed that the formation of Pakistan may have been a political necessity but it was not a logical outcome of cultural differences. Indian nationalism worked along a larger notion of the nation, that was above the difference in the two religions. Muslims were also a part of the Indian nation. Hindus and Muslims lived together within a homeland but with the partition the concept of the Indian nation shrank. Intizar Husain in his stories emphasizes the qualities which go to make a nationhood, "The fact of sharing, in the past, a glorious heritage... or the fact of having suffered, enjoyed and hoped together" (Renan 19). He deliberately makes use of the Hindu myths like 'Mahabharat' in "An Unwritten Epic" or refers to the joint celebration of festivals like 'Baisakhi' or makes it a point to mention 'the Peepal near the Idgah' or the harshringar, the flowers of which are offered to gods by the Hindus, being a favourite tree of Miyan Jani, only to emphasize that Hindus and Muslims are constructed as a category that always belonged to one country. The depiction of shared customs and commonalities in the two communities is an evidence of the discourse which emphasized pre-partition Hindu Muslim unity and the fact that the author belonged to India, that had a composite and syncretic culture. It was with the division of the country that the Muslim/Hindu community was viewed as the other by each one of them.

Thus we see how these stories forcefully raise several questions like how does the nation define itself? Where is home? Where does Imran Miyan belong? To whom does Pakistan belong? Do demarcated territories make a nation? In "An Unwritten Epic" Qadirpur is in India. Pakistan is Naim Miyan's and the narrator's country. But contrasted to this when Pichwa comes back to India and dies, India is referred to as his "former country." Where is then Pichwa's home? The pertinent question as to where does one belong stares one in the face.

Also the Subedar Sahib from India, writes to the narrator in Pakistan, "We are not strangers we are from the same place you are" (III: 77). In one stroke the territorial boundary of the two nations is diffused. India, Pakistan, Qadirpur, Jatunagar, where are these? Is then a nation only a state of mind? (Renan 19).

Similarly in "A Letter from India" the graves of the ancestors of Kurban Ali are in India. The family disperses across several territories but can such territorial divisions sever roots? Or erase memories and shared cultural history? Another very crucial issue closely linked with the nation is the self. How is the self defined? What happens to Pichwa's identity? Is the self annihilated or constructed in the event of dislocation?

Husain's constant questioning of these issues comments upon the agonizing reality of life where the individual is drawn towards the future but is unwilling to sever relationships with the past, where disruptions destroy instead of leading to new pastures. Dreams are meant for dreaming, fulfillment remains a distant and an unachievable goal.

Endnotes

1. These stories are included in the three volumes, *Stories About the Partition of India* (ed) Alok Bhalla, New Delhi, Indus, 1994.
2. Mushirul Hasan, in the introduction of *Indian Partitioned: The Other Face of Freedom*, New Delhi. Roli Books, 1995, 1997 2 vols., writes "In fact 'India' and 'Pakistan' were mere territorial abstractions to people who had no sense of the newly demarcated frontiers, and little or no knowledge of how Mountbatten's Plan or the Radcliffe Award would change the destinies of millions and tear them apart from their social and cultural moorings (I: 34-35).

References

Anderson, Benedict. *Imagined Communities: Reflections on the Origin and Spread of Nationalism.* New York: Verso, 1983.

Bhalla Alok. "Introduction", *Stories About the Partition of India*. (3 volumes, reprint in 1 volume). New Delhi: Indus 1999.

Bhalla, Alok. ed. *Stories About the Partition of India*. New Delhi: HarperCollins, 1994: 3 Volumes.

Hasan, Mushirul. *India Partitioned: The Other Face of Freedom*. 2 vols. New Delhi: Roli Books, 1995 and 1997.

Husain, Intizar. "A Letter From India", *Stories About the Partition of India*. Ed. Alok Bhalla, 3 vols. Vol. I. 1994.

—. "The City of Sorrow", *Stories About the Partition of India*. Ed. Alok Bhalla, 3 vols. Vol. II. 1994.

—. "An Unwritten Epic", *Stories About the Partition of India*. Ed. Alok Bhalla, 3 vols. Vol. III. 1994.

Husain, Intizar. *Basti* trans. Frances W. Pritchett. New Delhi: Harper Collins, 1995.

Kaushik, S.N. "The Two-Nation Theory and the Genesis of Pakistan, *South Asian Studies*, Jan.-Dec., 1976.

Renan, Ernest. "What is a Nation?" *Nation and Narration*. Ed. Homi Bhabha. London: Routledge, 1990.

10

Imperial Narratives
Dislocation and Power in Moodie and Duncan

Supriya Agarwal

Making use of location, history and time in its narration, Susanna Moodie's *Roughing It in the Bush or Life in Canada* (1862) and Sarah Jeannette Duncan's *The Simple Adventures of a Memsahib* (1893) reconstruct the story of dislocation and power in two entirely different ways. The two – that is migration to Canada and Australia and short spells of governance in the colonies – worked different at political and psychological levels. The Imperial dislocation which mainly occurred from the early to the late nineteenth century can be classified as that of the settler on one hand and of colonizers on the other. Families migrated to Canada in 1830s and later, when westward Canada became the great landmark for the rich in hope and the poor in purse. During the same time period the imperialists were spreading their rule over India, contesting power in the political and mercantile world. No doubt, better prospects, spirit of adventure and lure for money were obvious reasons for both to leave their homeland and both experienced the pain of dislocation but while the settler was completely uprooted the colonist was anchored and had roots in the homeland. In one case there is a new home waiting and has to be built with effort and labour and on the other there is the certainly of power but both processes have to negotiate with loneliness and isolation.

Both the works begin with accounts of travel on a ship and from there begins the dislocation – a moving out of familiar surroundings – necessitating a total readjustment with the outer world. *Roughing It in the Bush* is a first person narrative by the protagonist Susanna who has sketched her own experiences of emigration to Canada, accompanied with adventure and hardships for the new settler. With great effort and deliberation Moodie has given us minute details of the journey, the sense of loss and nostalgia for the homeland, the fascination for the new land and the practical problems which hinder them now and then. She relates the difficulties of bringing up the family and managing affairs in the absence of her husband and the gradual settlement after a lot of effort and labour.

The Simple Adventures of a Memsahib is a third person narration which gives an account of Miss Helen Peachey, the daughter of a clergyman who gets engaged to Mr. Browne posted in the Mackintyre Company in Calcutta. She comes to India, marries Mr. Browne and gains the status of "a memsahib" a dignity which is arrived to "through circumstances, processes and sometimes through foresight on the part of one's mama" (56). Mrs. Browne is introduced to the world of the Englishmen in India with their trail of *ayahs, khansama's, malli's, ticca gharvi's* and *burra khanna* as a necessity of the lofty state of their oriental existence. Rebecca Saunders in her article "Gender Colonialism and Exile: Flora Annie Steel and Sara Jeannette Duncan in India" reflects on this issue:

> In some deep sense, the British in India during British rule felt themselves to be in exile. The condition of exile resulted in people divided against themselves.... Much of the pressure of maintaining a balance between the needs so that imperialism could function properly was on the women. Not only did women have the problem of reconciling this conflict within themselves, they also had to take on the burden for men and for the culture at large. (304)

For Miss Peachey it is a matter of celebration to go to India and her family spends six months to collect reliable information and prepare a trousseau for Helen. India, to the imagination of the local English inhabitants was a vast sandy area filled with heathens and fringed with coconut trees which drew a great many young Englishmen away from their homes and their families "for some occult purpose connected with drawing pay in rupees" (14). Not only this, those like Mrs. Macdonald who had been to India, convince Miss Peachey's mother that "she will be sure to like it, everybody likes it. I'm devoted to India" (16). In fact Anglo-Indians saw themselves as the standard bearers of civilization. Their mission was to impose the order of their culture on the chaos of India but often the reasons for their presence in India were less than altruistic. Some came to escape poverty, overcrowded families, and unemployment in England and others came for adventure and for the challenge of exciting work. Fostering the cult of home was only one way in which wives and mothers eased the tensions and contradictions. Writers have focused amply on the Anglo Indian life. E.M. Forster's picture of the small-minded pompous Anglo-Indian in *A Passage to India* remains our dominant image of them while George Orwell in *Burmese Days* has also reflected on the role of the memsahib. Of Elizabeth he writes "She has an exhaustive knowledge of the civil list, gives charming little dinner parties and knows how to put the wives of subordinate officials in their place – in short, she fills with complete success the position for which nature had designed her from the first, that of a burra memsahib" (244).

But for Susanna Moodie who was shifting to Canada things were different, the ordinary motive being to better their condition and of escaping from the vulgar sarcasms too often hurled at the less wealthy by the purse proud. Commonplace people of the world, they went forth to make for themselves a new name and to find another country, to forget the past and to live in the future. To exult in the prospect of their children being free and the land of their adoption great. Trying to re-establish their identities by getting attached to the land, trying to cultivate it and metaphorically getting roots for themselves. Moodie and her husband work hard and it is for the first time they try their hand at field labour as their ready money gets exhausted. Moodie writes:

> I had a hard struggle with my pride before I would consent to render the least assistance on the farm but reflection convinced me that I was wrong – that Providence had placed me in a situation where I was called upon to work – that it was not only my duty to obey that call, but to exert myself to the utmost to assist my husband, and help to maintain my family. (352)

Thus it was a period of trial and exertion for the settler whereas in *The Simple Adventures of a Memsahib* Helen Browne's husband had a salary of rupees 500 a month – a considerable amount for a comfortable living alongwith which they enjoyed a established power of an imperialist – the white man. Mr. Sayter, an English gentleman, while talking to friends confides ironically "And for the misfortune of living in a country where I get my boots put on, I'm paid twice as much as I would be in England, and three times as much as I'm worth. Monstrous isn't it?" (198).

But although the colonizer has all power with him, he has the extra burden to maintain the imperialistic image of the white race and thus cannot be his/her true self. If the sahib took care of the sterner side of imperialism, the memsahib found herself in charge of the domestic arrangements. Her share of the responsibility is two fold, including both home and empire. She as a wife who is already confined to a secondary role, is doubly burdened, with this obligation. Mrs. Browne who has a love for languages earns her husband's disapproval when she starts speaking more of Hindustani to the servants in the house and she then never spoke a word of Hindustani again, so as not to displease her husband. The life of exile these memsahibs lived, even when it did not restrict them to the confines of the group, limited them by the conventions of the imperialist mentality. They had an interest in keeping the empire going, in perpetuating the relationship between colonizer and colonized. Duncan's work illustrates the depth of emotional exploitation felt by women in colonial experience.

The challenge in the writings of these women writes is that they cast local experience of settlers in a new land on to a universal scale at a time when their voices and views were generally left unrecorded and unacknowledged. They have also shifted the focus from men's problems to the sphere of home and hearth, exhibiting woman's sacrifice, tolerance and hard work which makes possible the settlement of the migrated family. *Roughing It in the Bush* is a pioneer story of settlement in a new land which establishes the theory of nation construction as explored by Homi K. Bhabha in *Nation and Narration*. We understand that a nation is constituted by the feeling of the sacrifices that one has made in the past and those that one is prepared to make in the future and origin of national traditions turn out to be as much acts of association and establishment as they are moments of displacement, exclusion and cultural assertions. The new identity achieved after dislocation is both complex and empowering and it can be considered as a process rather than a fixed, unitary, monolithic identity. Stuart Hall in his essay "Cultural Identity and Diaspora" says that identity is not an already accomplished fact, "it is a production which is never complete, always in process and always constituted within, not outside" (392).

In fact when people migrate, they build on their previous history and culture, taking and leaving, borrowing from and adding on to them. Thus identity becomes crosscultural or transcultural rather than fragmented, schizophrenic or hybridized. In the two types of dislocations which I have examined, not only is the attitude different but also the motives and experiences. Although in both cases memory and nostalgia plays a great role. Moodie records:

> the homesickness was sore upon me and all my solitary hours were spent in tears. My whole soul yielded itself up to a strong and overpowering grief. One simple word dwelt for ever in my heart and swelled it to bursting – "Home!" I repeated it waking a thousand times a day and my last prayer before I sank to sleep was still Home! (89)

Even Mrs. Helen Browne gradually gets bonded with the new home and stabilizes her identity as a memsahib. Cultural displacement as is conveyed by *The Simple Adventures of a Memsahib* involves the loss of language, family ties and social milieu. The confrontation of the Anglo-Indians with the oriental culture is sharp. Helen Browne finds herself confronted with "her little domestic corner of the great problem of India-the natives way" (86). But she had no language with which to circumvent it or remonstrate with it. Moodie in the Bush also encounters varied experiences which in the beginning are difficult for her to comprehend and accept, for example, the system of borrowing which was prevalent among the natives. Moodie records "Day after day I was tormented by this importunate creature, she borrowed of me – tea, sugar, candles, torch, blueing, irons, pots, bowls – in short every article in common domestic use while it was with utmost difficulty we could get them returned" (185). In the beginning she finds everything new, strange and distasteful. "We shrank from the rude, coarse familiarity of the uneducated people among whom we were thrown, and they in turn viewed us as innovators"(202).

Convention regarded women as weak and dependent while men were considered the explorers and settlers but these literary works portray a realistic picture of two different nations where the female protagonist works as the backbone behind the successful man settler and the dislocated family. In each of these literary works the author has a double focus. On the one hand they have raised issues about female identity and solidarity and at the same time successfully reconstructed the story of dislocation and power. Gabrielle Colu while talking about multiculturalism in her essay, "South Asian Women Writers in North America" says that "people react actively and critically in relation to other cultures and that their incorporation and adoption of certain cultural traditions or beliefs are more complex and reflective than is suggested by terms such as mimicry, schizophrenia or hybridity"(61). Thus we can conclude that empowerment consists in creating a new identity that allows the dislocated to identify with the culture that they live in without entirely abandoning the values and traditions of the culture of origin but finding a way to combine the two cultures and experiences.

References

Bhabha, Homi K. *Nation and Narration*. (1990). London: Routledge, 1991.

Colu, Gabrielle. "South Asian Women Writers in North America". *The Literature of the Indian Diaspora: Essays in Criticism*. Ed. A.L. Macleod. Sterling Publishers: Delhi, 2000.

Duncan, Sara Jeannette. *The Simple Adventures of a Memsahib*. D. Appleton and Company: New York,1983.

Forster, Edward Morgan. *A Passage to India*. (1924). Harmondsworth: Penguin Books, 1980.

Hall, Stuart. "Cultural Identity and Diaspora". *The Literature of the Indian Diaspora: Essays in Criticism*. Ed. A.L. Macleod. Sterling Publishers: Delhi, 2000.

Moodie, Susanna. *Roughing It in the Bush,* or *Life in Canada*. (1852). McClelland and Stewart: Ontario,1993.

Orwell, George. *Burmese Days* (1934). Penguin Books: London, 1989.

Saunders, Rebecca. "Gender Colonialism, and Exile: Flora Annie Steel and Sara Jeannette Duncan in India", *Women's Writing in Exile*. Chapel Hill: University of North Carolina Press, 1989.

11

Memory and Aesthetics
A Study of Margaret Atwood's *The Blind Assassin*

Sudha Shastri

The Blind Assassin (*BA* 2000) by Margaret Atwood contains a(nother) novel within its covers, also called 'The Blind Assassin'; thereby, already, diffusing identity in uncertain terms. Within the first-level novel is the memoir of Iris Chase Griffen, an old woman at the time of her writing. Her memoir is interrupted and enlarged with excerpts from the second-level novel, written ostensibly by her sister, Laura Chase, as well as from newspaper reports (*BA* 3, 14, 19, 24, 108, 113, 258, 273, 347, 357, 403, 410, 455, 456, 519) an alumni bulletin (31) and a letter from a doctor (405-406), which gives the impression that the presiding genius of the larger novel BA, is someone other then Iris herself.

Counterpoised with Iris's memoir is Laura's novel (called, as I have already said, 'The Blind Assassin'), which is a gory – if incredible – story of the rites and practices of a society hardened to cruelty and violence. Of more interest to a reader is the framework of this story, which consists of a series of clandestine meetings between a man and a woman, who has only a pronoun each for identity. The horrific tale of 'The Blind Assassin' is told by the 'He' (Alex Thomas, as we shall shortly figure out) to 'Her' (presumably Laura). As this story weaves in and out of Iris's own autobiographical recollections, the reader's interest accrues because the memoir chronicles the lives of both the sisters, Iris and Laura.

Since one of the initial responses provoked by Laura's novel is one of curiosity relating to the identity of the protagonists, Iris's memoir seems to offer itself, at least initially, as a clue-finder of sorts, to see what facts match and how. Iris relies heavily on memory to tell her eventful tale. As Iris's memoir unfolds, however, it befuddles rather than clarifies, since to a reader predisposed to 'find' things, the 'She' in the frame-tale appears capable of standing in for Iris (as well as Laura). And finally on page 512 (of a 513-page novel) Iris categorically discloses to her reader that the author of 'The Blind Assassin' is not her sister Laura but herself. By now the reader has already suspected as much, and has even received proof of sorts earlier, when Iris confesses to Laura that she and Alex have been lovers (488), a disclosure that drives her distraught sister to suicide.

The Role of Memory in Postmodernism

Memory is an already present 'given' in all narratives. The use of the past tense almost ubiquitously in storytelling, is born of the premise that the events have already happened, they are set in the past, and they are recalled through memory. Such an understanding of the storytelling process also assumes that the events of the past are fixed in a way that events in the present are not, that they are safely protected from the sort of fluidity which the present suffers from; or if you want to look at it from another perspective, that these events are denied an openness of possibilities that the present offers. The fixed nature of the past enacted in story-telling is viewed as a virtue from a pre-post-modern/realistic perspective.

Postmodernism of course challenges and subverts many of these assumptions, and *Blind Assassin* is one of those postmodern novels where this realistic assumption is sabotaged through the (mis)use of memory, the most fundamental of all tools in recalling the past. For a novel like *BA* this is a truly metafictional challenge to make. It is a challenge to the security and trust tacitly implied in all novels (particularly in the realistic tradition) narrated in the first person, and written – necessarily – from memory. The sense of authorial integrity that the first person conveys is eroded by Iris in her memoir in a subtle fashion; for she does not exactly lie, but lets a misleading fact stay without troubling to put the record straight till the end (she, i.e., lets the reader believe that the heroine of the second-level novel is Laura). Never in the memoir does she talk about her writing of the novel, except at the very end.

The use of memory to defeat its own fundamental premise (which is to bring the past back into focus with a clarity of outline) is, appropriately enough, achieved in the memoir, the genre most fitted to execute this fundamental premise. Iris recalls her past in the memoir in chapter after chapter. That a definite process of recall is at work is also made apparent to the reader, for most of the chapters of the memoir begin with a description of Iris's present surroundings, and then go consciously back to the past, in the manner of picking up threads from where they were left off.

There is more to come. In manipulating her record of the past, Iris sabotages more than one identity. While the reader considers her claim that she and not Laura is the author of 'The Blind Assassin', yet it becomes difficult for the reader to entirely discount Laura's presence as author-heroine too. Instead of the memoir replacing Laura with Iris, it simply throws doubt about either heroine being the sole presence in 'The Blind Assassin'.

The memoir becomes an important presence because Atwood juxtaposes Laura's novel with Iris's memoirs thereby destabilising the identity of the heroine in 'The Blind Assassin', whom all readers, including Richard, the husband of Iris, have taken to be Laura. It must not escape observation, therefore, that it is the larger novel, containing the memoir, that encourages the reader to observe that memory can be unreliable.

How Deliberate is this Misuse of Memory?

In Iris's defence, considering her advanced age, it can be maintained that her span of recall is very vast, and thus, she can be forgiven for occasional lapses of memory. She also shows evidence (besides drawing attention to her age and its attendant ills) of memory giving way. So for example:

> Where was I? *It was winter*. No, I've done that.
> It was spring. The spring of 1936. (368)

Here and elsewhere we find the tentativeness that is characteristic of a failing memory. But it is not an occasional tentativeness, or one which strives for the effect of Realism. For 500 pages the reader grapples with this tentativeness of identity that fails to distinguish between Iris and Laura. In fact, a good part of the reading experience consists of finding the answer to the question, is this Laura? Or is it actually Iris? I shall deal with the way in which this issue is negotiated, shortly.

To attribute Iris's strategy (of withholding the fact that Laura was the author of 'The Blind Assassin') to failing memory, is, thus, to be guilty of gross misreading. Her motive for keeping the fact back is surely not to create suspense; nor is it modesty which prompts her to declare, without a trace of apology or defensiveness, "As for the book, Laura didn't write a word of it. But you must have known that for sometime" (512). She adds: "I wrote it myself, during my long evenings alone, when I was waiting for Alex to come back, and then afterwards, once I knew he wouldn't" (512).

It is not however the intent of this paper to examine Iris's motives. Let us rather look at the effect of such a strategy.

What is significant, interesting, if you like, is that this candid declaration does not provide a satisfactory tying up of the threads that cross through the double-identity of the heroine of Laura Chase's novel. Despite Iris's assertion, it becomes impossible for the reader to replace Laura with Iris as the heroine of 'The Blind Assassin'. The problems that lie herein are partially created by Iris herself.

In the course of her memoir itself, Iris has raised the question, "is what I remember the same thing as what actually happened?" (217). The context is the hiding of Alex Thomas by the two sisters in the attic of their house. One day, when Laura is out of the house, Iris goes up to the attic and before she knows it, Alex is kissing her. In a kind of gnomic/generic present Iris reflects: "Had I expected this? Was it so sudden, or were there preliminaries: a touch, a gaze? Did I do anything to provoke him? Nothing I can recall, but is what I remember the same thing as what actually happened?" (217). In fact Iris defines memory in such a way that it gives her the power to reinvent herself and events the way she chooses to. Here is the answer she gives the above question, "is what I remember the same thing as what actually happened?" (217): "It is now: I am the only survivor" (218).

Memory is anyway unreliable; added to age, but what is worse, added to guile, it can be positively slippery. Yet the reader's impulse is to extract certainty out of a text that exploits the loopholes provided by memory to play tricks on the reader. This tension between the reader's desire for certainty and the text's teasing array of mutually contradictory meanings constitutes much of the brilliance of *BA*.

It is eventually Atwood – the overseeing author of the various levels of *BA* – who destroys the single-persona identity of the heroine of Chase's novel. But there is no doubt that she needs Iris to accomplish this design. So that, at the end of the novel, the reader is even more puzzled by the identity of the 'She' in 'The Blind Assassin' than she was before Iris's disclosure. It is a paradox of *BA* that after categorically disclosing the identity of the lady lover, it ensures that the reader is put into doubt about this identity – about the credentials of the narrator who fixes this identity. Memory, or so is the implication, gives licence for dislocation and a margin for error.

Public and Private Memory (the devices)

The presence of the newspapers adds to the role of memory in *BA*, as repositories of public memory. Also, the news excerpts inserted into the narratives provide a renewed glimpse of the public life of the Chases and the Griffens.

> Where am I? *It was winter*. No, I've done that.
>
> It was spring. The spring of 1936. That was the year everything began to fall apart. Continued to fall apart, that is, in a more serious fashion than it was doing already.
>
> King Edward abdicated in that year. He chose love over ambition. No. He chose the Duchess of Windsor's ambition over his own. That's the event people remember. And the Civil War began, in Spain. But those things didn't happen until months later. What was March known for? Something. Richard rattling his paper at the breakfast table, and saying, *So he's done it*.
> (368).

The newspaper is faithful to detail, but its bland tone gives the lie to the various seething emotions behind the events it so blandly describes. The character-sketch of Richard as presented in his obituary notice in *The Globe and the Mail* for instance (14) is at variance with the man, as we know him from the memoirs of Iris. Similarly, the report of Laura's escapade in *The Toronto Star* (258) is another instance where the public record is completely different from the private. The presence of these reports alongside the memoir, enriches the postmodern identity of *BA*, with the two forms of memory at variance with each other in factual detail, and thus creating tension.

Who is 'She'?

The author of 'The Blind Assassin' tantalises her reader with this question, best exemplified in the following instance. The hero of 'The Blind Assassin' reflects on his lover's name somewhere in the middle of the novel, as having "an electric aura circling it – a sexual buzz like blue neon" (275). Speculation can be endless whether it is the name 'Iris' or the name 'Laura' that has this quality.

I shall now take a closer look at the construction (destruction, perhaps, would be a more appropriate word) of the identity of the heroine in 'The Blind Assassin' through Iris's memoir. During the reading experience, almost progressively, Laura gives way to Iris as the heroine of 'The Blind Assassin'. Laura appears at the beginning by default thanks to 'public' information that she is the author of 'The Blind Assassin'. Things that point to Laura as the 'She', could become, in retrospective reading, things that are typical of Iris. Let me see if a trajectory can be traced of this progressive giving-(a)way.

There is the instance when the lover-hero asks 'her' how much time they have, to which she replies that they have a lot, for 'they' are all out. Doing what, he wants to know. "I don't know. Making money. Buying things. Good works. Whatever they do" (25). This could well be Laura speaking.

But well into the story, she reflects that "If caught, she would renounce him, before the cock crowed even once. She knows that plainly, calmly" (260). Betrayal would be unlikely where Laura is concerned; her instinct is supposed to lead her naturally to self-destruction, as events (including her suicide) eventually testify.

Here is ambivalence again, when she asks him if he is ever unfaithful to her. Evading a direct reply, he says, "No more than you are to me" (344-45). The answer is 'Yes' if it is Iris, and 'No' if Laura. Later on, he asks her: "Would you really leave? Would you leave him?" (360). If the reader has not been tempted to suspect that 'She' could be Iris, s/he could interpret this 'leaving' to mean, Laura leaving Richard's protection. After being told that Iris wrote the novel, this section of the dialogue makes a different sense, however. It also explains why the 'She' wonders what she would do for a living, which is something that would never occur to self-sustaining Laura. But there is really no comforting answer. For instance, at one juncture the hero refers to her as a "ruined maiden" (120). Of course being Alex, he could be merely mocking Iris. Yet the words literally apply to Laura rather than to Iris.

Even before Iris asserts (512) that it was she who authored 'The Blind Assassin', she has told Laura that she and Alex were lovers. But there are other hints too. At least one of them is a complete give-away. One of the books that Iris reads is *Perennials for the Rock Garden*. This title happens to form a part of the Prologue of 'The Blind Assassin', and it would be obvious to the reader that Laura could not have used it as a title, unless by a complete coincidence, since at that time she and Iris were almost completely out of touch.

And yet, a categorical picture is denied in the final analysis. Towards the end, 'The Blind Assassin' speaks of a telegram which arrives to the heroine, saying that 'he' is dead. She is amidst a group of people, presumably family, when she reads the telegram (466-67). It is likely that Richard is part of this group that consoles her. Since we are told that Richard has read the novel, it seems strange that he should not have realised after reading the novel, that his wife must have authored it. Yet he believes that Laura authored it. This is one instance perhaps of Atwood's ambition over-reaching itself, but in an otherwise flawless book it is tempting to find ways to get around this jarring note. A more positive argument to whether it could have been Laura (rather than Iris) is that we have been told in the memoir more than once that Iris finds sex distasteful. Consider this in the light of the fact that the lovers in 'The Blind Assassin' have a delightfully physical affair.

So it would seem that Iris's efforts to recall herself as the heroine of 'The Blind Assassin' has limited success, as she herself seems to recognise at the end. It is through memory that Iris superimposes herself on Laura as the heroine of 'The Blind Assassin' but memory, in the form of a photograph, turns the whole account into an Escher-like picture leaving the reader with the burden of understanding – but not knowing.

The Photograph

Apprehending the photograph as a symbol of man's acknowledgement of the value of the past as well as the blurring outlines of memory, Atwood imaginatively rests the answer to the question 'Who?' in a photograph.

The photograph is taken by Elwood Murray, and later Laura, who works briefly as his apprentice, steals the negative and makes two prints out of it. She makes different copies for Iris and herself, by cutting away the other sister's figure from each sister's copy of the photo. However, each copy has the hand of the other sister at a corner "scissored off at the wrist" (5). Though two separate photographs are produced out of one, the two overlap (significantly enough) at the hand. It is the photo of Alex with Iris that emerges at the end of the novel, but as Iris herself says, "Laura was my left hand, and I was hers. We wrote the book together. It's a left-handed book. That's why one of us is always out of sight, whichever way you look at it" (513).

The photo of Alex Thomas and the two sisters is a central device that can be used to construct the identity of the lover-heroine as either of two. The supposition is imaginary rather than possible – but as Iris has already made it clear to us, imagination is a fairly palpable driving force in BA – in Laura, in Alex's stories, and in the larger novel BA itself.

The Prologue (4-5) as well as the Epilogue of 'The Blind Assassin' (517-518) dwell on this photo. In the Prologue, we are told that "There's a hand, cut by the margin, scissored off at the wrist, resting on the grass as if discarded. Left to its own devices" (5). The Epilogue is more specific: "in the lower left corner there's a hand, scissored off at the wrist, resting on the grass" (517). This is definitely Iris's copy as she was sitting on the left side of Alex Thomas.

And yet...

Memory and Tense

'The Blind Assassin' (the story within the novel) is a story in the making and one that completely abjures memory, for the 'He' is making up the story as it goes along, in collaboration with, and based on feedback from, his lover. It is 'oral', but (paradoxically enough) without resting on memory as oral narratives traditionally do. It is fabricated ex-tempore.

The novel written of the same story by Laura-turned Iris, however, is based on memory. Yet it casts both stories, the story of the lovers and the story they tell, in the present tense.

Moreover, 'The Blind Assassin' is not only about the composition of 'The Blind Assassin' by 'him', but also about its publication; in instalments, just as the story was told. Its publication by Alex has a purpose that is crucial to his lover. After he leaves her, she searches for the story in journals to make sure that he is still alive. It is a kind of code between them. But when she reads the first instalment she realises that the printed version is different from the story that was told to her. It has digressed from the main story line. Either memory has deserted Alex, or he has decided, for some reason, not to take the straight route according to memory. When 'She' reads up to the night before the sacrifice, she wonders, "But where is the blind assassin? What's become of him, and his love for the innocent girl? He must be keeping that part for later, she decides" (400). So the story takes other directions, and the part about the blind assassin and his dumb lover does not make it to print. Not by Alex. It is preserved? Created? In the memory of Alex's ladylove.

In Conclusion

> The thing I recall most clearly from the voyage, apart from Laura, was the looting that went on, all over the ship, on the day we sailed into port. Everything with the *Queen Mary* name or monogram on it went into a handbag or a suitcase....
>
> What was the rationale for all this pillaging? Souvenirs. These people needed something to remember themselves by. An odd thing, souvenir-hunting: *now* becomes *then* even while it is still now. You don't really believe you're there, and so you nick the proof, or something you mistake for it.
>
> I myself made off with an ashtray. (379)

The above excerpt from Iris's memoir is an appropriate place to end my paper, if only because it shows the ubiquitous importance that the past holds for people. Iris speaks nonchalantly, perhaps even flippantly, about the ashtray – but of course what she has created – her memoir – is of greater and more personal significance in preserving her memory for posterity. But her attempt to hold on to the past through her memoir has resulted instead in creating an alternative reality, a reality that alters the present crucially by confusing identity.

Reference

Atwood, Margaret. *The Blind Assassin*. London: Bloomsbury, 2000.

12

Journey into Memory
Signposts of Dislocation

Mini Nanda

Margaret Atwood[1] in her poem "Journey to the Interior", writes:

> Mostly
> That travel is not the easy going
> from point to point, a dotted
> Line on a map location
> plotted on a square surface
> but, that I move surrounded by a tangle
> of branches, a net of air and alternate
> light and dark, at all times;
> that there are no destinations
> apart from this.

Journeys signify a quest, a modernist yearning to locate and fall back to the mythical patterns. They signify a search for innocence in a world full of violence and death and brings out the opposition and conflict between them. Journeys originate from the loneliness and the restlessness of the individual, who is unwilling to be trapped within circumstances. In much the same manner a character in Jean Arasanyagam's[2] story "Sanctuary", says as she retraces her steps to her childhood home, that they are rootless people, who have set out on unplanned journey without maps, with only the signpost of memory left behind by the past travellers, who have vanished into the leafy canopies of the jungles.

Jean Arasanyagam in her beautiful collection of seven short stories entitled, *In the Garden Secretly*, laments the loss of the garden, blighted by ethnic strife. Written in a crystal clear and evocative style, she paints Sri Lanka, the country where she lives, in the verdant landscape and, in sharp strokes goes on to sketch the feral, volatile war zone that it has become.

Born into a Dutch Burgher family (minority community) and married to a Tamil Arasanyagam, is the inheritor of a rich cultural tradition, "I have suckled on a breast shaped by the genetics of history". In her five volumes of fiction and ten volumes of poetry, she lends her voice to the wounded muffled moans of her people and refers to herself as an outsider. She knows (and writes) from personal experience how the common people become targets of suspicion and hatred in troubled times. In the bloody riots of July 1983, this "Outsider" and her family became refugees.

> It's all happened before and will happen again
> And we the onlookers
> But now I am in it
> It's happened to me
> At last history has meaning.

To the young Sinhala soldier in the title story "Into the Garden" violence appears meaningless. The army from the south has come up to the Tamil North victorious, but there are no garlands for the leaders, no victory banners, no grateful people around. They are greeted with an eerie silence, abandoned homes and devastation, for all the people have fled. It unfolds the dilemma of the soldier/pilot who from the clouds above, looks down at the ordered pattern of the city. It is his duty to destroy that pattern, but how does he differentiate the ordinary man from the terrorist? Even the civilians have bunkers in their gardens, where they retreat once the bombing starts.

After the victory the army from the South hoists its flag with the ensign of the Lion. The North has its own flag with the image of the Tiger. And the authorial voice notes perceptively that the two beasts are in perpetual combat, forcing the people deeper into the jungle and each time the endangered species is man. This spells out the bitter North/South divide and the way it defines interpersonal relationships. The young soldier is confronted by the important question of exile. Are exiles only those who fled from their homes in a hurry, or is he an exile too, who has left his home and family behind? The pervading thoughts that nothing matters but life itself, and the pitiful realisation that return is never possible, for not only is the home abandoned but also all the people who made it. In snatches of songs he realizes that he would have to start all over again:

> How shall me sing the Lord's song in a strange land?
> We wept when we remembered Zion. (15)

It also poses a second important question, the question of faith:

> Our lives become meaningful now only if we think of them in terms of parables. There's the parable of the good Samaritan, why isn't there a parable of an ordinary soldier? (16)

The soldier finds his reality at odds with his faith, his mission involves death, which is against the principle of the Bible; and they seek to destroy not forgive the enemies. He wonders whether anyone remembers Christ who shed his blood for mankind? The broken statue of Christ left on the mantelpiece symbolises a fractured faith. The statue seems to shed light on all the dark years of war. It brings to mind of the young soldier, memory of his friend Pali, shot in the arm and in the foot, but who had crawled to safety through his own blood, his faith had kept him going.

In the end the soldier pockets the broker icon as a memento to be carried away, leaving his hands ironically free to hold the gun. The milieu presses upon his consciousness, he is connected to this place by the memory of his own home. In the abandoned house he is trapped by his individual perception. Where is the 'garden' which the soldier had entered by stealth? Everything lies in ruins. Even the palmyrah leave fences are ripped apart, "as if by gigantic hands" (3).

In "Search My Mind" we have the chilling picture of the army which takes over civilian life. At presents a sharp contrast of time as "then" and "now". Memory forms a link with the past for the University lecturer who remembers that campus gardens which were once alive with the scattering of young boys and girls, full of canna lillies and colias. Now through the barred college windows only the soldier's encampments can be seen.

The routine life of the English lecturer is disrupted, when soldiers peremptorily order all passengers to disembark from the bus and show their bags. No one dare question a man with a gun. She shows the contents of her shabby, well-worn leather bag – text books, *The Merchant of Venice* etc., some fifty cents and one rupee coin. She sadly wonders what the soldier expected to find in a bag of a middle-aged teacher, a time bomb? firearms?

Violence punctuates campus life as well, the inexplicable killing of the university officials is followed by macabre reprisals. The fifteen insurgents beheaded and "their heads arranged around the ornamental pond at the center of the University campus" (23). Tyres and bodies burn on the roadside, students are shot, buses are burnt in a vicious circle of attack and reprisals.

The teacher questions her own role of teaching literature to students who leave classes to tear down monuments of the past. They scrawl their messages and slogans on charred walls. She tries to find parallels and relevance to this reality in her lectures. Colleagues discuss their experience of the previous night, the gunshots and the dead lying blindfolded with their hands tried in the morning. The milkman routinely passes the bodies lying unclaimed. This fear is echoed by Seamus Heaney in the poem, "Whatever you Say, you Say Nothing," of "the bangs/That shake all hearts and windows day and night."

> Is there a life before death? That's chalked up.
> In Ballymurhy. Competence with pain,
> Coherent miseries, a bite and sup,
> We hug our little destiny again

Which leads to the tragic destiny of Ricardo, a young poet and theatre director, who gave a riveting, lecture on *The Merchant of Venice* to a packed audience. He spoke of the play and of their lives and times, which was as fragmented for them as for the Venetians. Ricardo was abducted from home one night, tortured and murdered. His bullet-ridden body was dropped into the sea from a helicopter, later washed ashore and discovered by a fisherman. As Margaret Atwood writes "that Plato excluded poets from the ideal republic, it seems modern dictators shoot them".

Reality impinges on fiction here as Meenakshi Mukherjee[3] writes that Ricardo can easily be identified with a real person called Ricardo de Zoysa, a dynamic young broadcaster, actor, poet and journalist from Colombo. Whose life had a similar tragic ending in 1990 when he was barely thirty-two, In his death he became almost a mythic figure.

As the soldier "In the Garden Secretly" wonders:

> Will the war ever be over? When? Will we live to be old men?.... Is the history of a small island like ours important to the rest of the world? .... Death is an everyday fact I live with. All of us are caught up in this vast obsession with death. (9)

In Jean Arasanayagam's stories life and literature interweave in a strange melange as words flow from pain and experience, it informs her works. As Margaret Atwood writes that an art created from a sense of obligation is likely to be static. Here it is poignant for it unfolds the frustrations, the goals and aspirations of the common man. There is a knock at the teacher's house at night, the door is tentatively opened and she sees her student Saman, wounded and bleeding, begging for shelter for a night, for he trusts only her. 'Madam', he pleads 'Madam you taught us remember *The Merchant of Venice...* "The quality of mercy is not strained" ' (31) and her college-going daughter steps forward to continue the lines that Saman seemed to be too weak to quote.

> It droppeth as the gentle dew from heaven
> Upon the place beneath. It is twice blessed... (32)

The family opens the door wider and stretch out their hands to help Saman in.

The "Quail's Nest" becomes a metaphor for the teacher's home, which is constantly under threat, for she had married one of the 'others' a Tamil, whish is clearly autobiographical. The story connects beautifully to a Jataka tale narrated in it. About the weak quail left alone in the nest in the incidence of forest fire, while all others had fled and the courageous manner in which the frail fledgling, does not quail before the raging fire:

> I am not strong enough to fly away, And my parents and brothers have fled from fear of you. *Agni*, god of fire, there is no gift here worth offering you. So I ask you in the name of Truth, for which I have lived and now live, to turn back. The ferocious fire stopped. (40)

Memory of this tale, is fragrant in the teacher's mind, for it was a memorable evening, when she and her husband were the distinguished guest of the organiser – a Muslim owner of joss-sticks. There was a blending of Sinhalese, Tamil, Muslim and others. Now the perfume had evaporated, the violent mobs were on the scent of every alien ransacking and burning their houses.

The teacher's child lies ill in bed, and becomes the symbol of an ailing state as well. Much like the quail she does not want to leave her home, in fact she arranges for the safe passage of her English friend. The turbulent times test friends and neighbours alike, who demonstrate rare courage in sheltering others.

She feels branded and hunted because her marriage to a Tamil and wonders if she had done right to expose her children to this threat. Nevertheless she resolves that escape would turn them into strangers to themselves. In the end she resumes her evening walks by the river in an effort to pick up the routine of life.

In "Sanctuary" the writer creates an oasis, an astonishingly serene pond amidst the surrounding dark dread of the jungles. She creates the cadence of natural peace and beauty, as she culls images from childhood memories of the women, long since dead and gone, would bathe in the pond in the still evening hours. The tangle of pink and white *nelun* flowers would tremble and move as the woman plunged in the water, it appeared as if the net of flowers, held the women in a thrall. It was truly a world of enchantment.

As Edward S Casey[4] summarises this way of remembering, where all experiences "leave their mark". Such experience come marked for memory and marked by memory. They are marked to be remarked, they are made to be remembered. Heidegger speaks of the human conditions as being on the way to language – on the way to marking, that as signing in the basis of language.

The sanctuary becomes a metonym for her childhood world. It was from her father that she had learnt to seek out this sanctuary, where she could feel the peace within. He taught her to listen to the language of the birds and imitate their calls, in an endeavour to become a part of nature. As A.K. Ramanujan[5] writes in "The Ring of Memory" that 'A name is a metonym, a part that stands for the whole, especially a part that can be detached from the original and carried everywhere to conjure up the original at will' (99).

Thus Sanctuary with its riot of flowers, signifies the safety and sweetness of home for the narrator. She would retreat here once in a while and feels both rooted and rootless at the same time. For as a city dweller she no more feels connected to any other land its people.

In "The Crossing" the same rootlessness confronts the young engineering student. He studies in the University in the South and crosses over to the North to meet family of a father and a sister. He thinks, "I couldn't spent the rest of my life here. I was young I had no intention of being a martyr to the cause.... I have responsibilities, things to do" (79). Such as to get a degree and join his brother in Switzerland, to arrange a marriage for his sister abroad. He feels the sharp North/South divide. In the North his family's life is cut off from the South. It is ruled by LTTE, fighting for a separate state from his people, leading to the displacement of thousands of people. But human imperatives prevail. Parents leave the North to see their children in the South. Just as he headed North, with no quays where he could disembark, he would wade through shoulder high water to reach home. Where an old man and a young girl shared their lives, half of which was spent in darkness. The evening would plunge in darkness, as there was no electricity, oil lamps were used and oil was a very precious commodity.

In the South in the University they were not separated by racial identities. The lived together in halls of residence, attended the same lectures, took the same examination and gained the same qualification. No one was seen as an outsider. For him the crossing over was from one life to another but "both are mine" (82) he realises the journey nevertheless is hazardous, in the dark, they are all anonymous travelers going into a greater anonymity. The stretch of water he crossed marked the formal separation of his two lives. He can renounce neither, he travels with his double identity. Even in the south at some level the students are divided their external oneness "cracking under the weight of history" (91).

Against the salt of the sea studying the peruses and cuts of his skin, the young engineer dreams of constructing bridges over the water and of roads that lead directly to destinations. In an enigmatic sweep he covers all travellers – the student, the pilgrim, the soldier, the militia and the terrorist. For he only sees the imperatives of their mission and no other distinction.

On the other hand there is the journey of the mother from the North to see her son in the South. As she enters a *kovil* (temple) en route and finds that the spirit of bhakti pervades the place, she hums the hymns familiar to her, and the place appears like a sanctuary. As the *kovil* gleams with a golden hue, she thinks of gold as a precious metal inseparably linked to womanhood and brides. Today the young girls use gold as "a new kind of chastity", to buy guns with or passages to the South.

For the mother, the young bride and the fierce warrior represent the aspects of the goddess as Siva Shakti – the great mother of the universe and Kali who seems more powerful in the present day world, where young girls use themselves as live explosions. As the times are fraught with danger, she remembers the Biblical Exodus, when the water of the Red Sea parted for the Israelites to cross to the other side. Perhaps the present crossing presages another crossing, which could come to pass in the future? In the *kovil* as the mother removes her wet clothes, she sloughs off her fear, hunger and thirst as well. She is filled with a strange calm, her body miraculously altered into one of the deities. It is her faith, which had given her the courage to face the passage through water, land and jungle yet again.

From the journey within a country, I would move to another, journey to yet another blighted garden; undertaken by Sonia Jabbar[6] to Kashmir in her non-fictional essay "Spirit of Place". Where she visits Kashmir, symbolically in autumn to a place poised between the 9th and the 14th century of Kashmir's rich past. In the glorious sunshine she encounters the spirit of optimism and resilience, that has kept a handful of Kashmiri pandits in the valley. Nurturing their old relationship with the Muslim in times of war, politics and mistrust. Jabbar witnesses the abiding presence of the deity Kheer Bhavani in the lives of the Kashmiri pandits.

The people in the refugee settlement in Jammu had created an exact replica of the deity, smaller than the original, but faithful in detail. The Holy Spirit out of which the original temple grew, is here replaced by a tank filled with water. Homelessness becomes a means of self-fashioning and self-definition through spiritual bonding. Sonia Jabbar writes evocatively that "they missed Kashmir so badly that they had tried to replicate it here, like children with their doll's houses" (5).

The narrator wonders as she watches the displaced people whether it is worse to lose a beloved, to lose a father or a son, or to lose one's entire universe? The Goddess herself as the legend goes had left Lanka appalled by Ravan's evil deeds and had flown with her 360 serpents along with Hanuman to Kashmir, where a pious Brahmin had dreamt about her, he build a shrine to her and found the diving spring. It was believed that the serpents once surrounded the spring, now the bunkers of the B.S.F surround it. The women still take a holy dip in the dark water of Gangkhar. The writer experiences a feeling of homecoming with its relaxed, generous attitude. A unique phenomenon, a temple in India with a Muslim caretaker:

> We truly believe this is *Bhagvati's* place. We believe it is sacred. You will find Muslim coming here and offering milk to the spirit just like the Hindus. (22)

The caretaker believed that the springs turned black, first in 1984 after the assassination of Indira Gandhi, then pitch black during the Kargil war. Whenever things got bad the waters would reflect the situation. As the lady in Jean Arasanyagam's story 'The Quail's Nest' says as she walks by the river that each time she gazes into its fathomless depths, she feels she is drowning in the dark waters. Similarly Sonia Jabbar continuous her journey to Anantnag to visit Mattar Nag she is mesmerised by the "blueness of the water tessellated by the catfish specked with gold" (23).

She writes that water, spring, rock, cave, tree, mountains are all honoured in Kashmir by Pandit and Muslim alike and are imbued with the moving spirit. She feels that the differences are on the surface, deeper they faithfully follow their common ancestors.

Another political journey, marked by midnight, raids, brutality and murder follows this nostalgic and spiritual journey. Families are wiped out while sitting at supper, while other at prayers. This background of gore is defined by Urvashi Butalia[7] in her essay "The Persistence of Memory", where Bir Bahadur in his seventies undertakes a journey after fifty-four years, from Delhi to his village in Saintha in Pakistan. Bir Bahadur is a tall, statuesque Sikh with a white following beard, always dressed in white with a black turban and a saffron head cloth. As they ride across the villages, Urvashi writes:

> We could have been in India everything looked exactly as it would on the other side of the border in Punjab. (177)

As Bir Bahadur stops in Jhamali, the village from where his wife hails, the writer wonders how a small peaceful place, could be a witness to the terrible killings in March 1947. Memory plays an important part in recreating the horror of the death of his sister, killed in his presence by their father. There is an old pervasive silence, which forms the sub text, as Butalia observed that Bir

Bahadur glossed over any question about his sister and once he said that his sister died. At another level there is also the reconstruction of memory.

Bir Bahadur moves into the house of his childhood and the people of the two sides build up their past in bits and pieces. He remembers his sister as a martyr, who brought honour to the family. A feeling of compassion for the father dawns on him as Bir Bahadur sees his father as a helpless victim.

The journeys as Atwood had said were not easy, for any of these people. They were all travelling in a passage tangled with travail, trial and tribulation. The stories do not celebrate heroism, they deal with the aspiration, doubts and failures of the ordinary people as they hug their small destinies and remain outsiders in their own world.

References

Arasanayagam, Jean. *In the Garden Secretly and Other Stories*, New Delhi: Penguin Books, 2000.

Atwood, Margaret. "If you can't say something Nice, Don't say anything at all". *The Language in her Eye*, Coachhouse Press. 1990 and repr. *Meanjin*, Vol.54, No.2, 1995.

Butalia, Urvashi. 'The Persistence of Memory", *Civil Lines. New Writing from India*. Vol. 5.

Casey, Edward S. "Remembering Resumed: Pursuing Buddhism and Phenomenology in Practice" *In the Mirror of Memory, Reflection on Mindfulness and Remberance in Indian and Tibelan Buddhism*. Ed. Janet Gyastro. Albany, 1992

Jabbar, Sonia, "Spirit of Place". In *Civil Lines. New Writing from India*, 5. Ed. Kari Friese and Mukul Kesawan. New Delhi: India Ink, 2001.

Mukherjee, Meenakshi. "A Blighted Garden" Literary Review, *The Hindu*, April, 2001.

Ramanujan, A.K. "The Ring of Memory. Remembering and Forgetting in Indian Literature", *Uncollected Poems and Prose of A.K. Ramanujan*. Eds. Molly Daniels Ramanujan and Keith Harrison. New Delhi: OUP, 2001.

13
Alone Among Aliens

Ila Rathor

> ...And when she sang, the sea,
> Whatever self it had, became the self,
> That was her song, for she was the maker. Then we,
> As we beheld her striding there alone,
> Knew that there never was a world for her
> Except the one she sang and, singing made.
>   From *The Idea of Order at Key West*, by Wallace Stevens.

The Indian Diaspora is the largest with around 20 million Indians settled in different parts of the world. The Diaspora communities live in multicultural environments. In the process, the self is removed from its specific surroundings and what we have is a reinforced struggle for survival and re-identification. It is a process of re-constructing the self in a new surrounding, an alien environment. It has once again to establish its distance from the 'other'. The issue is one of relocation in the third space in a new multicultural environment. Moreover, social interaction has different norms in different societies.

The sense of an identity is very important for an individual both as an independent entity and in his social relationships. This sense of self provides the sense of having free will and also forms the basis of social control. It is defined through environment, past experiences, collective memories, possessions and even the lack of it. In this process the space occupied by, the place it is located in, is crucial to the construction of the self.

Social psychologists have classified self-types according to the behavioural patterns exhibited by them. Self is not only typified individual behaviour but one can also 'conceptualize the self as various types of dynamic systems' (*Self Types* 2). It can be conceptualized as based on the principles of exclusion. Rather than defining it in terms of what it is, it is defined in terms of what it is not. As such the self evolves as a boundary maintaining system. These boundaries may stop at the individual, as in the west, or may extend up to the tribal or religious community as in the east. Indians who migrated to Canada and America were essentially either those who lacked means and went in search of resources, or those who belonged to the affluent class and emigrated for the cause of better education or to add to their already affluent status. The demarcations between the 'self' and the 'other', fed by greed and self-effacement, are arbitrary in nature. Hence, the Indian immigrants found themselves in an unprivileged position.

> The bourgeois, then upon displacement from the nation of its origin, finds itself contained in the form of an immigrant community in a foreign country. In particular, the Third World bourgeois, as an immigrant group in the First World, finds itself in a position of subordination to the native bourgeois.
>
> (*Ex-Nomination*)

Therefore, due to the danger of being labelled the 'other' the immigrant community tries to underline the essentials and avoid being nominated the non-essential. Beauvoir felt that this duality is a necessary phenomenon as "no group sets itself up the one without at once setting up the other against itself" (*Second Sex* 17). This duality, the difference from and the opposition to the other reflect man's passage from the state of nature to the state of culture. It follows Hegel's perception of "a fundamental hostility towards every other consciousness" (*Second Sex 17*).

With the eastern emphasis on family and community, and the western idea of individual freedom, besides social discrimination, there was bound to be a clash. Discussing the effect of immigration on identity, Salman Akhtar, a psychoanalyst, states that the country of origin is idealized, and the new culture is devalued. The Indians in diaspora possessed a common past. Faced with this duality in the multicultural west, it took shelter in its tradition to define itself. Women who constitute the "inner circle" become emblematic of this common history. Traditionally, India is perceived as the abode of purity, chastity, and spirituality, and woman becomes the metaphor for this ancient spirit of India (Bhattacharjee). It is the

> woman who pays a price for the preservation of the essential (nationalist) spirit, always a woman who must keep smiling and hide her pain so as not to betray the fragility of this spiritual heritage, the high cost of its maintenance, and the euphoric security of its myth.
>
> (*Ex-nomination*)

Partha Chatterjee feels that this idea of feminity as embodying the attributes of self-sacrifice, benevolence, devotion and religiosity, stands as a sign for the nation. Due to this women have to function within the cultural confines in order to sustain the idea of nation beyond the geographical limits.

For centuries India has been a patrilineal and patriarchal society where the role of woman has been highly marginalized and her status constantly reduced. The 'otherness' of woman continues to play even among the highest Brahmanic castes. In the past few decades it has been seen that despite education and, social and scientific development the position of women has not seen substantial change. From these standpoints when we look at the Indian diaspora in the USA and Canada we find an attempt on the part of women to transcend the societal bonds and recreate the 'self' in a different culture. Relocation in another culture especially in North America, stereotypically associated with liberation for women from patriarchy, leads to the re-examination of gender roles. The west with a different culture and, seemingly, an entirely different set of norms gives her an opportunity to redefine her role. She casts off the parameters lined for her in the patriarchal set-up. But we need to study the experiences of the female protagonists to see how far multiculturalism helps or hinders their quest for a 'self' as they try to emerge out of their role of the 'other'.

I have studied the short story collections of Bharati Mukherjee[1] (*The Middleman and Other Stories*) and Chitra Banerji Divakaruni[2] (*Arranged Marriage*) to see the effect that this process of reconstructing the self has on the status of the Indian women and what happens when women are left alone in an alien space.

The west has always been presented as the land where dreams are fulfilled. Fairy tales are woven around the "handsome prince who took her to his kingdom beyond the seven seas" (*Arranged* 18). For Jayanti in "Silver Pavements" it is a 'no problem' zone. She is thrilled on her journey "to the land of Almond Rocas" and is filled with sadness for her friends who will never experience the world other than "Ramu's *pakora* stall, munching on the spicy batter-dipped onion rings that our parents have expressly forbidden us to eat"(36). Repeated confessions illustrate this need to overthrow the suffocating non-identity imposed by the patriarchal society. Akin to this need is also the desire to live the American dream. This longing for financial stability and the yearning to enjoy the moneyed status signals the beginning of an end to 'otherness'. Time after time the immigrant experience highlights the wish to break free the patriarchal fretters and embrace the so called western concepts of liberty, democracy and freedom. But the reality seems to be a bit different. In a multicultural society a greater need is felt by the Indian community to preserve its identity and avoid merging with the 'other'.

If the west is the land of opportunities, of dreams coming true it is also the place where the Indian immigrants have to face social discrimination. The 'self' has to be rehabilitated not only as different from the white westerners but also the black Africans. There is a repeated reference to the shock on being labelled the 'nigger'. While narrating the stories both the writers voice their own experiences and fears as well. Divakaruni writes about being taken for an African that "was such a shock to me, I realized that people didn't know who we were." And so does Mukherjee who stated in an interview:

> I am less shocked, less outraged and shaken to my core, by a purse snatching in New York City in which I lost all of my dowry gold – everything I'd been given by my mother in marriage – than I was by a simple question asked of me in the summer of 1978 by three high school boys on the Rosedale subway station platform in Toronto. Their question was, "Why don't you go back to Africa?" (C.J.S. Wallia)

In "Silver Pavements" the narrator, Jayanti, finds herself in a similar situation. She forces her aunt to take a stroll in the neighbourhood, something which the other avoids and her husband has forbidden.

They are attacked by a group of pre-teenage boys who shout "nigger" and throw slush at them. The two are badly shaken. It shows that the Indians seem to have lost their identity and are grouped together with the Africans as the 'other'.

The west with its never ending expanse of choices offers an opportunity to grow away from the constraining traditions in India. It gives them an opportunity to earn an independent income despite the pressures of the racist and exploitative society. Due to this they experience a greater degree of control over their own lives than they do in the traditional Indian setup. But they find themselves once again trapped in patriarchy as they are burdened with charge of maintaining kinship network and religious and cultural traditions. Invariably, the women writers of Indian diaspora reflect the fact that the multiculturalism gives them a chance to recreate their identities in a third space, in which they can hope to carve their own niche. But this recreating of the self has its disadvantages as it has also to give up the privileges enjoyed previously. Mukherjee is conscious that she has given up her superior Brahmanic status for the American dream. Likewise, Jayanti feels,

> Can't they see that I'm not black at all but an Indian girl of good family? When our chauffeur Gurbans Singh drives me down the Calcutta streets in our silver-colored Fiat, people stop to whisper, *Isn't that Jayanti Ganguli, daughter of the Bhavanipur Gangulis? (Arranged* 51)

Both Divakaruni and Mukherjee have built their stories around women who recreate their world in the third space all on their own. They are women who go their alone – Divakaruni's "Silver Pavements, Golden Roofs" and Mukherjee's "A Wife's Story" – or suddenly find themselves abandoned in an alien culture due to a painful separation – Divakaruni's "Meeting Mrinal" – or tragic widowhood – Divakaruni's "Clothes" and Mukherjee's "The Management of Grief".

The initiation of women into this multicultural society begins with their attempts to assimilate. It might begin with a change in name and continue through change in dress, accent, eating habits and trying to adapt to this new culture. The choices have to be made keeping in mind the need for acceptance as 'self' when there is a constant fear of being the 'other'. Ordinary choices become 'agonizing decisions', as we find in "Confessions":

Should I wear the colorful Indian clothes that I love, or should I quit wearing them in public because I am tired of being stared at? Should I keep my hard-to-pronounce Hindu name, or should I Anglicize it, like many Chinese had done? Should I celebrate Christmas, a tradition that I didn't grow up with or ...celebrate Diwali, the most important Indian holiday?

There is a need to become inconspicuous in the crowd rather than stand out. The Indian woman in her 'native dress' and with her vermillion mark is quite easily marked "as an embodiment of sheer otherness". As such they become the target for racial attack, as it happened when they were identified by the dot on their forehead and attacked by the 'Dot Busters' gang in New Jersey.

Clothes become an important statement. Divakaruni uses it for a metaphorical representation of the stages of hope, despair and reconciliation in the life of an Indian girl Sumita. She is brought up to sustain the Indian family structure with the ingrained belief that "a married woman belongs to her husband, her in-laws" (19). Her objectification is complete when she is presented before the groom's party and has to go through the bride-seeing ritual. That she is happy and excited about it reflects her unquestioning acceptance of these norms. She has not known a world other than this. Her husband Somesh fills her dreams with the details of the store in California. The store comes alive with its 'neon Dewar sign and a lighted Budweiser waterfall', brightly coloured cans and elegant-necked bottles, cellophane packages, and canisters of potato chips. The '7-Eleven' seems to recreate her sense of freedom which is a part of the world of abundance, a world that has not known dearth or scarcity. It spells financial stability for her. The brown case in the 'belly of the plane' is her unbroken link to the past. The 'thick Kanjeepuram silks in solid purples and yellows, the thin hand woven cottons of Bengal countryside' (24), preserved with a silk sachet of sandalwood made from her mother's old saris is her companion on her journey to the new world. It smells of her mother's hands and the fragrance has a calming effect. In the unknown world she feels the need for the familiar. But soon with jeans, sunrise-orange T-shirt, with *Great America* written on it, and lace nightie she starts dreaming of a different role.

> I want to stand behind the counter in the cream-and-brown skirt set... and ring up purchases. The register drawer will glide open. Confident, I will count out green dollars and silver

quarters. Gleaming copper pennies. I will dust the jars of gilt wrapped chocolates on the counter. Will straighten, on the far wall, posters of smiling young men raising their beer mugs to toast scantily clad redheads with huge spike eyelashes.

(*Arranged* 27)

The ironic reality is sharper as Divakaruni juxtaposes this narration with the fact that Sumita has never been to the store as her 'in-laws don't consider it proper for a wife' (27). The freedom remains a part of her dream world as she has to go through the paces of being a good daughter-in-law. She is conscious that with her head covered with the edge of her sari serving her in-laws, like a good Indian wife never addressing her husband by name and even kissing 'guiltily' in bed, her life is no different from that of her friends in India.

The 'inner world' is kept untainted by the multicultural world around as the jeans and nightie remain hidden in the darkness of her suitcase. The immigrant 'self' takes on the role of a boundary defining system and does not open its excluding limits to the other cultures. The effect of this dual existence can be seen in the second generation who does not have a collective memory to fall back on and has imbibed western values but do not have the freedom to live them.

Sumita's widowhood seems to bring an end to her hopes for a change in the situation and she is covered in widow's white. The multicolored dreams are shattered like bangles with the multicolored shards flying out. But the exposure, little though it may be, to the outside world stops her from giving in to despair. She has all along been conscious of the choices she might have if she is able to break free from the 'inner world' of sustaining traditional structures. She feels,

caught in a world where everything is frozen in place, like a scene inside a glass paper weight. It is a world so small if I were to stretch out my arms, I would touch its cold unyielding edges. I stand inside this glass world, watching helplessly as America rushes by, wanting to scream. (26)

This awareness of different options makes her reject the idea of going back to India where "widows in white saris are bowing their veiled heads serving tea to in-laws. Doves with cut-off wings" (23). And she wishes to experience America unencumbered by the burden of preserving the collective self of the Indians trying hard to maintain the defining boundary by preserving the past.

It is pertinent to add that the view of India held and projected by the immigrants and the immigrant writers seems to be anachronistic. The reality eludes description. The need to establish polarities makes them shun all western attitudes and create an artificial India much like the 'mock marriages'[3] held there. To resist the 'outer world' of the alien culture the Indians try to preserve as much India in their homes as possible. In doing so they try to live the myth which is a part of their collective memory. On reading these fictional and factual accounts one feels that the immigrants are talking about India which no longer exists. They seem to be out of touch with the changes, both social and attitudinal, that have taken place at a fast pace in the past few decades. The picture of a widow with her head covered serving her in-laws is more to be seen on the celluloid or soap operas than in Indian homes. What Gurinder Chadda questions in *Bend it Like Beckham*[4] is not limited to the NRIs but is a common issue in any Indian household. Apart from the occasional references to the *Great America* and the Budweiser, the west does not intrude the immigrant homes. The self has managed to maintain the boundary.

Shaila in "The Management of Grief" (*Middlemen*) takes a similar decision to cast off her past and take on the future. Unlike Divakaruni, Mukherjee tries to give India a chance. Shaila comes to India along with other 'relatives' after having lost her husband and two sons in the plane crash. She is unable to conform to the tradition in which her grandmother had her head shaved of when she was widowed at sixteen and saw herself as "the harbinger of bad luck"; lived in separate quarters and cooked her food with the servants. Shaila's parents are 'progressive people' who disagree with such a 'mindless mortification'. The gender bias is evident here also. The widowers are presented with new bride candidates and they find it easy to give in to the "call of custom, the authority of their parents and older brother". Working within the cultural confines suits them. Though we see the influence of cross-cultural experience as some men find the idea abhorrent, yet even the 'substantial, educated men of forty' find it difficult to fight the cultural conditioning.

In the process of managing the grief the Canadians prove as much ineffective as the Indians. The 'cut and dried' methods of the westerners are unable to grasp the problems of the immigrant ladies who are illiterate and ill-equipped, both psychologically and financially, to cope with such a disaster. The Sikh couple, with language and cultural barriers, is not able to understand Judith Templeton's desire to help them. Their living in Canada holds no meaning till they continue to believe in their sons being alive. Templeton cannot understand their 'duty to hope'. Their reactions do not fit in her systematic study of the stages of grief – "rejection, depression, acceptance, reconstruction" (192). Their distrust of all government agencies makes them fear that by signing a few papers they might be "selling their sons for two airline tickets to a place they've never seen" (193). Templeton has entered their homes but she is unable to reach them. Moreover, she cannot understand the divisions, marked by religion, that stop a Sikh couple from opening up to a Hindu woman.

Background and learning effect people differently. While Shaila feels that she has to distance herself from Indian conventions and continue what she had started with her husband, Kusum, another Indian lady who had lost her husband and her 'good daughter', takes refuge in the spiritualism of India. Her guru sends her to India and in a Himalayan village she finds a girl who is an 'exact replica' of her daughter. She looks for answers in the Indian spiritualistic tradition and finds them. The faith in Gurus and Swamis further reinforces the control of the family and community. It is meant to keep the disciples in a regressed position to keep individual autonomy at bay (Kakar chap. 2). Contrary to her faith, is the reaction of her 'bad daughter', a second generation immigrant, who is unable to relate to her Indian ancestry. She prefers a trip to Wonderland than to India. Free from the burden of family ties she easily gets on with her life, 'works in a department store, giving make up tips to Indian and Oriental girls'. She does not feel the need to exclude the west as she feels very much a part of the multicultural milieu and has no compulsions to remain distinct. Right from the beginning she is marked as different as, unlike her sister, she has failed to keep up the pretence of living the culture. The reaction of the two sisters to the immigrant situation carries an autobiographical touch as Mukherjee and her sister charted out different roles for themselves in their encounter with the west.

> My sister is an expatriate, professionally generous and creative, socially courteous and gracious, and that's as far as her Americanization can go. She is here to maintain an identity, not to transform it.... In one family, from two sisters alike as peas in a

pod, there could not be a wider divergence of immigrant experience. America spoke to me – I married it – I embraced the demotion from expatriate aristocrat to immigrant nobody, surrendering those thousand of years of "pure culture," the saris, the delightfully accented English. She retained them all. Which of us is the freak?... She is happier to live in America as expatriate Indian than as immigrant American. I need to feel like a part of the community I have adopted (as I tried to feel in Canada as well). I need to put roots down, to vote and make the difference that I can. The price that the immigrant willingly pays, and the exile avoids, is the trauma of transformation.

(Two ways to belong in America)

Similarly, Kusum resolves the crisis by ending her exile and going back to India while her immigrant American daughter severs all connections with it. Shaila realizes the futility of looking for answers in the country which had long ceased to be hers. Even religion offers little consolation. In an abandoned temple in the Himalayas she feels the presence of her husband. It may be her own alter-ego forcing her out of her stupor. Her brush with the sadhu who tries to molest her, inadvertently, shocks her out of passivity and she is ready to decide. The serenity of Kusum or the carefree attitude of Pam is not for her and she has to redefine her future away from the "religious and political feuding" of both the Indian and the Canadian worlds.

Women as a part of the cultural ethos cannot escape the gendered roles of passivity, acceptance, and subservience. Whether in India or the west they need to make choices which might prove to be a difficult task. Even in Canada and America the 'doors' might remain closed and they may continue to serve as 'inferior servants that acted occasionally as punching bags' ('A Manifesto'). This signals that the continuity of the Indian patriarchal system is preserved and sustained, at the cost of women, to mark the boundaries of the immigrant 'self' in the multicultural environment. But I may add that Divakaruni and Mukherjee both, while delineating the options, have taken care to stress the fact that a multicultural world might offer a range of choices to the Indian woman where previously she had none. And these options hold meaning for her, ironically, when she is left all alone without any encumbering relationships to destroy her sense of self.

Endnotes

1. Bharati Mukherjee was born in Calcutta in a wealthy traditional family. She got her Masters in Art and Ph.D. in English from the University of Iowa. She married a Canadian author in 1963, immigrated to Canada, and became a naturalized citizen in 1972. After 14 years she moved to the US and took US citizenship. She won the National Book Critics' Award for best fiction for *The Middleman and Other Stories*. She is currently professor at the University of California.

2. Chitra Banerjee Divakaruni, born in India, is an award winning poet and writer. She moved to Dayton, Ohio, to study at Wright State University in 1977 where she met her future husband. *Arranged Marriage,* her debut collection of short stories, was awarded the PEN Oakland Josephine Miles Prize for Fiction, the Bay Area Book Reviewers Award for Fiction and an American Book Award from the Before Columbus Foundation. She currently lives in Sunnyvale with her husband and two children while teaching creative writing at Foothill College in Los Altos Hills, CA. As she writes about the women caught in the two worlds she is convinced that, "the art of dissolving boundaries is what living is all about" ("Dissolving" 2).

3. Anannaya Bhattacharjee refers to the demonstration of a mock Hindu wedding at the Diwali celebration in New York City. "The actors were a smiling bride and groom dressed in traditional Punjabi wedding clothes, who were led by an understanding-looking and ever-smiling priest." She feels that this symbolic enactment "carried no trace of its concrete aspects such as the relations between the people concerned and their histories."

4. Gurinder Chadda's *Bend it Like Beckham* is a film on multiracialism and deals with cross-cultural interaction. It is about two eighteen year old girls, Indian Jess and English Jules, who want to play football for England like their idol Beckham. Jess has to face the objections of her parents: "Which family will want a daughter-in-law who can kick a football but can't make round chapattis?" It is Chadda's third milestone after *Bhaji on the Beach* (1994) and *What's Cooking* (2000).

References

"A Manifesto of an Indo-American Youth" by two Indo-American Youth, with a commentary by Sunil Khushalani. Online. Internet. Available. http://www.indiastar.com/anony.html.

Akhtar, Salman. "A Third Individuation: Immigration, Identity, and the Psychoanalytic Process." *Journal of American Psychoanalytic Association.* 1995: 1051-1084.

Bhattacharjee, Anannaya. "The Habit of Ex-Nomination: Nation, Women and the Indian Immigrant Bourgeoisie." *Public Culture,* 1992 fall (5, 1), 19-44.

Beauvoir, Simone De. *The Second Sex* (1949). London: Vintage, 1997.

Chatterjee, Partha. "Colonialism, Nationalism, and Colonized Women: The Contest in India." *American Ethnologist* 16 (4, 1): 622-633.

"Conceptualization of Selfhood". A Sociological Social Psychology: Self Types and Their Differences Across Generations And The Life-Cycle. Online. Internet. Available. *http://www.trinity.edu/mkearl/socpsy-6.html*

Divakaruni, Chitra Banerjee. *Arranged Marriage.* New York: Anchor Books, 1996.

— "Dissolving Boundaries." (1997): Online. Internet. Available. *http.//headlines.entertainment.com/boldtype.divakaruni.article$597.*

Jacob. "Othering the Other". Online. Internet. Available. *http://www.learntoquestion.com/vclass/galleries/facinghistory/essays/source/t-other-jacob.html.*

Kakar, Sudhir. *The Analyst and the Mystic: Psychoanalytic Reflections on Religion and Mysticism.* New Delhi: Viking, 1991.

Mukherjee, Bharati. *The Middleman and Other Stories.* New Delhi: Prentice Hall of India, 1989.

— "Two ways to belong in America". *New York Times,* September 22, 1996.

Narayan, Shobha. "Confessions of a Cross-Carrying Immigrant". Online. Internet. Available. *http://www.rediff.com/news/2000/jan/04us4.htm.*

— "Was it me or Was it my Sari?" *Newsweek,* March 2000.

"Profiles: Chitra Banerjee Divakaruni." Online. Internet. Available. *http://www.helloindia.com/profiles/profile-shtml.*

Wallia, C.J.S. Online. Internet. Available. INDOlink Book Review.*http://www.indolink.com/Book/marriage.html.*

14

History as Fiction
A Post-WTC Reading of Vassanji's *AMRiiKA*

Harish Narang

This paper is divided into two sections. In the first one, I discuss Vassanji's views about history since history rather than individual characters and events appear to be the real subject of all his writings – stories as well as novels. In this section, I also discuss his manner of presenting history. In the second section, I discuss his concern with history in *AMRiiKA* – this time it is American history – his *weltanschauung* and the relevance of his 'message' for a post-WTC (World Trade Centre) America. Towards the end, I have highlighted the latest on the conflict situation in the world, particularly the role of the American administration in foisting a war on Iraq and keeping quiet on the state terror unleashed by the government of Israel on the people of Palestine which in turn may trigger off a new phase of resistance and violence in the American society spawned by 'disaffection' and 'grievance' as highlighted by Vassanji in his *AMRiiKA*.

I

History fascinates Vassanji. In this he is with his senior African writer colleagues like Chinua Achebe and Ngugi wa Thiong'o both of whom have employed the history of their respective people to counter the colonial discourse and its most significant formulation that Africa had no history, no culture, no past. Vassanji too has employed history to highlight not only the discourse of hegemony as it evolved from its colonial avtar to the contemporary postcolonial period of domination of world politics by the United States of America but also to warn against the dangers inherent in its continuation.

If there is one common thread running through all the fictional writings of M.G.Vassanji – novels as well as short stories – it is his concern for history – history of individuals, history of communities and history of nations. Vassanji believes that fictional mode is a very valid mode – perhaps more valid than the mode of social sciences – for perceiving the history of a society, including that of its individual members. In this, he is with Karl Marx, who while paying a glowing tribute to the English novelists of the nineteenth century – Dickens *et al* – had observed that from them one could learn more about the history, politics and economy of Victorian England than from the social scientists of the time. Earlier, Engels had paid a similar tribute to the writings of Balzac who had claimed that he was acting as a mere amanuensis for the French society.

One cannot also help recalling, at this juncture, observations made by Aristotle in his *Poetics* about the similarity between the functions of poetry – representing all forms of writing, including fiction, no doubt – and history. In fact, Aristotle places poetry on a higher pedestal because it deals with not only 'what had been' – history does that too – but also with 'what might be' – this history does not do.

Vassanji finds the histories of individuals, communities and nations not only significant and insightful but also closely interrelated. Therefore, he structures his narratives in such a manner and chooses such modes of narration that would enable him to place all three of them – individuals, communities and nations – on the axis of simultaneity. Thus, in *The Gunny Sack*, through a simultaneous portrayal of the history of Dhanji-Govindji, his daughter-in-law Jibai and the narrator Kala nee Salim who is Jibai's grand nephew, Vassanji focuses on the history of the entire overseas communities of Shamsis that is in diaspora with India, having left the shores of western Gujarat – Kutch and Kathiawar, Junagarh and Porbandar – at the end of the nineteenth century and the beginning of the twentieth, to make East Africa their new home. This sense of simultaneity, so very crucial to Vassanji's world-view, is created by the writer by moving his narrative back and forth both in terms of time and space –

between the present and the past, between Bagamoyo and Junapur, between Tanzania of today and India of yesteryears. Thus while tracing the origins of Dhanji-Govindji, Vassanji traces, in the same episode in *The Gunny Sack*, the origins of the entire community by dramatising the moment of their conversion to a sect of Islam by a Persian Pir called Shamas:

> One quiet night they sat outside their doorways in little groups, gurgling hookahs and talking in murmurs....A tall bearded man came in sight, in a long white robe and a white skull cap. Pausing in the distance, his long wide shadow merging with the darkness of the trees and forest, he began clapping his hands in rhythm and dancing the *rasa*. He went one full circle, singing of hope. They listened....They formed a circle around him.Then, clapping hands and clicking fingers, together they danced the garba, a circle of singing men in motion around the white figure....Then the man initiated them into the secret. He taught them new prayers and he taught them songs....
>
> His name was Shamas, and they called themselves Shamsis. Thus was the village of Junapur in India converted to an esoteric sect of Islam that considered thundering Allah as simply a form of reposing Vishnu. (7)

Origins also fascinate Vassanji and he is always interested in beginnings. 'Begin at the beginning' is a favourite expression of Miss Penny nee Mrs. Gaunt, Kala's English teacher in *The Gunny Sack*. Beginning is also Vassanji's favourite site for perceiving the contesting identities of individuals as well as of communities if not of nations. For instance, there is quite a mystery that Vassanji weaves around the origins of characters like the Zanzibari woman, Bibi Taratibu and Huseini in *The Gunny Sack* and Nurmohamed alias Mzee Pipa, Mariamu and Akber Ali in *The Book of Secrets* and Rumina in *AMRiiKA*. And the way the destinies of these individuals get mixed with those of their communities and even nations to which they belong, shows once again Vassanji's fascination for viewing history as it rotates simultaneously on more than one axis. Dhanji-Govindji's obsessive love for his son Huseini, for instance, leads to his swindling the community of its funds and its eventual divisions into violent factions from which – the author suggests elsewhere – it could not recover for a long time. Similarly, Mzee Pipa's involvement with Mariamu in *The Book of Secrets* gets him mixed up with the

Anglo-German rivalry to control parts of East Africa during the first World War. Again, in the same book, Akber Ali's mysterious parentage – it is never revealed fully whose son he really is – leads to many a twist and turn in the fate of not only the Shamsi community located in the townships of Kikono and Moshi but of the British and German colonial rulers as well. Ramji's fascination for Rumina – part of which stems from her mysterious origin – leads to his involvement with Michel-Mehboob who in turn had to do with a terrorist act of bombing, leading to his – Ramji's – eventual destabilised state of mind.

Before we discuss *AMRiiKA* and Vassanji's ideological standpoint in the novel in detail, it may be of interest to observe here that Vassanji bestows mixed parentage on some of his central characters to signify the diasporic situation which for him – as also for many other immigrant writers – is a favourite site for the perception of merging identities of individuals, communities and nations. Thus Huseini in the *The Gunny Sack* is the son of Dhanji-Govindji's union – illegal – with African Bibi Taratibu that represents, among others, the hierarchy of social relations between immigrant Indians and native Africans in a typical colonial sandwich situation. In *The Book of Secrets*, Akber Ali represents a similar hierarchy but between the colonizer British represented by Alfred Corbin – the alleged father of Akber Ali – and the colonized Indians, represented by Mariamu – the mother of Akber Ali. And in *AMRiiKA*, Rumina is the daughter of Sheikh Abdala, the revolutionary ruler of Zanzibar and a Russian girl whom he had met and married in Moscow.

First person narration through the persona of the protagonists is Vasaanji's favourite narrative mode. In *The Gunny Sack*, it is Kala nee Salim, the grand nephew of Ji Bai and in *The Book of Secrets*, it is Pius Fernandes, a retired teacher of history. This kind of mode of narration – Vassanji also uses it for telling many a short tale in his collection of short stories, *Uhuru Street* – gives him an opportunity to not only move back and forth in time and space but also to embed tales within tales so that, as he put in *The Book of Secrets*, the tale "ingests us and carries us with it and so it grows" (2).

II

Vassanji's *AMRiiKA*, published in 1999, has all of these distinguishing features of his writings, namely, his fascination for history and his fancy for origins – of individuals, communities and nations. There is also this mystery surrounding some characters and hybridity built into the parentage of at least one crucial character. The mode of narration too is first person and the persona is that of a Tanzanian Shamsi from Dar es Salaam whose origins go back to Gujarat in India and who finds himself first studying at Tech in Boston and later settling down in the USA. There are, of course, also tales within tales – of Darcy, of Zuli, of Jamila and of Rumina and of Michel Mehboob.

But then let me begin, a la Vassanji himself, at the beginning. Let me talk first of the title of the novel.

The word *AMRiiKA* is in itself a phonological hybrid – a partly assimilated mutant – of the English word America that incidentally in turn has a hybrid inheritance as well. There could not have been a more appropriate metaphor for studying the global situation of the world that Vassanji analyses in the book. Again, what could be a more appropriate location – the title page and the title word – to announce his intentions. In fact, there is hybridity built into the very orthography of the word AMRiiKA – what with two dotted 'i's wedged between caps 'AMR' and "KA'.

As stated above, observing individuals, communities and nations on axes of simultaneity – of time and space – is of crucial significance to Vassanji for his objective – certainly implicit if not explicit – of perceiving and evaluating cultures and societies in flux. The beginning of the narration in *AMRiiKA* – the first 14 pages to be more precise – is truly a tour de force of both structure and style in capturing this simultaneity. Let me elaborate on this a little, citing some quotes from the novel.

The novel begins with the narrator – Ramji is his name and he is a middle-aged Shamsi of Indian origin who had migrated from Dar es Salaam to the USA as a young graduate student, studying hardcore science at the Tech – telling us that he is writing his memoirs "not without encouragement – to imagine beginnings, yes and more, to sustain them and guide them to my present conditions, here in the obscurity of these rented rooms near a beach". These memoirs, Ramji tells us further, will heal 'my wounds' and 'even save my soul from endless torments". If reference to 'wounds' and 'endless torments' to the soul are not enough to arouse our curiousity read on and know further about the narrator, we are also told these memoirs are also the subject of "the probing attentions of a certain representative of the law" who "does not interfere as yet but hovers just beyond the edge of my narrative" (2).

And then the narrator plunges into what he calls 'a constructed origin' – something that we know Vassanji relishes constructing for his characters – portraying 'a short stout old woman in a soft long dress with graying hair' who we are told was his "grandma...a singer and healer who...when she sang, she opened curiousity and old cupboards and strange premonitions and desires, even the desire to get away, leave everything behind" (3).

This, in fact, is what Vassanji himself does – opening 'curiosity' and 'old cupboards' – what he narrates next – of course, through the memoirs of Ramji:

> Our ancestors were Hindus who were converted to a sect of Islam and told by that refugee from Mongols to await the final avatar of their god Vishnu. In Grandma's words, the sun would arise that day from the west. How far was the west? Where did it begin? (3)

Before we've savoured these details fully – they are coming really thick and fast, thanks to Vassanji's style of writing in concentric circles – he has opened yet another window – the novel could as well have been called Windows 99 – for us, much in the same fashion as we go on opening them on a PC monitor screen:

> My people sought it first in Africa, an ocean away, where they settled more than a hundred years ago. But in time, this west moved further and became – America; or as Grandma said it: Amriika (3).

And then we are made privy to the scene of Ramji's departure for 'that El Dorado' – Amriika – at the Dar es Salaam airport – a scene that Vassanji no doubt creates to imply the next stage of the Indian-African diaspora.

> I remember going through the immigration checkpoint and turning around for one last look at Grandma: standing stiffly among the crowd, feigning sternness for grief, her right arm still raised in the goodbye she'd said minutes before, the hand closing and opening as if mechanically in one endless farewell. (4)

Portrayed as a typical airport farewell in an era when not so many travelled to the west – certainly not in big droves in which they do today – the scene still holds the strong emotive power for both those leaving and those staying back. But then that's Vassanji is best at – creating very dramatic, emotionally charged scenes from life that bring, at times, tears into the eyes of his readers.

What is, however, of more significance – certainly from the point of view of the narrative – is the revelation by Ramji of the year of his departure: August 1968. It is a date that facilitates Vassanji to 'crack open', for our view, a whole new vista of a world from the past – the America of the Spring of '68 when violence erupted across the whole nation. *AMRiiKA* is about America:

> ...the frightening America: dangerous streets, sex, drugs. Blackboard jungle, cement jungle, neon jungle...and the death's head of technology: ICBMs and MIRVs, marvellous and terrifying. (9)

This America – 'a fucking fascist country' (8), as Ramji's roommate Russell described it on Ramji's first night in the new land – was a "land of multiple choices, where even ice-cream comes in thirty one different flavours and where every city had a colourful baseball team and there were a dozen television channels to flick through" (82).

The America to which Ramji looks back after twenty seven years, was a nation of weird tastes where university bums named their cats shamelessly after renowned philosophers – Kate's cat was called Husserl – and where donkeys delivered the lectures of seminal scientists – Peter Bowra's mechanical donkey wrote the formulae and drew diagrams with its tail. It was a strange nation where middle aged women seduced young men their son's age with full knowledge if not complicity of their husbands and grown up sons – remember Ginnie seducing Ramji on the new year night.

America of those days, as the author tells us, was a market place of ideas where 'everywhere, gurus, pirs, psychologists, zealots of every stripe were fishing for disciples' and where revolutionary radicals supported the Vietnam war through the organization of sexual orgies. Looking back, Ramji the drifter protagonist locates the failed cause in the spurious revolutionary zeal and sham radicalization of upper middle class white American youth. Shawn Henessy's book *Dissent to Nowhere* told it all.

The real significance of *AMRiiKA*, however, lies in its portrayal of the process of alienation of immigrants like Ramji and Sona – coming as they do from societies rooted in tradition and community cultures – who are unable to adjust to extreme individualism of the majority on one hand and the ruthless marginalization of the minority on the other and who are sucked gradually into the vortex of a more radical, more intolerant, more fundamental version of their own religious ritual:

> This semester there were two other newcomers, students at Harvard, who had already begun to undermine Sona's prestige by insisting that proceedings at the mosque were not being done in the proper Islamic Way. (155)

And again –

> As Sona concluded the hymn, with the king putting down his sword and saying, Queen, tell me about this Faith of yours, one of Sona's detractors spoke up: "But Sona, where is Islam in this song you sang?" (156)

It is this double alienation – their failure to acquire the value system of their new land of adoption and at the same time their inablility to fight the onslaught of more radical types from their own community – that leads to both Ramji and Sona – in their separate ways – to get involved with violence, the consequences of which are horrendous. A family of three is wiped out in a bombing of a bookstore in Ashfield, Michigan, apparently because of extreme hatred and intolerance that such fundamentalism had spawned. Both Ramji and Sona – the two primary wayfarers from the postcolonial third world – come to be involved in this extreme hate crime.

The core of *AMRiiKA* therefore deals with that most turbulent period of not only American but world history since the end of the second world war when the agenda for peace, for civil and minority rights including rights of blacks and women were foregrounded and hopes raised for a more just and democratic world order in which war – whether cold or hot – will have no place and in which the infamous Monroe doctrine of American hegemony will have little relevance.

How that dream turned sour, dashing hopes of a new dawn into a frightening nightmare is what the novel portrays through the life of Ramji. At this level, *AMRiiKA* is the story of an immigrant to America and his efforts to negotiate the identity crisis triggered by the gap between the anchoring spiritual values brought in the cultural gunny sack from back home – to practice faith daily, not to drink, not to succumb to sexual temptations – and the sheer materialism of his new homeland. This is aggravated by the yawning chasm between the romantic notion of America, nay AMRiiKA, of his adolescent school days' imagination – Elvis Presley, John F.Kennedy and his brother Bobby were its human icons and the landing on the moon was the ultimate symbol of its supremacy in the fields of science and technology – and the harsh, blind reality that he finds himself into on arrival there – a realty in which the Industrial-Military Complex pursues its economic agenda relentlessly, completely oblivious of its impact on the lives of people both within America and without. It is as a result of his inability to skirt around and negotiate this chasm between his dream and reality that Ramji becomes a drifter – both in personal life and professional career – pursuing girls and gurus, changing jobs and wives and converging, finally, towards an organization – Inqalab International – which seems to be pushing a fundamentalist agenda in the garb of ethnicity and radicalism – 'Inqalab was the Urdu-Hindi word for "revolution"' (271). In portraying this, Vassanji examines Ramji's historical roots – both in Africa and India – very critically and does not absolve the past of its responsibility in the resultant mess that Ramji makes of his life in the USA. So far so good, since this is what Vassanji had done previously too – in *The Gunny Sack*, *No New Land*, *Uhuru Street* and *The Book of Secrets*.

At another level – and this to my mind is more significant, ideologically, since it sets *AMRiiKA* apart from Vassanji's earlier books – the novel turns the gaze from the past back in Bagamoyo or Dar es Salaam in Tanzania or Kutch and Porbandar in India to the present in Boston and Chicago in America, examining critically the socio-politico-cultural goals and objectives being pursued by the government of the United States of America vis-à-vis the ideals enshrined in its Constitution. And it is here – in turning the gaze within – that Vassanji's world-view, his ideological standpoint about America manifests itself. Choosing, as he does, the sixties of the last century – a very volatile period in the history of post second world War America – Vassanji portrays very dramatically through some of its most prominent frozen frames – a grief-stricken Jacky clad in all black standing at the Arlington cemetry before the burial of her assassinated husband, John junior, all dignity, saluting his father's coffin, a napalm-hit Vietamese girl, aflame, running naked on a street in Vietnam – his critique of a society divided vertically on the questions of civil and other minority rights and on the manner of pursuing and realizing its ideals and goals.

Thus, in *AMRiiKA*, Vassanji has chosen to tell the truth, his truth, about the America of the sixties and the seventies. But why now – at the fag end of the millenium? Why rake up the past – and an unsavoury past at that? Drunk on the reality of being the sole superpower in a unipolar world, the post-Iraq was United States of America has become brash and arrogant, showing absolutely no tolerance of not only of its present acts – ruining of Iraq on the basis of unfounded grounds as also total and unashamed support to the acts of terror and occupation inflicted by the Israeli government on the landlocked, hapless Palestinian population in total defiance of the world opinion is a testimony of this – but also its dubious past. What is, however, of more substance and significance is the implicit ideological insight provided by Vassanji in his novel that the recent spread of religious bigotry and fundamentalism and its militant manifestation in various parts of the world that the USA apparently opposes so vehemently, may have been spawned by its own acts of intolerance against its own people beginning in the late sixties.

As is evident from some of his writings – non-fictional – Vassanji has been very disturbed by the growing intolerance – both in intra-national and inter-national relations. We find him commenting repeatedly on violence and intolerance of Asian, Arab and African immigrants in North America including in Canada, of ethnic cleansing in Bosnia, Chechenea and Gujarat, of political repression in Africa and Asia. He feels that such intolerance has increased manifold in world politics after the disappearance of the former Soviet Union and the Eastern Block and the arrogance of the United States of America after it became the sole super power. According to him, the worst manifestation of this was the Gulf war. Somehow, he has not been able to reconcile in his mind the two images of America – one of the world's biggest democracy, possessing world's most wealth, claiming a very sophisticated education and health system for its citizens, boasting of an absolutely open society which permitted total freedom to dissent and the other that of a solo but vengeful superpower which boasted of having bombed a modern prosperous Iraq back into stone age, forcing millions of innocent Iraqi people –

women and children included – to pay either with their lives or by surviving at subhuman level, for the sins – if these were sins at all – of the ruling forces in Baghdad. In a very lengthy discussion with this scholar sometime in 1997, Vassanji had expressed his grave concern against the growing insistence on purity – of race, religion and region – and the accompanying sense of intolerance, violent intolerance, of which the Gulf war was perhaps the worst manifestation after the end of the Second World War.

But then why did Vassanji choose to invoke the late sixties and the time of the Vietnam war for critiquing this sense of political arrogance and intolerance of contemporary America? Perhaps the parallel would not have been lost on him. In the post-second world war period that saw the sudden rise of America's role in world politics, the period of the Vietnam war was the only time when American foreign policy dominated by the military-industrial complex was at its brazen worst, attracting universal condemnation from not only most members of the United Nations but also the American people at large. The famous photograph of a Vietnamese girl with her body on fire from a napalm bomb hit, crying and running naked alone on a lonely road – splashed world-wide which also won the best photograph award for the year – became the icon of this barbarity, making the American administration a political pariah. In a post-Vietnam war debacle analysis, the demoralization caused by such strong criticism by the American public was cited as one of the major reasons of their defeat in Vietnam. In fact, during the Gulf war, fearing similar repercussions, the American administration imposed very strict censorship on the media – both print and electronic – against reporting the war in a manner detrimental to the American military interests.

It is this sense of alarm about the growing intolerance in both inter and intra national relations that must have prompted Vassanji to focus his last novel on America and its role in destabilizing the world socio-politically. And looking for a parallel in the past, he would have found the America of late sixties to be an ideal situation to describe. Also, this is one part of American history that he is personally so familiar with, having lived through it as a graduate student in one of most volatile American campuses – M.I.T.

But then what is the message for contemporary America that he builds in his novel. Let me go back to a situation described quite early in *AMRiiKA*. When Ramji, the protagonist-narrator of the novel, moved into Rutherford House, a dorm for graduate students at the Tech, he contributed to the décor of the room a khanga – a bright printed cotton cloth with a message in black running across it:

"Wayfarer, look back". (32)

This crisp concatenation of just three words is constructed in a manner of aphorisms of wisdom in the Sufi or Bhakti tradition that more often than not construed the world to be a serai and human beings mere passers by. And very much like those doubly distilled words of wisdom that ancient India was known for, the saying inheres in itself the potency of meaning various things to various people, communities and nations at various locations on various occasions. However, the semantic core of the saying remains more or less constant, reminding the wayfarers to plan their future by locating their present in their past.

At the most obvious and literal level, the saying exhorts individuals like Ramji and Sona, Zuli and Jamila, Darcy and Rumina to 'look back' to their past in Africa and even their past past in India and Persia for getting out of the mess they find themselves in their brave new world. But at another – and more diffused level – the Khanga saying exhorts the world at large – America included, of course – to look back to the wisdom of ancient India and its message of tolerance. As Vassanji put it in his essay "Life at the Margins":

> And so I have come to accept a condition that my ancestors found quite natural: that of agglomerating all one's experiences, not denying anything in the interest of "purity" but always being wary of the purifiers – religious, national or ethnic "fundamentalists". Life at the margins has its comforts, and IN MULTIPLICITY THERE IS CREATIVITY AND ACCEPTANCE. (Bahri and Vasudeva, 120, emphasis added)

The message is of special significance after what happened in the USA on September 9, 2001. In a way the events of 9/11 were anticipated by Vassanji in his novel *AMRiiKA* in the episode – of course, very minor as compared to what happened on 9/11 but the comparison would not be lost on all those re/reading the novel after that date – involving the bombing of a bookstore in Ashfield:

> On the night of January 20, 1995, a Friday, in the main street of the town of Ashfield, Michigan, a bookstore was bombed. The blast demolished the front end of the store and a portion of the

residence above it, killing all the occupants, a family of three. (317)

Vassanji's message of exhorting the wayfarers – in this case the American administration and also the white American population at large – to realize that 'in multiplicity there is creativity and acceptance' has a special relevance in the wake of what happened in the USA and Canada immediately thereafter by way of reprisals against all non-Europeans. Bearded Sikhs from India were mistaken for bearded followers of Osama Bin Laden and attacked, even killed. Incidentally, the brother of one such Sikh victim was also killed in America a year later. The message has more relevance in the wake of what was done to Afghanistan immediately after 9/11 and to Iraq later under what the USA called Operation Pre-emptive Action. What is at stake is – this is what Vassanji seems to be implying – what the French people had in mind when they gifted the Statue of Liberty to the people of America – symbolizing a society based on liberty, equality and fraternity – hoping that these ideals would become the corner stones of the founding of that great nation. I read this interpretation very clearly in Vassanji's choice of the epigraph for *AMRiiKA* from America's most powerful and prophetic poetic voice – of Walt Whitman:

> "But where is what I started for so long ago
> And why is it yet unfound?"

Let me conclude by referring to a rare insight that Vassanji bestows on one of his inconsequential characters – the investigator of the hate crime at Ashfield. Speculating on the possible causes of the violent incident, he observes:

> Disaffections lurk right beneath the surface of our democracy...grievances against history and fate threaten to tear at its fabric; these defects in our pluralist society have to be understood by the guardians of its security. (408)

The million dollar question is – will they?

References

Bahri, Deepika and Vasudeva, Mary, *Between the Lines*. Philadelphia: Temple University Press, 1996.

Vassanji, M.G. *The Gunny Sack* (1989). New Delhi: Penguin Books India, 1990.

—. *No New Land* (1991). New Delhi: Penguin Books India, 1992.

—. *Uhuru Street*. Toronto: McClelland & Stewart Inc., 1992.

—. *The Book of Secrets*. Toronto: McClelland & Stewart Inc., 1994.

—. *AMRiiKA*. Toronto: McClelland & Stewart Inc., 1999.

15

Re-Configuring Identity
Suniti Namjoshi's Diasporic Journeys

Alka Kumar

> I did not/come into being/a full-grown lesbian/with a knowledge of English
> a trained brain/and sexual politics/inscribed upon it
> These native modes/these shades of feeling/return me to an element that feels
> Like home/In the west I burn/here/when my lungs give out/I cannot breathe.
>
> Suniti Namjoshi[1]

The conflictual pulls of the contemporary historical moment bring to the literature of our time its unique dynamism and energy. In this age of globalization, Diaspora studies become a crucial site that manifest just these contradictory and vibrant pulls, simultaneous and in opposite directions.

The first section of this paper articulates the conceptual parameters of this ever shifting signifier, showing thereby also how the essential ingredients of the diasporic sensibility give to this literature its unique critical position, dynamic thematic energies and diverse plural forms. The second section locates Suniti Namjoshi within the theoretical grids conceptualized in the first part, attempting to read in her fiction some of the resonant tensions that enrich her writing with power and meaning. The paper reiterates the multiplicity of her inheritance, diversity of the personae residing within her which shape her inventive, irreverent and transgressive self. The paper traces this unique myth-maker's creative journey from her first home in India, via McGill University in Montreal to Devon, England where she now lives. The lesbian-feminist perspective in her work as also the quicksilver nature of her multiple sensibility, both mirrored richly in her texts, derive, to a large extent, from her diasporic journeys through her many homes as they do too from the mythic traditions of the land of her birth, namely India.

The word 'Diaspora' derives from the Greek – *dia*, 'through', and *speirein*, 'to scatter'. According to Webster's Dictionary, diaspora refers to a 'dispersion from'. Hence the term implies the notion of a centre, a locus, a home from where the dispersion occurs. Thus, the word necessarily invokes images of journeys and displacements, wherein diasporic journeys essentially imply putting down roots in other, alternative homes. Both the situations of leaving home and the circumstances of arrival in a new land as also the ways in which these new settlings intersect with other social relations determined by class, race, ethnicity, racism, gender and sexuality are important factors that configure a diaspora, and subsequently its literature, in a certain manner.

The heterogeneity that constitutes the diaspora is underscored by the construction of a common 'we' which, although it is at best an 'imagined community', to borrow Benedict Anderson's term, it certainly has its far-reaching forgings in the processes of identity formations. Diasporic populations scatter globally across and their networks of belonging transcend transnational and transcultural boundaries. When home becomes a mythic space of desire it becomes also a place of no real return. Home then can be seen to have many versions, as the actual geographical space of 'origin', refigured and reinvented through the imagination, as also the lived experience of present day reality with its local sounds, smells and sights. There is a paradox at the heart of this formation and that may be one of the reasons for the conflictual tensions that energise literatures of the diaspora. This paradox is that in the specific context of this literature, the writer's identity shapes the text in crucial ways. Since generally identity formations are dependent on concrete and tangible everyday realities, like one's allegiances to a nation, culture and family, in this case the writer's emotional rootings are in a reality that is distanced and imaginary, thus it has crucial implications for the text. The multicultural contexts within which the diasporic writer is located in the present day impinge upon and influence the narrative structures of this literature, the choice of genres and forms employed by the writers.

The discourse of the diaspora that underpins literary writing in this genre – both creative and critical – draws its impulses from the interconnections between the unique specificity of a life and the sense of belongingness to a community at large. Although the contexts by which the term has been articulated have often been clearly defined it remains an elusive descriptive and analytical category. There are many reasons for this. For one, any umbrella term, despite reiterations of inherent diversities, attempts to homogenise. In the case of the diaspora this will simply not do as it is impossible to encapsulate the dynamic energies that seethe therein under any one single rubric. Besides, as diasporic movements are located at the heart of cultural encounters and often crucial historical junctures, and these variables are themselves in a state of continuous revision and flux, it becomes increasingly difficult to categorise and pin down a complex term like diaspora. Thus it is essential to problematise the basic formulations innate in this central notion, first by trying to understand its varied ramifications, going on to examine perhaps some of their inadequacies, suggesting ultimately the impossibility of finding fixed and unchanging definitions in the contemporary multicultural scenario.

The sense of belonging to a common homeland and the unifying experience of displacement and colonization have established strong ties among scattered communities. Naipaul says of diasporic communities, that, cut off from India by distance, diasporic Indians "developed something they would never have known in India, a sense of belonging to an Indian community." [2] And although diversities abound and there are no homogenous or monolithic notions of home, any number of variations on the twin themes of identity and home can be easily read into this literature. The tones swing between nostalgia and anguish, anger/cynicism and love, reconciliation and acceptance. The themes are often social and political concerns and the contradictions that the writer perceives mirrored in the contemporary fabric are perhaps a reflection of his or her own contradictory psychic pulls. The uncertainties with which a writer who has left his homeland speaks about it can hardly be the same as those of one located securely within it. The act of leaving home and settling elsewhere shapes then both the writer's sensibility and the text. Chelva Kanaganayakam writes, "For writers who have not chosen to leave, the epistemology of home is hardly ever problematic." He examines too the case of political and other exiles, discerning in the literature thus produced a sense of impassioned indignation or outrage, 'literature of resistance' he terms it, with a clearly 'definable political agenda'.[3] Moving on to voluntary leave-takers, the expatriates, that is, he writes of their perennial outsider status, their alienation awarding them a special fluid space wherein memory can intervene to create unreal and often distorted images. Rushdie's writing is a case in point, his peculiar positionality determinant of his thematic preoccupations as also the literary genre that he employs, which in fact makes his writing what it is. The self reflexivity of metafiction that is the stuff of his writing is a result of his inability both to look at home in real terms and also to look away from it. Arnold Itwaru writes, "this sense of estrangement ...touches upon the very notion of home, the lands and the places of our birth. For that land, that region, lives in us as memory and dream, as nostalgia, romance of reflection, that which defines us as different, that to which we think we belong but no longer do."[4]

Literature of the diaspora is about sensibility rather than space, and readers often come up against questions like the absence of real-life spaces in the writing, either the new home or country of origin or earlier settlement. This question, however, has been debated with great interest ever since diaspora studies became the focus of attention. It has been resolved too (if 'resolution' is ever possible in literary and cultural contexts) as other aspects of the text that locate it within such a theoretical grid emerge and evolve in obvious ways. Issues of identity, home, dislocations, relocations, rootlessness and belonging, often predominate as thematic pegs while multicultural contexts provide settings. It is impossible to generalize, homogenize or universalize a complex and ever developing concept like the diaspora, pointless too, as historical moments are neither static nor closed, and never ready for a last analysis. However, where there are references to a bygone home there are rootings in nostalgic harkings back to a past caught in a time warp, and such a vision is necessarily regressive. Backward looking stances of this kind dissipate assimilative energies, precluding attempts at relocations of the mind.

The latter section of the paper draws attention to Suniti Namjoshi's fiction. The theoretical issues raised in the essay need to be conceptualized through and located within, her writing. For instance, the following questions seem significant. How does cultural value get encoded through myth and gender stereotype? Does the act of mythologizing, the way it is done by Namjoshi, raise questions about the role of the writer, (woman writer?) and the dilemma of being a woman? Besides, are the subversive strategies used by her for re-inventing identity indicative of her location in the real world as well as the inability to speak in other ways? Are all acts of reading, re-thinking and re-inventing conventional children's stories, fairy tales, myths and the like then political acts, both of exploration as well as reconfiguration?

Through a reading of *Conversations of Cow* as well as references the writer makes to her personal journey in *Because of India*, the paper focuses upon the dilemmas of being Suniti Namjoshi, her lesbian, feminist, Indian, immigrant identities conflicting, coalescing, fuelling her texts. Questions of diasporic consciousness, and the ways they emerge from a blending of India and the west in her work present themselves in ways that are both baffling and seductive. The novel begins in the following manner:

> I'm down on my knees, waiting for the goddess to manifest herself. When I open my eyes, The Cow of a Thousand Wishes is standing before me...[she] is a Brahmini cow....Cow and I walk the length of the park. We would like some information about our future partners, but where to begin? 'When did you come to Canada?' I ask. 'Oh, a few years ago. How did you know I was an immigrant cow?' ...'Well, it's your horns,' I continue. 'That astounding curve. It is not typical of Western cows.'...I note she uses certain Americanisms. We amble along.[5]

Besides, her feminist ideas though shaped in the west evolve out of Indian thinking systems and Indian influences from the realms of Hinduism and Hindu mythology find their way into her writing in the shape of ideas about transgressions and flexibilities in gender boundaries as well as between the two worlds of humans and animals, same sex relations, women's sexuality and her location in a world governed largely by men. Thus, 'Asian', 'Canadian', 'lesbian' 'diasporic' are all crucial, overlapping and simultaneous perspectives that help the reader understand the separatist and celebratory tenor of Namjoshi's important work.

Her ideological stance is clear from her conversations and interviews. In a dialogue with Pratibha Parmar she says that her consciousness is a "lesbian feminist one and an Indian one in some curious way." She believes that "now feminists in their own writing must necessarily transform the power balance and write for a female readership, allowing men to eavesdrop if they choose to."[6] Responding to a question by Brenda Brooks if she considers her audience to be exclusively lesbian she replies: 'Absolutely. And, for a change,[let] the rest of them eavesdrop...Let them sympathise with what we consider to be our question: "what does it mean to be a lesbian?" By which we understand: "What does it mean to be human?" Let them exercise their imagination and let them see the universality of the theme in this.'[7] Her writing, then, is hugely "concerned with deconstructing a literary canon and an ontology that insisted on privileging patriarchy."[8] The writer's commitment to such a political stance is obvious in *Conversations of Cow* where the Brahmini cow is the principal actor in the drama. She is in command, she sets the terms of the partnership with Suniti, and among other things, although the furniture is constructed primarily for humans she has no problems in suggesting 'Let's go to your place and talk' while Suniti is hesitant, uncertain and tentative in her questions and her suggestions. Obviously then, in a world supposedly designed and controlled by humans, she subverts the given structures, assuming and appropriating power legitimately not hers. When Suniti and Cow visit the 'Self-Sustaining Community of Lesbian Cows' the human has to establish her credibility by producing evidence of affiliation to SPCA, Greenpeace, vegetarianism etc. The metaphor is easily extended to the gender paradigm which is yet another parameter that is subverted in the text. The later sections of the paper offer some detailed comments on this theme.

Dualities, paradoxes, simultaneities abound and complexities deepen. The *Conversations of Cow* is at the same time both a work in the novelistic tradition as well as a subversion of the tradition. Further, although it makes a deliberate connection between the author and the persona in that both are Suniti, women of Indian origin, academics by profession (both teach English Literature), the character functions really in a mythical, allegorical, and counter-realistic framework rather than in the classic realist tradition. This is not to insist upon a hegemonic 'novelistic' tradition or to claim that writing such as in *Cow* is more unlike (than like) our expectations from a genre like the novel. It is to point out that in being what it is, the text in fact does many things simultaneously. As it challenges patriarchal hegemony by reading such a point of view as given, so too in questioning the novel tradition while being inside it, it provides a perspective that has its double edge and thus enhanced value. Namjoshi's account of her evolutionary journey, in *Because of India*, traces her coming to feminist articulation and political consciousness. She writes: {'I hadn't properly understood the structures of Western society, or even of my own. I remember making one remark that still troubles me. It went something like this: "Here in the West, all that seems to matter for social status is gender and money. But in India several other factors operate: caste, class and family background. An Indian woman who has all these factors operating for her certainly isn't oppressed. And it seems to me that such women are far less awkward and far more assured than many of the women I've seen here." There's more than one kind of stupidity in this remark. First, there's the tendency to regard being oppressed as somehow ignoble. But what really appalls me now is my utter disregard of the women who had all the factors operating against them.'}[9] It is this spirit of interrogation (of her own earlier position) and growth that makes for qualities of authenticity in her text. The myth-maker and fabulist in Namjoshi explores feminist ideas, using familiar patterns and systems of thought, Western and Indian, through forms that are playful, ironic, transgressive and surreal. About the ingredients that made *Cow* she writes:

> ...I had been asking...what was my place in a world that often seemed absurd to me? All right, I was a lesbian, a lesbian feminist. But what was a lesbian? What was her relation to other people?...identity isn't only a matter of self-definition. It also depends on the identity other people attribute to one. I played with the notions of identity and alienation in *Cow*; but there was an additional ingredient that entered into my thinking. Personal immortality is not one of the tenets of Hinduism, as it is of Christianity. Identity is arbitrary in the sense that who you happen to be this time around has to do with who you were last time around and who you wanted to be. ..the very framework makes it possible to ask: what would happen if one let go of the identity one clings to so desperately?

The question of identity then, for Namjoshi is both philosophical as well as 'real', as she concludes in this section:

> It's apparent that the components of core identity change from place to place and period to period. Today the main components seem to be based on gender, skin colour, and sexual choice, as well as other factors such as nationality and religion, which are more or less important in different places. Any threat to the sense of self causes a violent reaction. But then how are we all to live? (*Because of India*, 83-84)

These questionings are foregrounded in *Cow*, a feminist, lesbian, separatist utopia where humans (Suniti, they want to shorten it to Sue) and cows (Bhadravati alias Baddy, (the Brahmini cow, who sometimes throws on a turquoise and gold Benarasi stole across her shoulders), Boudicea, Cowslip, Lou-Ann, Ariadne, Sybilla easefully negotiate thought, borrow vans and drive together in them, eat pizza and drink scotch. Cowslip explains the system that guides the world: 'The world...is divided into Class A humans and Class B humans. The rest don't count. How they look, walk and talk depends on television, but there are some factors which remain constant for several years. For example, Class A people don't wear lipstick, Class B people do. ..Class A spread themselves out...Class B apologise for so much as occupying space...[former] stand like blocks, never smile, [latter] look unbalanced, smile placatingly twice in a minute...'(*Conversations* 24). Later in the text, duties and obligations of the male, and the female partner are suggested, the former being 'strong, successful, right and noble' and the latter, 'the complementary ones' being 'weak, incompetent, uncertain and inferior' (100-101).

The patriarchal world as norm is assumed to be a given, satirically commented upon through strategies that use both allegory and irony. In *Conversations of Cow*, an alternative world is constructed where identities are far more fluid and strange things happen though completely matter-of-factly. A brown lesbian woman befriends a Brahmini lesbian cow who later (due to anger towards her woman friend) metamorphoses into an abusive white-American-pizza-chomping-male. It seems essentially a diasporic world, where questions of identity are most significant, a world where strange creatures are able to transform themselves to be what they choose, they travel and meet others, have adventures and new experiences. Baddy dresses up as Class A human and Suniti puts on make-up to look like Class B, and making a charming couple they go for a walk. The text goes as follows: 'An elderly gent tips his hat at us, his elderly wife beams at us. Everyone seems to approve of us. I feel so good, so safe, so respectable...I belong!' However, those moments of fun go by and doubts return 'what about our identities? Aren't we being false to our true selves?' And Suniti dreams: "Bhadravati and I have undergone plastic surgery. We have the faces of women and the hindquarters and legs of Brahmini cows and we wear top hats like true gentlemen...Then our wings slide out and we drift heavenwards" to which B responds mischievously, "Well, now we know who you really are...Saint Suniti without her top hat" (31-33). Another dream: B turns into a beautiful woman wearing a sari and Suniti into a well-kept poodle. And although morning comes and with it goes the dream, B keeps her new form. Through these playful and transgressive situations/adventures serious questions are being raised regarding the fixedness of identity and the normativeness of givens. The tenor of the text, interrogative, challenging and subversive, turns the tables on what may be considered the only truth.

In *Cow* then, where identities are fluid and arbitrary, the characters are easily able to choose their metamorphoses, effortlessly moving across shadow zones. Reincarnation and transmigration are referred to and there is a suggestion that people could become what they eat ('if one has eaten a great deal of beef, or a great many snails...it offers one a measure of self-determination...and constant control, the sense that destiny is in one's own hands' (40). There is an obsession to 'be', Suniti thinks and talks about 'being' a goldfish, a bear, a sheep, a poodle, a misogynist, (she also wants to be a cow, feels very duck-like and at another time looks like a owl) and both B and Suniti talk about going on a journey of exploration, to go through ordeals, 'and then find out who I really am.' "I already am. Tomorrow I become...I can be anything, anyone, or no one" (76). The last section 'Conjuring Cow' gets deeper and more complex as Suniti is duplicated, Suniti and S2, and B is nowhere. There is a strange sense of 'constant contiguity' as Suniti finds another of herself. She feels too a sense of unfairness in the fact that she is accountable for all actions of S2 as though she performed them, as also a curious empathy, or true fellow feeling as she feels stiff and tired although S2, and not herself, has been driving. Finally Cow comes home and Suniti's split self becomes whole again, coming together in the form of 'scribe Suniti' who is content to faithfully record 'The Conversations of Cow.'

Morris writes of being embarrassed by 'the dialogue and plot' and "the child-like allegorical mode, which turns painful adult problems into a simple narrative."[10] Smith's comment on the novel reads as follows: "The *Conversations of Cow* is a pleasant little work with a sixties feel to it...It's probably saying something about sexual roles and the nature of love, but not a lot."[11] Kanaganayakam points to the overt use of artifice in the novel, the allegorical and mythical resonances that 'draw in a whole field of intertextuality, including the ideological stance of feminist utopian separatism. "Further", he writes, "it is a diasporic novel involving a brown woman in a white society, with the consequence that the homogenization of feminist or lesbian identity is resisted from the very beginning...a binarism that borders on essentialism is deliberately invoked and even sustained, but neither Suniti nor the cow Baddy fit into any dualistic scheme" (132). In fact unless the novel is read as highly allegorical and working through metaphor its validity as challenge/subversion cannot be appreciated.

Namjoshi, in an interview with Kanaganayakam, discusses several issues, significant in the general context of her writing and particularly with reference to *Cow*. She refers to the dual traditions contained in her head as also the complexities of straddling multiple and diasporic realities, "one is Indian and the other is a language which holds another tradition."[12] Also there is an intriguing coming together of sensibilities in *Cow*, in that clearly articulated notions like pantheism, polytheism, personal immortality, all derived from Hinduism, give inner form to her text while there is too a simultaneous and paradoxical individualism which is a consequence of her having lived and internalized a western language, tradition and sensibility. Besides, being a fabulist and myth-maker, possibilities for ambivalence, innovation, experimentation and transgression in the form she uses are limitless. She acknowledges the pervasive presence of the landscape of Maharashtra as also the deep resonances of the tone of Marathi in her work.

The easy communion between animals and humans in *Cow* and the effortless transformations that frequently occur in this text can be understood within allegorical and non-realist paradigms when the 'novel' is read in a novelistic tradition, particularly if the reader brings to the text a western frame of reference. However, according to Hindu tradition there is nothing unusual or counter-realistic in such a depiction. In fact, Hindu myths and religious stories are replete with instances where animals converse with humans, befriend and help them out of difficult situations. A well known example from *Ramayana* is that of Jatayu, a huge bird, (friend of King Dashrath) who tries to save Rama's wife, Sita, from the clutches of the evil Ravana. Although he is injured and fails to prevent the abduction, he is able to inform Rama of the direction in which Ravana has fled with Sita. Another myth which is an integral part of the popular imaginary is that of Hanuman, the monkey god who, along with his army of monkeys (Vanar Sena) played a crucial role in the destruction and downfall of the evil empire of Ravana. Lord Ganesha, the elephant God known for his auspicious aura, is another case in point.

Besides, for the western reader, *Cow* is a quest for identity. However, the novel could as easily be read as a reiteration of the maxim that identity is arbitrary, fluid and unstable. Namjoshi says: 'I once told a Christian friend that only a Hindu could have written *Conversations of Cow*...Hinduism is pantheistic. The West has tended to think that we worship idols but really polytheism is an offshoot of pantheism...This means that you don't have to think twice before seeing a God or something sacred in anything'(*Configurations* 49). Thus there are curious re-imaginings of old stories, local flavours get added on and fill the imagination with religious faith and fervour. In India small shrines and temples, often just an idol here or there, can be found in obscure towns, small villages, highways, dotting the landscape anywhere and everywhere.

In *Conversations of Cow* come together the dilemmas and multiple inheritances of being Suniti Namjoshi. A 'novel' such as this could perhaps only have evolved from a generous coming together of the diverse range of locations to which the writer belongs. Her work grows out of the following: a Hindu sensibility, an Indian cultural ethos (being a Brahmin, hailing from Maharashtra), being part of the mainstream in more ways than one, also as part of the prestigious power corridors in being an officer in the Indian Administrative Service, later moving to Canada and growing as student and Professor of English Literature, finding poetry as predominant form of response, coming to political consciousness as feminist and lesbian, moving on to England and seeking more ideologically conscious forms of expression.

India, Canada, England...Namjoshi has a varied heritage of identities and thus many confusions as well as many burgeonings. The term Diaspora is doubly relevant in her case, both as an Asian located in England, having made her path through double migration, from India via Canada, but also more holistically, 'diaspora' read also as metaphor. This may be understood to mean a simultaneous belonging to multiple locations, being aware of one's plural heritage which, though stable, constantly reconfigures itself through intersections with the ever evolving contemporary, multicultural scenario. Concepts and questions of nationalism inhere in these locations, the diasporic writer carrying within her a multiplicity of cultural traditions, a sense of many homes and more than one affiliation. These rich anarchies of her diasporic sensibility coalesce and weave together with the imagination of her partner, Gillian Hanscombe, with whom Namjoshi lives in Devon. The following lines, written after their visit to India, fascinatingly and aptly encapsulate their shared experiences of a shared country:

> And so you said, "Well, which goddess then?"/I replied, "Come to the country of which/my bones are made up, I mean the minerals,/the dust and ashes, the named chemicals. Our gods/inhabit birds and beasts and our ruined temples are still functioning." So we went to India/where a stone is a god – if you say it is – and where a great many stones are carved with gods,/but just lying about, because as I told you,/the whole country is a gigantic junk heap./When we walked about, both reverent and casual,/you were undisturbed. How shall I say it?/You were like me. Did you exercise caution/O my dearest love? You did not question my kinship. (*Because of India* 114)

Besides, Namjoshi's location as academic adds another important dimension to her 'being', and in that role one can perceive a coming together of theory and praxis, ideology translating into reality. The following statement is important. Namjoshi writes:

> I hadn't really thought about humanism much, except to say, "Look, women matter too." If pressed I'd have probably gone along with the vague humanism of the university atmosphere I was immersed in. It was only when I tried to imagine creating entire courses with a female literary tradition at the center, and making these courses, rather than the traditional ones, the core of the English curriculum, that I realized that in the vague

humanist terms I was used to, I would have been committing heresy. The implication of this was that humanism probably couldn't be separated from a male-centred consciousness. As for a feminist humanism, did I really want women to be separated from the rest of creation?...trying to understand what kind of sense the world makes to a lesbian consciousness, and in the very process of writing we are trying to deal with the fact that language creates worlds. (*Because* 113)

Although her writing is not in the realist tradition and there is an absence of overt social, sociological or political comment, the reader is never in doubt about her ideological stance or political location. Her novels, fables and her poetry are a scathing attack on the unjust and non-egalitarian patterns that define the contemporary world. Both in terms of form and thematics, *Cow* is a subversive and powerful comment on the exploitative, and real, world in which we live. Namjoshi has pointed out that aesthetics is for her more important than the communication of a certain political perspective. The reader, however, can hardly remain in doubt about the power and conviction of that message while the work retains its value and appeal as a well written 'novel.' In fact, the mythical-allegorical format of the narrative assumes a huge range of meanings, and through these plural significations it is possible for the text to work simultaneously at many layers/levels.

In the Afterword to *Because of India*, the writer offers a justification for giving biographical information in a systematic and chronological order. She states: "particularly for us as lesbians, the personal, political and poetic or intellectual development is interlinked. The process of trying to arrive at an awareness of how our thinking has shaped us is, in my opinion, more important than the particulars. If these notes prompt you to ponder on your own experience, then they'll have served their purpose" (124).

The *Conversations of Cow* is significant in its reiteration of the concept of fluidity, of identity, of perception, also of the sense of home. The section 'Interlude' that deals with the story of Spindleshanks is a good example to illustrate this. There is an air of uncertainty in Suniti with regard to her own feelings in that she does not know for sure whether or not she is happy. She wonders too, as she looks around herself and sees a pine, a cricket, a moon, a forest, two women etc, 'Who am I, B?' she asks. B answers, 'Sometimes I think you're a baby.' B then goes on to tell her a story intended for babies in an atmosphere that is one of intimacy. This is a story about Spindleshanks, the cow who has a hollowness and blackness within, and an incessant craving. In an attempt to become 'substantial' she decides to eat everything she sees, 'pots, pans, kettles, crayfish, cabbages and turnips, articles of clothing, houses and furniture… animals, men, women, pigs, parrots, tiny babies.' As the contents of the world began to diminish due to her greed "the earth began to lose shape and looked more and more like a pock-marked lump" and the creatures who had survived her hunger were afraid to be next. Finally the cow ate all that remained, "the very last handful and the last clod of earth." Nothing was left, "only Spindleshanks and Nothing. Nothing and Spindleshanks. She began to scream…screamed and screamed until she burst and had turned herself inside out. Then the world spilled out of her, and not quite the same world as it once had been because it had been processed by Spindleshanks and Spindleshanks permeated everything." Although blackness is now both inside and outside her, so goes the story, which has no ostensible and obvious moral, as B reiterates, it is a frightening story and challenges all givens. In the face of chaos and anarchy where violence takes the place of harmony, and fragmentation reigns where wholeness could be, one is left feeling helpless but also certain that possibilities of order lie in fact in one's own hands. The 'higgledy-piggledy' world that spills out of Spindleshanks' insides is of her own making, a result of her greed, actions will indeed have consequences, and there will be disharmonies if evil prevails. And yet collective hope emerges once again, born as always of life and love between individuals, man and woman, woman and woman or in this case lesbian woman and lesbian cow. All borders are eliminated, subverted too as gender, race, the species to which one belongs, become irrelevant. This short section is both disturbing and affirmative, indeed a beautiful interlude, and it ends as follows: B asks, 'If you were to cut me open, Suniti, what would you find?' 'Blood and guts, a functioning body, a living creature.' 'Will it do, Suniti?' 'You know it will.' That night B and I became lovers. The birds wake us up the next morning. They're hunting for food. They are very noisy. They are celebrating the fact….well, they are celebrating the world' (80-86).

Home too, wherever it may physically be situated, is a metaphorical and conceptual space and for the diasporic person and particularly for the writer of the diaspora, is being increasingly configured in ways that are hugely diverse and affirmative. A sense of coming home in distant lands sets the tone of recent diaspora literatures. Again it is difficult and limiting to generalize or homogenize. In difference nestles life and vibrancy. In the contemporary moment when moving populations are norm rather than exception, configurations of home, homecoming, identity, alienation, loss, forgetting, memory, rootlessness, etc, become truly real and global issues. It becomes crucial then to seek valid and viable thinking parameters that may help combat the sense of loneliness and exile that of necessity accrues from such nostalgia. I am tempted to conclude in the words of the 12th century mystic, Hugh of St. Victor:

> The man who finds his homeland sweet is still a tender beginner; he to whom every soil is as his native one is already strong; but he is perfect to whom the entire world is as a foreign land. The tender soul has fixed his love on one spot in the world; the strong man has extended his love to all places; the perfect man has extinguished his.[13]

Endnotes

1. The poem is called 'But you like what you see' and is part of the collection *Because of India*. Namjoshi selects the poems for this volume, interspersing them with autobiographical narrative that provides extremely useful contexts that help locate and elaborate upon the many landmarks in the diasporic journeys of her 'self.'
2. V. S. Naipaul, *India: A Million Mutinies Now*.(New York: Viking, 1991) 7.
3. Chelva Kanaganayakam, 'Exiles and Expatriates', in Bruce King ed. *New National and Post-Colonial Literatures: An Introduction*. (Oxford: Clarendon Press, 1996) 206-207.
4. Arnold Itwaru, 'Exile and Commemoration', in Frank Birbalsingh ed. *Indenture and Exile: The Indo-Caribbean Experience*. (Toronto: *Toronto South Asian Review*, 1989) 202-6.
5. Suniti Namjoshi, *Conversations of Cow* (London: The Women's Press Limited, 1985) 13-14.
6. Pratibha Parmar, "Interview with Suniti Namjoshi". *Women's Review* 1 (November 1985): 18-20.
7. Brenda Brooks, "Words Invent the World." Interview with Gillian Hanscombe and Suniti Namjoshi. *Rites* Dec.1986/Jan. 1987: 14-15.

8. See Chelva Kanaganayakam's *Counterrealism in Indo-Anglian Fiction*. (Waterloo: Wilfrid Laurier University Press, 2000)123.
9. Suniti Namjoshi, *Because of India: Selected Poems and Fables* (London: Onlywomen Press, 1989) 78-79.
10. See Patricia Morris' "An Object of Desire", Review of The *Conversations of Cow*. *African Concord*, 17 April 1986, 41.
11. See Anne Smith's review of the novel in *New Statesman*, 20 September 1985, 30.
12. See Kanaganayakam's *Configurations of Exile* (Toronto: TSAR, 1995), 49.
13. Supriya Chaudhuri's review of Milan Kundera's *Ignorance* (Biblio, Vol VIII Nos. 1&2) raises well some interesting and important issues in the context of home and the loss of it.

References

Anderson, Benedict. *Imagined Communities: Reflections on the Origin and Spread of Nationalism*. London: Verso, 1983.

Birbalsingh, Frank. ed. *Indenture and Exile: The Indo-Caribbean Experience*. Toronto: TSAR, 1989.

Brah, Avtar. *Cartographies of Diaspora*. London: Routledge, 1996.

Brooks, Brenda. "Words Invent the World." Interview with Gillian Hanscombe and Suniti Namjoshi. *Rites*, Dec.1986/Jan. 1987: 14-15.

Kanaganayakam, Chelva. *Configurations of Exile*. Toronto: TSAR, 1995.

—. *Counterrealism in Indo-Anglian Fiction*. Waterloo: Wilfrid Laurier University Press, 2002.

King, Bruce. ed. *New National and Post-Colonial Literatures: An Introduction*. Oxford: Clarendon Press, 1996.

Naipaul, V S. *India: A Million Mutinies Now*. New York: Viking, 1991.

Namjoshi, Suniti. *Conversations of Cow*. London: The Women's Press, 1985.

—. *Because of India*. London: Onlywomen Press, 1989.

Parekh, Bhikhu. *Rethinking Multiculturalism: Cultural Diversity and Political Theory*. London: Macmillan Press Ltd., 2000.

Parmar, Pratibha. "Interview with Suniti Namjoshi". *Women's Review* 1 (November 1985): 18-20.

Smith, Anne. "Review of *Conversations of Cow*". *New Statesman*, 20 September 1985, 30.

16

On the Edge of Animation
Pakistani Women Poets in Their Own Voice

Anisur Rahman

> Even the most unemotional get excited.
> So here I am, on the edge of animation,
> A dream, a dance, a fantastic construction[1]
>
> Moniza Alvi

Desired Existence: A Dot on the Canvas

In quoting the above lines from a poet born in Pakistan, raised in Britain, and now working and writing there, I wish to underline the remarkable sense of confidence she exudes in constructing and celebrating her identity. Born of a Pakistani father and English mother, she inherited both the elements of the native and the non-native, weighed and balanced the two together, found a voice of her own that is lyrical, mnemonic, eerie, and yet so very certain about itself. With the poems contained in her curiously titled anthologies – *The Country at My Shoulder* (1993) and *A Bowl of Warm Air* (1996) – she repositions herself in a plethora of spatial, temporal, cultural/multicultural references. The poem entitled 'I would Like to be a Dot in a Painting by Miro', from where the lines have been taken, may be read as her credo. This credo strengthens her position in being a dot, 'barely distinguishable from other dots'. It is only real, and affords her a chance to survey the linescape, and reflect on her placement in relation to the other concrete images. Placed otherwise, she would not have the joy of realizing her own significance. She is happier further on not being a perfect circle for it holds no curiosity, and not being so makes her more interesting. The poem is an address of belonging, a certain way of apprehending herself in relation to her time and place. It would become all the more significant if one remembered that the Spanish surrealist painter and sculptor, Miro (1893-1983), acquired his meaning by shifting focus to the open space rather than the concrete image which has its relevance only in relation to the space left seemingly open and unused. Thus, being a dot in Miro's painting is being important for the poet in her new spatial context. Swinging back and forth in time and space, she collects a variety of images to compose a larger canvas of peculiar contradictions drawing close to reconciliation. In yet another poem ('Presents From My Aunts in Pakistan', *ADITS*: 404-6) salwar kameez, embossed slippers, candy-striped glass bangles, silver-bordered apple green saree, received as presents from the aunts in Pakistan find a place, in this half-English girl's home, alongside her denim and corduroy. The aunts from Pakistan, sending the country-made presents abroad, request for themselves foreign-made cardigans from Mark and Spencers. The off-shore presents, however, do not impress her school friends and she continues living her life in striking a reconciliation, and seeking an identity of 'no fixed nationality'. She remains at ease with the changing dynamics of the world around, its remarkable intermixing, and with her place in it. Thus, in yet another poem ('The Double City', *ADITS*: 406-7) she does not find it inconvenient to reach out to Indus, Trafalgar Square, Southall, Kiranjit, Lord Taylor, Ramayana, Ram, Sita with ease, and strikes an affinity with them in her effort to create and recreate an imaginative and real space of belonging for herself. In this process, several identities of her being a Pakistani-British, an Asian-British, a half-Muslim, and a half-English, apart from many others possible, merge in her being quite naturally. As such, she does not appear to be anxious about establishing her identity; it comes out without making a conscious effort.

Moniza Alvi, however, is only one case in point. There are several other women poets like her living in or outside Pakistan, for whom identity is not a cause or source of crisis and who do not work deliberately towards creating one, or labor hard to acquire a voice[2]. It would appear from a general survey that the second and third generation writers[3] living outside Pakistan seem to have completely resolved and finally forgotten the issues of why they have chosen to write in 'English' and acquire a new 'address'. They have been able to answer the questions posed by history, memory, location, and their individual lives. In the case of those at home, it would appear that in spite of the efforts made they are not marginalized on account of their gender, region, or ideology; they have constructed, claimed, preserved, and celebrated their selves, their identities. An attempt is made here to read some examples of this new literary manifestation in some of the more prominent women poets of Pakistan writing in English and other languages, and to see how they problematize their new and shared history, and configure their society and culture.

Pakistan: A Site of Contestations

The Pakistani nation-state is a historical phenomenon, a curious combination of disparate elements. English is its modern medium of expression, Urdu its adopted national linguistic identity, while Punjabi, Saraiki, Sindhi, Pushto, Balochi are its regional languages. All these languages have established themselves as the medium of literary expression in Pakistan. As they have also brought with them their own cultural baggage, they have emerged as the languages of power for the creative writers and the people. Written in various linguistic literary registers, these literatures in Pakistan remain at best an expression of the essentialist concerns of the land.

Two more important points must be added here. First, there is a significant literary tradition of Urdu writing in India which is shared by most of those writing in Urdu and which helps them develop their own modes of expression. Second, English has been the common colonial heritage of all these writers and this language has shaped their sensibilities to a very great extent. Since poetry constructs a more indirect narrative, and the poets in question represent a variety of cultural and linguistic backgrounds bearing curiously upon each other, it would be interesting to read them together to identify an underlying principle of coherence and continuity. This should not, however, create an impression that all Pakistani literatures constitute a single whole; in fact each one of them has an identity of its own but, taken together, they seem to represent the aspirations of a nation in more general terms. One may, for the sake of illustration, say that several of the contemporary Pakistani poets and writers writing in English and other languages are quite concerned about the experience of migration as such but it does not hold the same meaning for all of them. Those based in Pakistan, and belonging especially to the first generation of migrants, are concerned with the consequences of migration following the partition of India. This great event changed the course of life and times in the subcontinent, while those writing in English outside Pakistan are more concerned with their new experience of migration to greener pastures. Both create their own diasporas and their own tensions. One could call the former 'primary', and the later 'secondary' migration, which the people of the same nation experienced during a brief period of history. In the same manner, it may also be said that those writing in English outside Pakistan are more concerned with the multicultural motifs, while those at home have their own myths to explore/create in their own socio-political set up. Both, however, seek a condition of harmony with the world around rather than be at conflict with the custodians of power and politics. Both seek their identities and for both of them it is a relative condition. It shifts too frequently at given points of time from a mother, to a wife, to a colleague, to a citizen, and so on, in a single day of their lives. In the process of acquiring this identity/self, the poets and writers fill the gaps created by time and place to produce a semblance of continuous existence. And finally, it must also be added that the poets writing in English and those writing in other languages have two distinct literary hinterlands to draw upon. While one group cannot disengage from the English and the European sources, the other group has a vast and rich sub-continental heritage to fall back upon. In spite of this, the poets have frequently drawn upon each other's resources. Further, most of the poets have been extremely mobile, refurbishing themselves to think and write modern. An appropriate case has been made, though not along these lines, for the vitality of Pakistani literature by some Pakistani writers and critics. They refer to the quality of its cross-pollination, its non-self-conscious character,[4] and its emergence to power over a period of the last fifty years,[5] which are surely some of the other important factors concerning Pakistani literature in English to be taken into consideration.

So, poetry written by women poets like Moniza Alvi is only one facet of this rich phenomenon. There are several other important women poets in that country who deserve serious critical attention for a variety of reasons. These poets writing both in English and other languages of Pakistan have very certainly created a space for themselves. They have explored new contexts for their survival by challenging the mechanics of power and patriarchy, and making a hole in the principalities of dominance. A critical study of their preoccupations would reveal that these poets are essentially concerned with the issues of female bondage/confinement, political injustice, their status as women, impatience with their current predicament, desire for independence, and the vast sprawling multicultural world around. A remarkable group of women poets in English has made its way by discovering a certain idiom and an identity for itself. Works by Maki Kureishi, Hina Faisal Imam, Farida Faizullah, Gulzar Bano, Mona Hasan, Perveen Pasha, Shahbano Bilgrami, Soofia Ishaque, Zeba Hasan Hafeez bear it out quite well. Urdu poets like Zehra Nigah, Kishwar Naheed, Fehmida Riaz, Nasreen Anjum Bhatti, Sara Shagufta, Azra Abbas, Shaista Habib, Ishrat Afreen, Saeeda Gazdar, Neelma Sarwar, Mansoora Ahmad, Noshin Gilani, are remarkable for their heavy and compelling presence, their strong commitment to feminist issues, and the for their view of literature as a by-product of their lives and times. Another literary tradition, represented by Sindhi women poets like Razia Khokhar, Pushpa Vallabh, Attiya Dawood, Sultana Waqasi, Tasneem Yaqoob, Munawara Sultana, Sehar Imdad is of no less consequence, as is the tradition represented by Punjabi women poets like Bushra Ejaz, Sarwat Mohyuddin, Afzal Tauseef.

No Exit: The Experience of Confinement/Bondage

A remarkable number of women poets, based in Pakistan, have made some of the most powerful expressions concerning female confinement/bondage, as the problem concerned them much more directly than others. The consequential 70s, which brought forth the issues of Islamization and curtailment of democracy, had a far-reaching impact on the socio-political complexion of the land. The segregation of women from all visible sites (literature, art, painting, media etc.) by going hoarse for *chadur and char-diwari*, the promulgation of the Hudood Ordinance, and its implementation by the Federal Shariat Courts[6] led to severe controversy and large-scale opposition. Women organizations,[7] poets and other creative artists, raised voice against this repression. Zehra Nigah's poem 'Hudood

Ordinance', dedicated to the girls suffering imprisonment under the ordinance may be read in this context:

> In this tiny cell
> I am both fettered and free.
> There is a tiny window
> Almost as high as the ceiling.
> When the sun is about to set
> it passes just above it
> a handful of rays beam through the window
> they form a kind of path
> for me to tread on
> so I can go home. (*PL* 222)

This sense of imprisonment and the desire to seek a release is further aggravated as the victim girl innocently remembers her baba, ma, apa, and bhai, all of whom do their bit for her. The poem takes a grim turn at the end when the mother picks pebbles, talks to the birds, and thinks the birds understand her message. The message here lies in a Quranic allusion[8] where birds, with pebbles in their beaks, ravaged the oppressors on the earth, which the mother thinks the birds will do now as well. The poem ends pathetically, underlying a woman's helplessness, and in her seeking God's intervention. Another poem 'Chadur and Char-diwari' by Fehmida Riaz may also be referred to in this context. The poem begins on a note of questioning and surprise: 'Sire! What use is this black *chadur* to me?/A thousand mercies, why do you reward me with this?' As it progresses, it denudes the sire who deserves the veil himself and ends on a note of great confidence:

> These four walls, this *chadur* I wish upon the rotting carcass
> In the open air, her sails flapping, races ahead my ship
> I am the companion of the new Adam
> Who has earned my self-assured love. (*PL* 228)

There are many poignant, extremely angry, and devastating poems centred around the problem of male order/hegemony, social constraints, and political super-structuring that one may read in the Urdu and Sindhi women poets. Some examples may be seen here: 'I sat down naked behind the sun/Both my feet were in one shoe/And both my arms in one bracelet' (Nasreen Anjum Bhatti, 'Banishment',

PL 248), 'How merciful and sympathetic are those who kill,/They avoid killing in each other's presence/After all, they observe propriety' (Shaista Habib, 'No Exit', *PL* 254), 'If my hands are freed/then I will blacken/the walls of this earth.../and place this world/on the palm of my hand/and crush it.' (Azra Abbas, 'If My Hands Are Freed', *PL* 259), 'Every daughter of Eve/Who steps into this world/Must be made to wear/Shoes of iron' (Mansoora Ahmad, 'Centuries Back in Time', *PL* 268), 'Whatever the season/Be it of confinement or oppression,/Of wastelands or forests,/This prisoners breathes' (Noshin Gilani, 'This Prisoner Breathes', *PL* 274), 'Where can I go/This way or that/To find freedom?' (Munawara Ahmad: Sindhi, 'In Captivity', *PL* 283), 'That you love me, there is no doubt/But don't turn that love into a slave ring around me' (Attiya Dawood: Sindhi, 'The Boundaries of Love', *PL* 288). The extracts quoted here represent a body language, a gesture of disapproval, supported by strong verbal expressions. They underline the poets' need to speak up. They are the internal mechanism of their self-defense, unreserved expressions of their anger, and proclamations of their self-confidence. The spirit of utter rejection enlivens them. Nowhere do we have a sense of fear, despair, or self-pity. They are ruthlessly ironic; they put forth a challenge and make a claim. This is a condition, which unites them together irrespective of linguistic or regional barriers. Languages and regions, insofar as they represent people, invite them to get together and construct an identity, which these examples amply demonstrate.

Buy My Flag: The Fall of Political Imperialism

Another aspect of this anger may be marked in poems with a clear political intent. Enraged at political injustice and efforts made to marginalize them, the women poets register their protest in clear terms. This protest has the elements of irritation, resentment, bitterness and deep irony in varying degrees. Tired of ruthless subjection, Shahbano Bilgrami ironically represents a stark picture of the fourteenth of August, an important day in Pakistani history. The speaker, on this day, ironically seeks her personal freedom as she calls for selling her flag:

> Buy my flag! Buy my flag
> So that I can pull myself out of

> Searing flames of engine heat
> And hellish, gnawing need,
> So I can cool my face,
> Hide from the heavy weight
> Of the immovable sun,
> Retreat into some silent,
> Full-stomached sleep
> In a country of my own. (*AA* 88)

The green and white, star-studded flag of her land, fluttering on that day, is no better, for her, than the meaningless market wares. It makes no promise, offers no pride, and it seems too insignificant before a real ten rupee note. The poem has an important subtext of disaffection and it has a history behind it, which presents itself rather murkily even without any verbal expression by the speaker. In another poem, dramatically constructed with voices, questions and answers, Gulzar Bano, brings out the pathos of rape, women have been subjected to in all times and places, in spite of the regulatory social order, legal deterrents, and religious injunction. In her poem entitled 'The Rape of Macharanwali', the place represents all places where such crimes are committed, and the women stand for all women who have suffered this ignominy in all ages. The poem employs stark images of chadur, char-diwari, adalat, kafan, Bichuanwali, sappanwali to create a condition of insufferable pain. It begins on an extremely depressing, yet a very sure female voice throwing a challenge:

> Land of my fathers and their mothers
> Clothed with proud Begs and silk scented Begums
> Broadcasting grand Commissions, Forums, Ministries
> We are the daughters of a naked land
> Bring us the ashes of our garments from Macharanwali (*AA* 30)

This part of the poem called 'Death Cry' is followed by 'Consolation', and a 'Second Cry', and subsequently 'Questions' and 'Answers'. The dramatic structure of pain and suffering is brought to an end with a 'Passive Confession', 'Third Cry', and 'Active Response' where the poet offers 'individual collective shame' and expresses faith in tomorrow that may reverse their fate. It is a typically multiple text reflecting sadly on the personal and the social, the cultural and the political. The poem can also be approached as a stock response to a predicament, irrespective of time and place, even though it particularizes the crime in relation to a given time and a place.

Various other poems may be quoted to show the deep concern of the women poets with their society, and the historical process of the configuration of a nation as a good, bad, or indifferent space. Some examples should illustrate the point: 'In those times when the camera could not freeze tyranny for ever/only until those times/should you have written/that history/which describes tyranny as valor' (Kishwar Naheed', 'Censorship' *WSW*/51), 'This law is a rag/Worthy of the dust/Off the rebels' feet/Dictatorship is a curse/This government of/Ordinances/We shall shred/in a public square' (Fehmida Riaz, 'The Interrogator', *WSW* 83), 'You snatch from me the status of a human being./I refuse to give birth to you' (Saeeda Gazdar, 'Twelfth of February 1983', *PL* 246), 'The thesis for the search of affiliations/Is in the last show-case of the museum,/So that future generations may go through it/And prepare notes on history' (Shaista Habib, 'Do Not Question', *PL* 257), 'A greater punishment than hanging is to bear a borrowed life/the ace of spades does not prolong the game; it finishes it/it finishes all claims' (Nasreen Anjum Bhatti, 'Ace of Spades', *FAR* 286), 'We shall search the globe/to find a NEW homeland./We shall hold the right/to look anew', (Hina Faisal Imam, 'The New World Order', *PL* 302). As these poems reject the existing order, they also dream of establishing a new one. They nurture the hope for a new community of reconcilable beings, which may not be an ideal one, but the inhabitants may share respect amongst themselves. It may be a small island of survival, not a jungle for perishing.

I Cannot be Sublime: The Status of Women

The status of women is an issue essentially relative in nature but a major one by any standards. The poets have related to it at a personal level, as also at the social, political, and cultural levels. The poems in this category have the elements of anguish more than of ease, as the poets are quite conscious of their present status and have little hope for amelioration. This comes out quite clearly in Shaista Habib's 'I cannot be Sublime':

> Lady Caroline Lamb was really brave,
> She thought life was in Byron's shoes
> And in waiting drenched in rain'
> She was well versed in living death

But she was blamed even then
For she could not be sublime
Lady Caro!
Smoke and chew betels,
No, no, all intoxicants are alike –
I am drunk on the love of my being
And I adore my existence
In which is dissolved the alcohol of tears.
Come, let's clink our beings and drink this cup
In the name of all lovers
Who cannot be sublime. (*FAR* 328-29)

The sense of independence the poem expresses has a streak of pride as also of helplessness. It is a queer feeling for them to be a woman in the given context, marked by uncertainties and fears. Expressions of confident womanhood may be heard in the poets we have been discussing. Kishwar Naheed's self-confessedly 'We Sinful Women' is, in fact, a declaration of this womanhood characterized by a rare conviction. Ironically called 'sinful', these women do not sell their lives, bow their heads, fold their hands; on the contrary, they warn the hands from raising the demolished wall. Her other poems, 'A Palace of Wax', 'Who Am I?', and 'Nightmare' (*WSW* 37/43/47) have similar notes of faith and courage. The essential question of woman's identity emerges in a different ways in different poets: 'She is a woman impure/imprisoned by her flowing blood/in a cycle of months and years' (Fehmida Riaz, 'She is Woman Impure', *WSW* 97), 'In my very first breaths it stirred/the bitter poison of defeat as I heard/'O, it's a girl!'/A girl!' (Ishrat Aafreen, 'The First Prayer of My Elders', *WSW* 151), 'My man you are an infant/Fresh from your mother's womb/What do you know what a woman is', (Mona Hasan, 'My Foster God', *AA* 56), 'Ever since I opened my eyes, I was taught:/'Society is a jungle and the home a shelter/Man is the owner/And woman its tenant/Who pays the rent/By obedience, by fidelity' (Attiya Dawood, 'Autobiography', *PL* 286). These poems represent a variety of irreconcilable moods, as the women are sometimes impatient with life, while at others in love with it, in spite of all the attendant contradictions around. They proclaim independence and express their innermost desires as human beings. They represent themselves as beloveds, mothers, daughters, and citizens. Scared of the inevitability of pain in a woman's fate,

Sara Shagufta advises her daughter: 'Whenever anyone causes you sorrow/name that sorrow – daughter' ('For Sheli, My Daughter' *PL* 264) but Ishrat Aafreen chooses to be too expressive in her defiance when she says: 'She belongs to the tribe of Ego/This ruthless girl/And lives way beyond/The bounds of your territory'. In yet another short poem, she maintains that gesture when she proclaims: 'I grew/Taller than my father/And my mother won' ('I'/'Dedication', *WSW* 143/141). The poems may have notes of protest, rebellion, and negation but they do not, by any means, create a sense of nihilistic pleasure or of negative enjoyment. They are strongly reminiscent of many of the western feminist and confessional texts. They, however, do not represent those conditions but they certainly recreate the essentialist concerns of the women and the women writers as such. They need to disengage themselves from the fetters of conditioned response in their own respects, and acquire a self, a personality, and an individual independence while being a part of the system. They represent a condition of a desired existence, and project themselves as intellectually alive and socially engaged human beings.

An Endnote

The women poets discussed above are easily distinguishable for their iconoclasm and an independent feminist stance in the apprehension of their lives and their conditions. They neither necessarily blow out the traditional norms of a society, nor violate the conventional poetics or flaunt their offbeat stances. They try to achieve a precarious balance with the existing norm but they do not give up when it betrays them. In writing themselves, they write a new social and literary order. They extend the possibilities of language as they speak in an entirely new idiom, while drawing upon the tradition, and making radical improvisations upon them, without valorizing themselves. This owes much to their mobility and their ways of intermixing the real with the mythic. Several of these poets have had an eventful career of taking bold stances, speaking without fear, and getting punished, as if, under 'a foreign code of conscience'. What sustains them, however, is the genuineness of their experience and the honesty of their expression. The women poets of Pakistan are remarkable for the unique difference they make in their apprehension and expression and the new canon they create. It is a rare group of literary artists and social activists the likes of whom are not to be found anywhere in South Asia.

Endnotes

1. 'I would Like to be a Dot in a Painting by Miro,' *A Dragonfly in the Sun: An Anthology of Pakistani Writing in English*, Selected and edited by Muneeza Shamsie. Karachi: OUP., 1998, p. 403.
2. Women poets have been discussed in the subsequent parts of the paper. One may, however, like to look at the male composition. Among the male poets writing outside Pakistan mention may be made of Zulfikar Ghose, Adrian A. Husain, Shuja Nawaz, Waqas Ahmad Khwaja, Tariq Latif, Sheryar Singha. Among those at home, Alamgir Hashmi, M. Atar Tahir, Abbas Husain, Moeen Faruqi, Ghulam Fariduddin Riaz, Masood Amjad Ali are more especially mentionable.
3. Consider, for example, this illustrious familial line of descent: Attiya Hussain>Muneeza Shamsie>Kamila Shamsie. While the grandaunt Attiya Hussain (*Sunlight on the Broken Column*) chose to migrate to England, Muneeza Shamsie ('Shahrazad's Golden Leopard') stayed mostly in Pakistan, and her daughter, Kamila Shamsie (*City by the Sea, Salt and Saffron, Kartography*), born in Pakistan, is based in US. Like the locations, their attitudes and sensibilities are remarkably different. There are many other third generation writers who have found a home away from the ancestral home and have become a part of the new soicio-cultural-literary order. It must also be added that opinions regarding their degree of adaptability vary as there is a belief that even the second and third generation writers have not been able to identify themselves with their locations fully. This is, however, a debatable point.
4. See Huma Ibrahim, 'Transnational Migrations and the Debate of English Writing in/of Pakistan,' *Ariel*, Vol. 29, No. 1, January 1998, pp. 33-48.
5. See 'Introduction' to *A Dragonfly in the Sun*.
6. Hudood Ordinances were promulagetd on 10 February, 1979. They were directed towards imposing maximum punishment (as per the *hud*: limitation) on the acts of offence like theft, drunkenness, bearing false witness, and adultery/rape. Federal Shariat Courts were established to see their implementation. Since it gave an open license, there was fear of its being used indiscriminately, which several cases proved true at later dates. The case of a couple, Fehmida and Allah Bux, is one in point that shook the women organizations around and brought them together.
7. Shirkat Gah (site of participation) an important pressure group brought several organizations together. Women's Action Forum (WAF) was established in Karachi, then in Lahore, Islamabad, Rawalpindi, and Peshawar. All Pakistan Women's Association, the generic organization, endorsed the actions of WAF.

8. See the Holy Qur'an, Sura CV (*Fil*). 1-5. Introduction and summary to the Sura reads as follows: 'This early Meccan Sura refers to an event that happened in the year of the birth of our holy Prophet, say about 570 A.D. Yemen was then under the rule of the Abyssinians (Christians) who had driven out the Jewish Himyar rulers. Abraha Ashram was the Abyssinian Governor or Viceroy. Intoxicated with power and fired by religious fanaticism, he led a big expedition against Mecca, intending to destroy the Kaba. He had an elephant or elephants in his train. But his sacrilegious intentions were defeated by a miracle. No defence was offered by the custodians of the kaba as the army was too strong for them, but it was believed that a shower of stones, thrown by flocks of birds, destroyed the invading army almost to a man. The stones produced sores and pustules on the skin, which spread like a pestilence' Abdullah Yusuf Ali, *The Meaning of the Glorious Qur'an*, Vol. 2, Dar Al-Kitab Al-Masri, Cairo and Dar Al-Kitab Allubnani, Beirut, nd. P. 1791.

References

Ahmad, Rukhsana. ed. and trans, *We Sinful Women*. New Delhi: Rupa and Co., 1994. (*WSW*)

An Anthology. Karachi: OUP, 1997. (*AA*)

Pakistani Literature, Vol. 3, No. 2. 1994, Islamabad, Special Issue on Women's Writing (*PL*)

Rahman, Anisur. ed. and translator, *Fire and the Rose: An Anthology of Modern Urdu Poetry*. New Delhi: Rupa and Co., 1995. (*FAR*)

Shamsie, Muneeza. ed. *A Dragonfly in the Sun: An Anthology of Pakistani Writing in English*. Karachi: OUP, 1998. (*ADITS*)

17

Not White and Also Women

Race, Gender and Multiculturalism in South Asian Canadian Women's Poetry

Sudha Rai

> If we, who are not white, and also
> women, have not yet seen that here we live in a prison,
> that we are doing time, then we are fools, playing
> unenjoyable games with ourselves.
> —Himani Bannerji ('doing time')

I

Canada was the first country in the word to adopt multiculturalism as an official policy in 1971. Himani Bannerji, in *The Dark Side of the Nation (2000)*, offers convincing arguments to show how the Canadian policy of multiculturalism is flawed in practice. The discourse of openness and acceptance in the said policy, is only a facade, accepting coloured immigrant peoples in "cultural" terms but basically denying them equality and status in "political" terms. "Whiteness", as Bannerji posits, continues to be accorded value and power making the Canadian multicultural policy discriminatory in practice:

An element of whiteness quietly enters into cultural definitions, marking the difference between a core cultural group and other groups who are represented as cultural fragments. The larger function of this multiculturalism not only takes care of legitimation of the Canadian state, but helps in managing an emerging crisis in legitimation produced by a complex political conjunctive evolving through the years after the second world war. (Bannerji 2000: 10)

Bannerji, in the same work, pleads for attention to "the task of forging a real anti-racist feminism" (173) which will make it possible "to enter our politics through the door of particular "women's issues" (174).

This context of organized women's resistance to the Canadian multiculturalism policy becomes the social text that illuminates the representation in poetry, of the politics of race and gender in contemporary. South Asian Canadian women's poetry in English, that will be discussed here. The text of the racial and gendered South Asian woman subject fleshes out the poems of 'othering' and the specific issues of violence against the female body. The poems of Surjit Kalsey, Himani Bannerji, Lakshmi Gill and Uma Parameswaran interrogate the rights of immigrant subjects, that include the right to work, the right to dignified treatment, the right for redressal and action in calamities, as well as the right to information and truth. The extracts gleaned from these poets bring before us the politically aware consciousness of immigrant women poets, protesting against the rhetoric of policies and documents, interrogating the hidden crevices of veiled realities.

South Asian Canadian women poets see themselves as catalysts of social change, turning away from nostalgia to rebuild an authentic multicultural society by negating the opposition of races, classes, cultures or sexes. Indo-Canadian diasporic women's poetry is an expression of resistance to their condition of othering – both because they are 'women' and because they belong to the racial category 'non-white' as Bannerji's poem 'doing time' effectively evokes. The interrogation of hegemony and patriarchy is within the changing Canadian contexts of multiculturalism, feminism and postcolonial consciousness.

The notion of 'double colonization' indicating the condition of coloured women being colonized twice over – by both imperial and patriarchal ideologies gained currency in the 1980s. (Ashcroft

1997:250) Recent feminist postcolonial theory has insisted that the critiquing of authoritarian structures must be contextualized and historicized, refusing essentialisms of race and gender, emphasizing local politics and specific forms of resistance. Kirsten Holst Petersen points out "that universal sisterhood is not a given biological condition as much as perhaps a goal to work towards" (Ashcroft 1997: 251). "The relationship between 'woman' – a cultural and ideological composite other constructed through diverse representational discourses (scientific, literary, linguistic, etc.) and 'women' – 'real material subjects of their collective histories' – as Chandra Mohanty (Ashcroft 1997: 259) establishes becomes central to the problematic of the 'self'. Historical processes activate the journey of self-discovery of the racial women subjects, compelling the diasporic reconstitution of the self through an apprehended distinction between 'native homeland' and 'adopted home'.

Three of the historical fields within which the feminist critique of Canadian multiculturalism is conducted, which I will substantiate through selected poems are *the Air India Kanishka Tragedy (1985); the Canada – U.S. (hidden) ideological alliance in the Vietnam war and the issue of job discrimination against immigrants in Canada.*

These three situations test the awareness of outsider immigrants and their 'action' as responsive Canadian citizens. The onslaught on the female body subjected to a compounding censure of the "male gaze" (and the attitudes and power it stands for) and the racist gaze (which shatters the esteem of the non-white self), and the subsequent perceptions, become the poetic vehicle for eroding the Canadian multicultural premise of equality, and the critiquing of the gap between policy and action in Canadian social reality from the 1970s onwards. As members of a group who migrated to Canada in search of academic and professional opportunities in the 60s the voices of Surjit Kalsey, Lakshmi Gill, Himani Bannerji and Uma Parameswaran articulate the interplay of the factors of race and gender in impeding their growth as individuals and professionals. These third-world perceptions voicing protest can provoke Canadians to rescrutinize their political ideologies and self-image.

Though not constituted as a movement, or a genre of political poetry, Indo-Canadian women's poetry stands out as an exercise in social consciousness raising, as a counter discourse indulging in a deconstruction of terms and language exposing the racist underbelly, and as a didactic mode, mapping the lure and the trap of the myths of freedom, equality and creative fulfillment in Canada, for the colonized non-white, offering counsel and sage advice. Questions, issues and some solutions that emerge in the poems are problematised, highlighting the forms of feminist protest.

II

"Quantitatively and qualitatively, poetry is the best genre produced by South Asian Canadians" in the opinion of Diane McGifford and Judith Kearns (1990). In her article "South Asian Poetry in Canada: In Search of a Place," Arun Mukherjee identifying distinguishing features of this poetry emphasizes that "racism is one of the predominant concerns of South Asian Canadian poetry", that it is "a violation of proprieties and that "it bears the character of a rhetorical appeal even when it does not address the reader directly." Within this genre South Asian Canadian Women's poetry is a forthright articulation of their consciousness of gendering which they bring with their traditional Indian moorings. The new searing consciousness of the victimization of women at the level of race and gender and protest against racial and gender discrimination is their feminist contribution to critiquing state policy and apparatus in Canada. The poetry evaluates the failure to live up to the "hope" that Pierre Trudeau, former Prime Minister of Canada, cherished as an ideal for the country:

> It is my deepest hope that Canada will match its new legal maturity with that degree of political maturity which will allow us to make a total commitment to the Canadian ideal. I speak of a Canada where men and women of Aboriginal ancestry, of French and British heritage, of the diverse cultures of the world, demonstrate the will to share this land in peace, in justice and with mutual respect.

As counter discourse to the rhetoric of official policy, women's poetry probes the invisible aspects of marginalization, contrapunting the emotional and psychological realities of insult, neglect and rejection in the country of adoption, spreading awareness that the racial divide has not ended. In Surjit Kalsey's poem "Speaking to the Winds" the persona voices the fear of the unknown, which accompanies the immigrant's choice, through the analogy of entering "a deep well half-covered with a board." The disappointment with the racist encounter is figured in images of torture: "Whenever I went/to become a part of them/they stripped off my flesh from my fingernails/eyes pierced my being like poisonous thorns." Metaphors of flight and homelessness, show up the lack of fulfillment in the diasporic choice: "the flight begins to die slowly in our wings" and "no sun/no earth/where to look at what to look for." The erosion of the female self through imprisonment in the "invisible cage" makes a recovery of home impossible. "This is a real loneliness/This is a real barrenness" admits the speaker in "I want my Chaos Back", acutely aware of the physical and psychological distances between Toronto and India, the 'I' admitting: "Today I am three thousand miles away/from throbbing bubbling figurines of/my flesh ...."

Himani Bannerji deconstructs language, even vocabulary, to capture racial discrimination as in the poem "Apart-hate". Brimming with a savage irony "apart-hate" evokes the word "apartheid" through echo-connotations of sound. Canada the "white land" of the poem has laws that translate as "apart-hate". The racial other – "Chinese coolies, black slaves, indian indentures" is contained through a battery of procedures like "immigration head tax, virginity tests." The racial subject in Canada, represented as the female prey, is exploited and nullified. The poem is a no-holds-barred denunciation of white racist policies:

> In this white land
> Skin is fingered like pelt
> Skin is sold and the ivory of her eyes
> the category human has no meaning
> When spoken in white
> Apart-hate

In Bannerji's "Paki Go Home", the impact of verbal racist contempt is embodied through the woman subject, doubly condemned because she is "too visible":

> And words run down
> like frothy white spit
> down her bent head
> down the serene parting of her white hair
> as she stands too visible
> from home to bus stop to home
> raucous hyena laughter
> "Paki go home."

A rejection of the Canadian idea of progress is the vital issue in Lakshmi Gill's "Letter to a prospective Immigrant" for the speaker warns: "This is no cotton candy country/no penny arcade." One observes the didactic, moralizing strain in the poem, as valuable and necessary insights, moving between the "they" of white Canada and the "you" of the desirous immigrant, are passed on. The stark wisdom in the closure of the poem: "hell does not give but takes", endorses the negative imaging of "Canada the cold," or a "they" who are seen to "deal with devil commerce."

In Gill's poem "me", the traits of "visibility" and "otherness", (Mukherjee: 1994) are vividly rendered in a two-stanza self portrait. The construction of the racial other in the white imagination as "Aha! she's Asian" or "Ha, ha, the Oriental" is parodied by the speaker who knows that "the mind clicks in all/the notions of orientalese (like some disease)". In Gill's "Fredericton Highway Bridge" the persona stands in a hostile relationship to the environment which has made her "fallow" – "All around me this arid country/stretching from the stretch marks of my belly to beyond my reach".

Uma Parameswaran's poems evoke in her view "a way of apprehending the world that is different from the male, white engagement with it." The footnotes which Parmeswaran attaches to several of her poems are factual histories of women's struggles to resist and overthrow gender discrimination in the Canadian context. The poetic text contrastively, is utilized to deal with the gender issues in symbolic and connotative ways.

Parameswaran strikes back at gender discrimination against coloured women in the area of employment, in the two poems "The Interview" and "Vigilance," exposing the racism implicit in the process. "The Interview" narrates the outcomes of a recruitment process. The placing of an ad for office supervisor ends in the rejection of the candidate of colour, despite her having the necessary bilingual and supervisory skills. The whites are satirised under the fictitious personae of "Walrus" and "Grendel's mother." In response to the interviewer's questions, vetting her ability to "toe the line" the candidate answers defiantly that she will continue to wear the "placards" they so dislike: "And she answered with even keel: All my placards, buttons, pins. Always say the same thing – Equality." The poem's refrain of "I am your problem," is a frontal attack on a power-wielding other. Various gender issues from racist policies, to sexist harassment are highlighted and the powers that be are depersonalized, with only truncated reference to their body parts – "four mouths that spoke at her" or "And four silent hisses breathed."

The poem ends on a note of defiance and courage (flat and one-dimensional as far as poetic meaning, one must point out) affirming "words and voices that will ring again and again/Even though you shoot down my friends and me,/words and voices that will echo and resound/For our time that is yet to come."

The footnote to the poem "Vigilance" reads "a public tribute to women activists and a private tribute to the signatories of a systemic discrimination complaint against universities. The euphoria of their youthful days as activists ("raised hell on campuses". "stormed citadels of power") has now crystallized into the grim knowledge that for women, there is a long vigil before resistance produces results. The names of women of diverse backgrounds, who have come together (connected by resistance to gendering) are strung together in the poem – "Wilma, Susan, Anne-Marie, Michele, Sonia, Genevieve." Female bonding is affirmed despite the thorny obstacles set by Canadian multiculturalism: "We now start the day holding each other/in thought or over telephone wires to say. Take heart, Hang in there."

III

Canada's role as negotiator between the US and Vietnam, serving on two international truce commissions, as recent rewritings of history reveal (Levant 1998), was not neutral; in fact Canada is reported to have aided and abetted the US by supplying aid and medical supplies only to South Vietnam. Lakshmi Gill's "Beneath the Purple Lantern" is a taunting exposure of Canada's cowardice in toeing the US policy line, while publicly proclaiming its distance from the US. The persona exhorts – "O Canada emerge from the bowels of the land/with a battle Hymn/why must you sit on your haunches/and howl at your neighbour's deeds?"

The poem is an address to Canada to endorse an authentic independent pacifist mission through her actions and to overthrow imperialist Big Brother. The critiquing of Canada's internal policies, shows up latent racism and cultural imperialism:

> And Canada refuses to send troops
> because this is a holy nation
> because it doesn't want to be involved

because it doesn't believe in force
because the women want the needed population
to till the prairies
and fill up the Yukon Territories
instead of these lousy immigrants
who mess up the Canadian Identity Puritans.

IV

A third political intervention South Asian Canadian women's poetry has made is in the context of the delayed investigations of the Kanishkha crash, of 1985, when Air India Flight 182 crashed into Dunmnus Bay, Ireland. The 329 victims were mostly Indian Canadians.

Uma Parameswaran's Kanishka poems (Parameswaran 2002) – "On the shores of the Irish Sea" and Surjit Kalsey's "Voices of the Dead," are elegies for the specific group who were killed. The elegiac mode fulfils the larger purpose of commemorating the Indian diasporic community and formalizes the act of mourning and reverences. Vijay Mishra (2001) theorizes the sociological significance of the mythologising of loss in the lives of diasporic peoples, even when it is an "impossible mourning":

> In theorizing diasporas we need to be conscious of the ways in which mourning and trauma do acquire historical depth, and are significant elements in the social lives of diasporas. This is not an essentialist argument it is one that addresses the kinds of discourses that frame the lived experience of diasporic peoples. (46)

The Kanishka tragedy stimulates a protracted exercise in self-searching, especially of the rightness or wrongness of choices made earlier, especially that of immigration. The delay in bringing the perpetrators of the tragedy to book is attributed to several causes – namely, "that an agent of the Canadian Security Intelligence service (CSIS) destroyed key audio tapes.... because of the turf war going on between the CSIS and the Royal Canadian Mounted police, placed in change of the investigation". As one opinion suggests: "There is a feeling in many quarters, including the families of the victims, that if the victims were mostly 'white' Canadians the government wouldn't hesitate to set up a judicial inquiry" (Correia 2000). The story of the crash, and the human aftermath for the families of the dead has subsequently been widely represented in books, documentary and video, and live dance performances, especially by Lata Pada who lost her own family in the crash.

The narrator who reminisces the Kanishka tragedy in Surjit Kalsey's "Voices of the Dead" invokes the 329 dead in the fatal plane crash. The elegy for the dead Indians, is an attempt to initiate dialogue on the closed chapter of the tragedy. In a country where racialism preempts adequate honour to the dead from another race, Surjit Kalsey captures the fragmentation of communities, families and the very body through clinical, staccato phrases: "Fragile/arrow/ this side up/handle with care/secret is assumed safe in this black box (43).

Death appears to become even more tragic, even more final for the South Asian immigrant community. Life abroad is fraught with new risks (other than those of an inclement climate and discriminating policies) – as immigrants become targets of terrorism. The dilemmas of the immigrant choice are confronted afresh, this time in the new context of international terrorism. The manner packs is an aphoristic twist in the line: "Black box can keep the secret only not the truth."

Parameswaran's poem "On the shores of the Irish Sea" echoes Wordsworth's lines from "Tintern Abbey" to dramatise reverberations of the tragedy, in chaste poetic diction: "Fifteen years have passed/Fifteen summers with the length of fifteen long winters". The elegy narrativizes important milestones in the history of Indian diaspora in Canada such as the Komagatomaru incident of July 23rd, 1914, and the insensitive lapse on the part of Mulroney, Canada's Prime Minister in not including Indian victims of the Kanishka crash as "Canadians" but rather pointing out their loss in a condolence statement to Rajiv Gandhi, as "Your great loss". The elegiac history shames the Canadian government for indifference and delay in bringing justice, even fifteen years after the disaster.

> Cry rivers
> June 23rd, 2000, dark day of ignominy,
> when the criminals who sent limbs and hearts
> hurtling through the sky into the Irish sea,
> have still not been brought to book.

The poem rises to a crescendo of affirmation, commemorating the continuity of spirit of the immigrant community:

> and to sing dirges to the dead, who,
> denied funeral pyres
> shall glow forever
> in history books and hearts
> of all who live from sea to sea.

V

As a cross cultural feminist contribution, South Asian Canadian women's poetry is "pledged to the micropolitics of context, subjectivity and struggle, as well as to the macropolitics of global economic and political systems and processes (Mohanty: 2003). For these women poets, every feminist struggle in the Canadian context anchors the self in a reality divested of illusions. As Himani Bannerji affirms in "Upon hearing Beverley Glen Copeland".

> Civilization of Greece and Rome
> The England of Hawkins and Victoria
> A heap of soiled clothes fell from us
> Discarded in the new night of history.

South Asian Canadian women's poetry not only represents the personal traumas of racial and gender marginalization through spatial metaphors or imprisonment and foregrounded images of the female – racial body as a site for violence, but also breaks the female "culture" of silence to denounce the shortfalls in the ideal of Canadian multiculturalism. The deconstruction of racism in the Canadian context, and the deconstruction of cultural symbols of gendering – such as "wife" and "mother" are processes that mutually strengthen the feminist critique of nation.

Formal features of the poetry include didacticism, use of the elegiac mode, letters, deconstruction of power centres through fragmented language, counter discourse, and dialogic modes for social protest. The rewriting of history from alternative perspectives and an alignment of the angry, ironic voice with those who have been cheated out of their human rights, makes South Asian Canadian women's poetry a political contribution to the rebuilding of a vision of a new Canada, cleansed of racism, embracing the leadership of women.

Endnote

The poems by Surjit Kalsey, Himani Bannerji, Lakshmi Gill and Uma Parameswaran discussed in this article are from the anthologies *Shakti's Words* eds. Diane Mc Gifford and Judith Kearns (1990) and *Sisters at the Well*, Uma Parameswaran (2002).

References

Bannerji, Himani, *The Dark Side of the Nation: Essays on Multiculturalism, Nationalism and Gender*. Toronto: Canadian Scholar's Press Inc. 2000.

Correia Eugene, "A tragedy that won't go away, rediff.com (US edition), June 22, 2000. (Online)

Levant, Victor, "Canada and the Vietnam War", *The 1998 Canadian and World Encyclopaedia*, McClelland and Stewart (Online).

McGifford, Diane and Judith Kearns. eds. *Shakti's Words*. Toronto: TSAR 1990.

Mishra, Vijay. "Diasporas and the Art of Impossible Mourning," *In Diasporas* Ed. Makarand Paranjape. New Delhi: Indialog Publications Pvt. Ltd., 2001.

Mohanty, Chandra. "Under Western Eyes: Feminist Scholarship and Colonial Discourses", *The Post-Colonial Studies Reader*. Eds. Ashcroft, Griffiths, Tiffin. London and New York: Routledge 1997.

—, "Under Western Eyes Revisited: Feminist Solidarity through Anticapitalist struggles," *Signs*, Vol. 28, No. 2, 2003.

Mukherjee, Arun, "South Asian Poetry in Canada: In Search of a Place" *Oppositional Aesthetics*. Toronto: TSAR Publications, 1994.

Parameswaran, Uma. *Sisters at the Well*. New Delhi: Indialog Publications Pvt. Ltd., 2002.

Peterson, Kirsten Holst, "First Things First: Problems of a Feminist Approach to African Literature", *The Post-Colonial Studies Reader*. Eds. Ashcroft, Griffiths, Tiffin. London and New York: Routledge 1997.

Trudeau, Pierre Elliott. "Canadian Multiculturalism" www.pch 9c.ca (Online).

18

Enclaves of Otherness Within Larger Cultures
Lee Langley's *A House in Pondicherry*

Veena Jain

In January 2003, when twenty million strong NRIs from fifty-five different countries gathered to celebrate the *Pravasi Bharatiya Divas*, they were here not so much for the celebrations but for the occasion that accorded them the chance to align themselves to their roots. "There is a singular force uniting the diversity of this diaspora, a love for India", commented the *Times of India*, (New Delhi, January 11, 2003).

Moving a little further than mere celebrations or the government's foreign exchange building move, one wonders if the *pravasi* stands at the point of no return in spite of his strong urge to come back to his roots. Does the emigrant live with a permanent sense of loss, as is expressed by some writers? Salman Rushdie, an expatriate Indian, writes, "The past is a home and the present a foreign country" (quoted in Viney Kirpal, 3). Another Fiji-Indian writer, Satendra Nandan presently living in Australia in exile writes, "The loss of any paradise is a sad and saddening narrative .... They say exiles live in one place and remember the reality of another. One belongs where one cannot be, and one is where one does not belong" (Introduction, *Requiem for a Rainbow*, Intro, 4). The colonizer's experience may differ but he feels equally threatened when the colonized begin to aspire for freedom. But for the immigrant, after an initial sense of loss, the freedom movement begins, the second stage could be one of adjustment or merger, a kind of settlement with one's surroundings. The third stage with the next generation and the youngsters stepping in, could be a point of no return, when the ties with the past are sufficiently snapped.

And yet the pull always remains. The *pravasi* preserves his identity by preserving his cultural heritage, although he may harmonise into the political, social and economic life of the host country. The question then arises, does the concept of multiculturalism in any way help groups of minorities living in Europe and America? Since the paradoxical stance of the divided self of the migrant is an undeniable factor, it raises many issues of identity, nation state, minority status, psychological and social adjustments and cultural crisis.

The term multiculturalism, basically a by-product of globalisation or global commodification, was initially used as a resistant force to decentre discrimination against minority cultures in Europe and America. It was also used as a tool to avert or dislodge antagonism brewing inside minority cultures because of discriminatory practices. In this way, it tries to conceal racism and exploitation. Avtar Brah calls multiculturalism "diaspora space". She feels, multiculturalism "marks the intersectionality of contemporary conditions of transmigrancy of people, capital, commodities and cultures. It addresses the realm where economic, cultural and political effects of crossing/transgressing different borders are experienced; and where belonging and otherness is appropriated and contested" (242).

The discourse on multiculturalism takes two positions. Ideologically speaking, multiculturalism is a potent force that can create a harmonious world where difference is preserved and narrow mental boundaries of caste. creed and nationality obliterated. Writers like Rushdie, Homi Bhabha, Gayatri Spivak[1] celebrate multiculturalism. But there is another stand that questions multiculturalism on the ground of ignoring vital issues of nationalism, statehood, minority rights, woman status and community identity. Writers like Aijaz Ahmad[2] and Timothy Brennan fall in this category. Practically speaking, absolute multiculturalism is only a theoretical illusion as there is always the danger of larger groups or entities subsuming smaller or minority communities. In India where we pride ourselves on its multicultural and democratic base, we have incidents like Godhra and repeated religious riots. After September 11 incident, the repercussions were experienced by the Asian immigrants and the non-white population in America. Politics may create rifts and divisions but such incidents put a question mark on our ideology of multicultural and secular existence. The identity, rights and status of minority culture are threatened and it is expected to merge with larger national cultures. Even writers who aim to project multiculturalism in their writings through their international characters and who consciously want to obliterate boundaries, unconsciously fall a prey to their divided self and cannot but portray smaller groups who remain enclaves within larger cultures. One such writer is Lee Langley, an Indian-born British writer who feels,

> Looking back over my books, I see a preoccupation with outsiders – of enclaves of otherness within larger cultures. This sense of otherness, of not belonging, has always been there – sometimes without my realizing it at the time – like a shadowy reef lying beneath the surface. The characters are often people who don't fit in.
> (Author statement www. contemporary writers.com)

II

Lee Langley's three novels, *Change of Address*, *Persistent Rumours* and a *House in Pondicherry* are about India. *Change of Address* was shortlisted for Hawthornden Prize and *Persistent Rumours* won the Writers Guild/Macallan Best Novel Award. Lee Langley was born in Calcutta and having spent her childhood there, she carries with her a sense of loss and uprootedness experienced by all migrant writers. This feeling of exile, sometimes leads to an idealistic stance by the writer. Having left behind a place one loves, its recreation is in the form of utopia. Langley's preoccupation is with history and she creates characters who are filled with an 'unspecified yearning', a sense of displacement "with an awareness of the fragility of human bonds".

Her novels span more than two centuries. Her latest work, *Distant Music* (2001), spans six centuries. It begins in the 15th century on the Portuguese island of Madeira and ends in London in the year 2000. *A House in Pondicherry* (1995) spans three centuries, beginning from the 18th century French settlement to the end of 20th century that is 1992 India. The vast panorama of her writings bring out sharply the contrast between past splendour and present urbanity. Historical changes, upheavals and wars change the future and fortunes of her characters. There is 'love and loss'. The setting of her novels is exotic, abounding in lushful greenery giving the feel of the Garden of Eden.

A House in Pondicherry picturises Pondicherry in the rich splendour of the French Empire, its natural beauty spread with its palms and coconuts, cashew blossoms and "an imposing promenade that curved the length of the bay, straight streets lined with trees, houses spilling bougainvillea down their white walls, gardens filled with flowers and shady fragrance" (7). But there is a strict demarcation between the Indian and the French Pondicherry, "At the West bank India began" (8). The glorious past of French Pondicherry comes to an end with India's independence and its merger under the Indian flag. So does the fading stucco of Hotel de France signify its rundown state. Oriane's life is entangled within these two historical forces.

At the outset, Lee Langley's work seems to advocate multiculturalism. We may even call her transnational or international to borrow Gayatri Spivak's phrase. She makes a passionate plea for a more humane existence where her work rises above nation or culture. Langley uses the setting of Pondicherry as a background for different cultures and nationalities. A combination of history and fiction, culture and mysticism, the book gives a curious chiaroscuro effect of multiplicity, of mixing of realities and lives in a tiny tropical French part of India that is Pondicherry,

But beneath this strong desire is the ambivalence of uprootedness that the central character Oriane experiences at every turn of her life. Oriane is to be sent to France to be removed from the Indian influence. The war disturbs the plan. She writes to her cousin Marie Helen in Rouen: "This is my home and I am not happy to think of leaving it" (14).

As a child she shows her assertion and asks the Mayor to give protection to Aurobindo Ghose under the French flag in the French territory when the British were demanding his extradition. She dreads going to France if kicked out of India. France is the grey North while Pondicherry has warmth, coconut trees, the palms and scents. Anglo-Indians are half-castes and are called the 'touch of the tar brush.... . "Nobody wants them," the man said, "not the Indians, not the Europeans. Yet surely they belonged to both?" ' (74). With the merger, the French tricolour is replaced by the Indian flag. When in December 1962 with the 14th amendment in the constitution, Pondicherry is announced a union territory, Oriane exclaims, 'Thank God. We've kept our independence!' Oriane refuses to leave Pondicherry for France with her parents and stays back alone.

It is the French Pondicherry that Lee Langley is interested in. India as a larger world poses a threat to this French part of India. Hence India's colonial past during the British Raj is merely used as a backdrop in the novel. The account of India's history begins only in 1909 at Alipore with the imprisonment of Aurobindo. Gandhi's Satyagraha movement and civil disobedience movement leading to independence. 1947 announces India's freedom and Pondicherry witnesses scenes of jubilation. 1950 is the year of Aurobindo's death and 1954 sees the merger of Pondicherry with the Indian Union. 1992 again brings us to the Indian democracy with its anti-Hindi agitation and BJP riots in Madras where Arjuna Shetty loses his life.

In contrast the account of Pondicherry's history begins with the arrival of de L'Espirit who sailed from Rouen in 1527, for the Malabar coast. Pondicherry's survival is discussed in detail with attacks and sieges by Alexander, Napoleon, the English and Germans. Ranga Pillai's diary provides an account of the glorious days of French empire in Pondicherry. Beginning from 1736 it chronicles the growth of Pondicherry in the hands of Dupleix, its French governor and his wife Madam Dupleix, Jeannie, whose mother is half-Indian. The nawabs are entertained "with great pomp. with a roll of drums, clanging of cymbals", mentions the diary. "The procession has fifty soldiers, horsemen, dancing women, tomtoms, horns. drums, pipes... (97)". Anand Ranga Pillai's friendship with Dupleix formed a strong link between the French and Tamilians. Pondicherry's present is seen in the Aurobindo Ashram, a haven of peace.

At the heart of the novel is the relationship of Oriane de L'Espirit, the French girl, whose parents own Hotel de France and Guruvappa, a young Tamilian Hindu Brahmin boy, returned from England, ten years younger to her. He is researching the history of palm leaf books and the surviving manuscripts which contain coded messages exchanged between the colonizers and colonized. Oriane's and Guru's friendship is strengthened with Guru's lessons in French translations and their love further blossoms into maturity with the translation of Ranga Pillai's diary from Tamil to English and French. His marriage makes little difference to their relationship. During their translation lessons, Oriane comes across Tamil love poems

> ... You and I
> How do we know each other? Yet like rain and red earth
> Our hearts have mixed together. (119)

— And wonders about their relationship.

The love relationships that blossom in the novel are mainly crosscultural. Thomas Ettridge marries the Burmese girl Kyung. Dupleix is French and his wife Jeannie is half-Indian. Finally Oriane plans to build a city called Auroville, 'a place for love and peace. Utopia, perhaps' (123).

With the death of Aurobindo, Oriane regrets a wasted life. The strong feeling of displacement which she had felt after India's independence perhaps transmutes itself into her dream of Arcadia. It is the Mother's vision of oneness after the death of Aurobindo. The place is bare and cursed according to an old legend. But it can breed life if people from across the place come and plant trees. Raymond, an architect from France who is Marie Anne's (Oriane's cousin) son, comes to build the city. Life begins with planting of new trees and the building of huts. 'The scent of cashew blossom was the scent of Auroville. It combines the sweetness of first sight with the burning bitterness of experience' (146). People from all over – the British, French, German, Italian – come and help in the building of this place. A *matri mandir* is built in Auroville, with the greatest crystal in the world. Raymond and Judith make love. But Auroville has its own share of hardships too. Judith returns to England disappointed. Charlotte their daughter comes to the city of dawn Auroville in 1992. South India is disturbed by riots and the anti-Hindi agitation move. Pondicherry is also partly affected by these disturbances.

Charlotte witnesses the changes that have taken place in Hotel de France. It is now the Pondi Beach Resort. Only some French names in the library and its cuisine reminds one of Hotel de France. Oriane has become old and her ageing runs parallel to the fading remnants of French culture in Hotel de France. Before leaving, Charlotte finds a snapshot of Oriane and Guruvappa laughing in a moment of complicity, "Across the years Charlotte could hear their laughter" (273).

Oriane, in her youth, had felt that "cultures are not completely grafted like apples or roses. Ultimately rejection takes place" (112). Now, towards the end of her life she asks Guru, "Shall we become a part of the place, grow into a couple of small unimpressive trees?" (273).

The novel then is a utopia of oneness, of tolerance and love. The French English, Tamilians and Indians come together and accommodate other cultures. Through the translations of Tamil poetry, French poets and Ranga Pillai's diary Lee Langley has established connections in language, geography, history, culture and religion across the centuries In spite of the paradoxical stand boundaries have tried to merge. Auroville is not an imaginary utopia but a real place as the author says in her acknowledgement. And so is the Ashram in Pondicherry. The novel should be read not only for its expression of oneness but also for its evocation of beautiful scenes and lyrical writing that bares hidden truths.

Endnotes

1. Rushdie privileges the migrant writer on the ground that he can see both from inside and outside which the indigenous writer cannot do ("A Dangerous Art Form" 4). Homi Bhabha talks of culture as a strategy of survival in *The Location of Culture* (172). Gayatri Spivak in *Outside in the Teaching Machine* asks the 'Indigenous Elite' or the 'metropolitan marginal/not to produce a merely antiquarian history which seeks the continuities of soil, language and urban life in which our resent is rooted...' (64).

2. Aijaz Ahmed in *In Theory* favours cultural nationalism calling it the 'constitutional ideology of the theoretical positions from which these issues are raised' (67). Brennan is quoted by Viney Kirpal in her comprehensive introduction to *The Postmodern Indian English Novel (3)*. She says, "Brennan in *Salman Rushdie and the Third World* demolishes persuasively the claims that the cosmopolitan writer empowers the diasporic communities when he or she writes from the interstitial perspective of the contingently-acquired hybridity."

References

Ahmed, Aijaz. *In Theory*. Bombay: Oxford University Press, 1992.

Bhabha, Homi K. *The Location of Culture*. London and New York: Routledge, 1994.

Brah, Avtar. *Cartographics of Diaspora*. London: Routledge, 1996.

Kirpal, Viney. ed. *The Postmodern Indian English Novel*. Bombay: Allied Publishers, 1997.

Langley, Lee. A *House in Pondicherry*. London: Heinemann, 1995.

Nandan, Satendra. *Requiem for a Rainbow: A Fiji Indian Story*. Introduction by Kavita Nandan. Canberra: Pacific Indian Publications, 2001.

Rushdie, Salman. "A Dangerous Art Form." *Third World Book Review* 1, (1984): 3-5.

19

Living With the Trauma of Cultural Displacement in Naipaul's *Half a Life*

Anu Celly

"At school we were told that it was important to read, but it is not easy for people of my background and I suppose yours to find books where we can read ourselves... I feel that I had to write to you because in your stories for the first time I find moments that are like moments in my own life, though the background and material are so different. It does my heart a lot of good to think that out there all these years there was someone thinking and feeling like me."

That is how a character from *Half a Life*, the latest novel by Naipaul describes the experience of reading books. *Half a Life*, perhaps, clinched the Nobel for Naipaul precisely due to such qualities of readership and not for his alleged predilection for certain caste-based formulations or his professed abhorrence for religion-based fundamentalism. The felicitous turn of phrase that converts the title into such a telling insignia of an autobiographical documentation of the hyphenated existence of the migrants in today's world, also earns him a place of indisputable distinction among the galaxy of writers of Indian origin who have migrated abroad. The diaspora comprising of literary dons like Salman Rushdie, Vikram Seth and Amitav Ghosh, have all traced in their works the predicaments and paradoxes haunting the lives of individuals who traverse across continents in the aftermath of the great project of decolonization.

As the progeny of a generation that migrated from India to the West Indies in search of labor as slaves to the dictates of the British imperialistic regime, Naipaul remained a protean in spirit, a wanderer whose quest for gentility and education took him to England, while the lure of knowledge, experience and heritage had drawn him to India in the 60s. In a letter from Trinidad, dated 24.11.49, addressed to his sister Kamla, who bears an uncanny resemblance to Sarojini, the sister figure in *Half a Life*, Naipaul had affirmed, "I am longing to see something of life. You can't beat life for the variety of events and emotions. I am feeling something about everything about this amusing and tragic world".

Half a Life is a narrative of dislocation and self-recovery that attempts to make explorative excavations in colonial history and addresses the self within each of us and the sense of displacement that we cannot escape in today's world, while presenting a chronicle of individual life, that of Willie Chandran, who bears an uncanny resemblance with the writer. The novel may be considered as a kind of picaresque *bildungsroman,* charting the growth and regression marking the life of an individual, while spawning the phenomenon of cultural colonialism and its imprecations with the aesthetic brilliance characteristic of Naipaul's narrative style. The story of Chandran's life is irrevocably intertwined with the facts of migration, cultural adjustment and critical appraisal of the relationship between self and society, that is so integral to Naipaul's life.

In a narrative style which is neat, compact and rhythmic in its tenor and a narrative content which may appear nihilistic, but is searing in its impact of confession and honesty, Naipaul means *Half a Life* to be an unalloyed saga of cultural collusion, self-confrontation and the putative acts of mimicry which the people of erstwhile colonies practice in relation to the imperialistic powers that be. Willie Chandran, whose sense of being a cross-breed of colonial hangover and nativist acknowledgment is implicitly evident from his name, is the son of high-caste Hindu who gets married to a low-caste woman on the principle of an ideological stance against the rigid stratification of caste, class and economic stature rife in the pre-independence society of a little South Indian hamlet. The sense of personal degradation, class discrimination and economic deprivation suffered by Chandran early on in life correlates with the seething anger of his mother against the predominant forms of cultural hegemony which drives a 'dalit' woman like her to inconsequential inanity, "'Willie Chandran's mother learned that in the world outside aluminum was for Muslims and Christians and people of that sort, brass was for people of caste, and a rusty old tin was for her. She spat on the tin" *(Half a Life* 38).

Willie's decision to migrate to UK at an early age is guided by a clear perception of his goals as well as antecedents and is unmarked by any sign of an embattled consciousness. However, since "all landscapes are in the end only in the imagination" as per the protagonist of *A Rag on the Island,* it is on the canvas of consciousness that Naipaul plays out the drama of "half a life" torn between such acts of mimicry and revulsion towards colonialism, enacted by Chandran who is buffeted by the legacy of colonialism wherever he goes. His sensibility is besieged by the schism of divided loyalty as he strives to come to terms with sense of alienation amidst the curious admixture of aristocratic decadence and crude modernity marking the life of a species of Londoners in a phase of transition. Chandran's feeling of debilitating despair accruing from a state of spiritual/emotional non-cognition and physical isolation may be considered as a pertinent reflection of a typical predicament facing the contemporary generation of migrants, "He was unanchored, with no idea of what lay ahead. He still had no idea of the scale of things, no idea of historical time or even of distance. When he had seen Buckingham Palace he had thought that the kings and queens were imposters, and the country a sham, and he continued to live within that idea of make-believe" (58).

Chandran's urge to be a writer, like that of Naipaul who termed writing to be "a great cherishing of the self", is symptomatic of his desire to refashion his identity and insulate himself against the pejorative offshoots of caste and class based deprivation still clinging to him as a reminder of his parentage. "'He could as it were, write his own revolution. The possibilities were tizzying. He could, within reason, re-make himself and his past and his ancestry" (60), confesses Chandran/Naipaul. Writing empowers him with a sense of self-control and transcendence over the petty concerns of survival, security, and employment faced by his compatriot groups of Caribbean, African and Asian migrants swarming the run-down and chirpy district of Soho in London.

The blatant mode of degradation inflicted on Blacks and Asians by sections of churlish Englishmen and the gaping gulf between riches and poverty, splendor and murkiness marking the life around Chandran, evokes in him outrageous resentment as he sets out to counter the mounting tide of anger within him by writing farfetched stories about characters far removed from the nebulous reality of his present life. An insight into Naipaul's abhorrent reaction to the practice of cultural, economic and political predominance on the part of British people colludes with his ire against all forms of neo-colonialism, which, in turn, goes contrary to his much-berated preference for West-oriented ideology and establishment. To echo his words from an essay called "What's Wrong in being a Snob?", "The sad fact about prejudices, between classes, castes or indeed races is that they are an accretion of observations and can't be destroyed by simple contradictions ... To create classless society you do not deny class differences. You ceaselessly wage class war" (Hamner 37).

In this context, the words of the English editor in *Half a Life* may also be quoted as a critique of white-dominated Eurocentric supremacist precepts defined more often than not as the prevailing norm of socio-cultural and economic relations in the colonial world, "Not many people want to know about us nowadays. But we have played our part in history. Our factories made goods that went all over the world, and wherever our goods went they helped to usher in the modern age. We quite rightly thought of ourselves as the center of the World. But now the world has tilted, and it is only when we meet people like yourselves that I get some idea where the world is going" (98). Ironically, within this statement, there is an in-built and incisive denunciation in the authorial expression of a myopic view of colonialism that negates the expansive and progressive turn of colonial regimes and that does not shirk from an acceptance of the all-pervasive prevalence of corruption, civic strife, sloth, mediocrity, nepotism and many other casualties of postcolonial history Chandran begins to feel restless and discontented amidst the dingy clubs and lonely pavements of post-war London and yet he can't pluck up the courage to go back to India, since it continues to epitomize to him an enslaved adherence to norms of indigent conservatism in matters of sex, marriage, occupation and community life. "'I have lived like a free man. I can't go back to the other thing ...'" (117), muses Chandran, with a scornful diffidence over the hypocrisy and double-standard inherent to the Indian approach towards sexuality, rife with incest and dubious indulgence in sexual infantilism. Chandran's own casual encounter in a sexual liaison with a prostitute leaves him with the taste of a lacerating shame, further compounded with a loneliness accruing from his friend Percy's departure for Panama.

The archetypal wanderer within Chandran yearns to take an odyssey to seek refuge in a place that would lend sustenance to his individuality and erase his dilemma over the "feeling of difference" and whether he can use it as a weapon. The country that comes closest to his compulsive yearning for India is the African continent and he decides to travel to an African Portuguese settlement along with a woman of mixed racial heritage, Ana, who falls in love with him. Chandran's journey to Africa is dotted with intense moments of self-realization wherewith he envisages "another self inside him, in a silent space where all his external life was muffled" (133).

Eighteen years of a challenging life amidst the rugged and sturdy landscape of Africa exhaust his energy as he decides to leave his wife Ana in quest for a land and life which would be all of his own. A chance encounter with some young and vibrant Tamilian boys from India make him feel ashamed of his cowardly denial of self-appraisal. "They have proclaimed who they are and they are risking everything for it. I have been hiding from myself. I have risked nothing. And now the best part of my life is over" (138), speculates Chandran with a hard-hitting sense of remorse. As the bedrock of love and faith that he has shared with Ana begins to shake, the narrative, at this point, takes on the tone of intimate eloquence, as the writer addresses the reader in the first person. The evocative view of postcoloniality, viewed across the arched stratum of "the tract of experience", now begins to ease him into "a state of knowledge" dependent on the trope of exile that reaches a point of apocalypse towards the end, framed by actual leave taking and imagined return. As Chandran derides to shed the skin of his grafted existence as a migrant who has lived through the life of others, prepared to discover within himself the fledgling motion of a self that draws sustenance from the anchorage within.

The feeling of contentment and tranquillity predominates over the vigor of narration as it begins to assume the shape of a stream of consciousness, its labyrinthine movement colludes with the peace-making crevices of the author's mind. For the first time in his life, Willie Chandran finds complete acceptance in "that regulated colonial world" (145) that makes one accept that "such a reasonable life could be extracted from such an unpromising landscape, that blood, in some way, had been squeezed out of stone" (149). The complete acceptance that Willie Chandran feels in the response of the Portuguese makes him feel at home, perfectly attuned to his inhabitation in Africa, which all but intensifies his sense of being an Indian.

Willie Chandran starts cherishing the self within him, even while subsuming his individuality to a sense of acculturation within the mainstream of settler races. "Just as no man can truly wish to be somebody else, since no man can imagine himself without the heart and mind he has been granted, so no man of a later time can really know what it was like to live on the land in those days" (150), affirms Chandran as the ground below his feet begins to move with a shaky exposure to shelterless vulnerability. The feeling of alienation returns as he loses his passport and along with it a legal sense of authority over his own identity, too. The enormity of a schismatic reality of the horde of migrant people around him begins to strike him – those who neither belonged to old world nor to the new, those who have striven for economic freedom through political acquiescence, those who can't afford to embrace the vision of 'a world of concrete" and just cannot shed the influence of "the frail world of straw" (165). Naipaul's description of this "half and half world" (160) sounds uncannily similar to his response towards decolonization in the new world.

One of the few incidents in the novel which could almost be ignored by a preoccupied writer is the one in which Chandran takes up a practice of shooting, setting up targets which seem to him like his Brahmin ancestors, "'the starveling servants of the great temple" (168). Such an incident provides testimony to the epigrammatic brilliance of Naipaul's narrative art that uses episode as an expressionistic co-ordinate of the state of mind. The ring of satire combined with a scathing critique of the prejudice and exploitation inherent to plutocracy as the guiding forces of the postcolonial world, finds expression through another incident in which Correia, a comrade of sorts to Chandran suffers a betrayal at the hands of a rich Portugese, all his new-found riches confiscated by the latter, while he is banished to an ignoramus darkness. As a representative of 'the half and half world', Chandran feels united with Correia in spirit and in the reflexes of his bewilderment towards life in Africa. Chandran goes ahead to redeem his sense of self-esteem and sanity through a series of casual sexual encounters, yet again. As he begins to get tired of living under Ana's shadow of protection, Chandran's reckless moments of sensual adventurism with a pack of African dancing girls acquaints him a sense of gay abandon and impassioned energy as a marker of "'something in the African heart that was shut away from the rest of us, and beyond politics" (186). Chandran feels haunted by the ghosts of past as he subjects himself to what he terms "a child's fear of being in Africa, at having thrown myself into a void" (189), in an attempt to gain through "sensual education" what he calls "a new idea of myself" (195).

Chandran's voyage of self-discovery continues as he makes a trip to an abandoned castle built by a German migrant to Africa which brings him face to face with the living insignia of his own condition. The residual nostalgia for his homeland that drives home with startling immediacy the symbolic reverberations of certain indigenous aspects of India's cultural riches. Chandran's growing intimacy with Grace enhances not a sense of fulfillment, but that of guilt, treason and self-disgust, as he feels himself drawing back towards his wife.

An incident that hinges on its pivotal value as the most intense manifestation of the title and the theme of the novel is the one in which Chandran encounters an outlandish possession of his wife's brother: a live snake, who lives in a narrow green-tinted bottle. It's a spitting cobra spitting at all bright objects, arousing in Chandran's sensibility, a sense of reflexive aversion, resembling an inhabitant of the postcolonial world, who can neither extract himself nor remain content within the matrix of a closet delimitation inherited from history. Finally, the sanctimonious mythological associations if the snake with a deity are transcended to lend to it a postmodern signification as a symbol of suppressed wrath, an envious third worldist act of "'spitting venom" that aims to convert erstwhile mimicry into a pro-active contempt for the hegemonizing structures of entrapment inflicted by forms of neo colonialism and the maladies of civilization. Perhaps, one could quote here, the insight of Naipaul's father, from a letter written by him to Naipaul in July 1952, where he says, "What gets us sick is our wrong ideas. The whole illness is often the outcome of a conflict between the demands of man, the animal in Nature, and the demands of Man, the creature of civilization .... Consciously or unconsciously we think we have done wrong; we want to run and hide. We cannot face reality .... But there is no sin but society makes it so. Cure lies in re-education".

Both Willie Chandran and the snake bear an uncanny resemblance with V.S. Naipaul who could never identify himself fully either with India, the land of his origin or with Trinidad, the land of his ancestors' exile. "I have been hiding for too long", ruminates Chandran on behalf of the writer, rearing to come out of the stifled constriction to look for his roots again and with it the wholeness of life, a "totality" (Lukacs' term), of being, of life and of the world without and within.

References

Bryden, Ronald. "New Map of Hell". *Spectator*, 8 (Aug. 3, 1962), 161.

Hamner, Robert. *V.S Naipaul*. New York: Twayne Publishers, 1973.

—, ed. *Critical Perspectives on V.S. Naipaul*. London: Heinemann, 1977.

Naipaul, V.S. "London". *Times Literary Supplement* (Aug. 15, 1958), 7.

—, *Area of Darkness*. London: 1964.

—, "What's Wrong in Being a Snob?" *New York Review of Books* (May 18, 1972), 30.

—, 'Conrad's Darkness". *New York Review of Books, 21* (Oct. 17,1974), 18.

—, *Half A Life*. London: Picador, 2001.

—, *Letters between a Father and Son*. Intro. Gillon Aitken. Great Britain: Little Brown and Co., 1999.

Thorpe, Michael. *V.S Naipaul*. Writers and their Work Series. Ed. Ian Scott-Kilvert. Essex, UK: Longman Group Ltd. for the British Council, 1976.

20

Identity, Home and Culture Through Dislocations

Jasbir Jain

I
Routes of Passage Dabydeen, Bissoondath and the Naipaul Inheritance

The title of the section, with its play on 'routes' and 'roots', signifying a two way movement reflects the complexity of the multiple dislocations as they work through successive generations and each successive shift. When migrations take place does history remain the same or does it alter? And as the past recedes, what is it that one chooses to remember? In most of the epigraphs selected by writers of the West Indies, the past remains a factor to be considered. George Lamming begins *The Pleasures of Exile* (1960) with a quotation from James Joyce, "History is a nightmare from which I'm trying to awaken". Naipaul in *The Middle Passage* (1962) hearkens back to James Anthony Froude and Anthony Trollope[1], while Cyril Dabydeen, in his most recent work, *My Brahmin Days* (2000), frames it with a quotation from L.P. Hartley, "The past is a foreign country/They do things differently there" (*The Go Between*).

Difference becomes a defining category for an immigrant. The difference in his perceptions and remembered pasts from that of the man at home in his surroundings, the difference of colour or language in alien surroundings, the memories of landscape and climate and the association with the flora and fauna. These are the differences which mark him: he merges where he feels different and stands out where he wishes to merge. And even as he senses the necessity of recalling a past (*FC* 9), for blankness does not work, he recognizes the inevitability of forgetting.

The immigrant's narrative despite this pull/attraction towards or fear of the past is a linear narrative. It contains within it the impossibility of return. There is no going back in time or place, (only in memory); there is no possibility of belonging once again even as the past controls the present. How does the writer then construct his narrative and his 'self'? I propose to take up some stories from Neil Bissoondath's *Digging Up the Mountains* (1985) which also happens to be his first collection of short stories (published at age 30) and some from Cyril Dabydeen's latest collection *My Brahmin Days* (2000).

Bissoondath is Naipaul's sister's son, and perhaps is consciously rejecting the Naipaul inheritance – he moved to Canada (at the age of 18) instead of England, studied French instead of English and has rejected multiculturalism because it essentializes and ghettoizes the immigrant. His work *Selling Illusions*, critiques the policy of multiculturalism as one which subverts the idea of individual identity. Dabydeen grew up in British Guyana and now lives in Canada. Dabydeen has also, like Bissoondath, explored the meaning and construction of a Canadianness which would include the immigrant. They are both East Indians from West Indies, both have a Brahmin inheritance and memories of recitals from the *Gita* and the *Ramayana*. Thus both of them, as they write their identities, have constantly to negotiate the memories of an inherited past as well their contingent present. A third additional factor which each has to negotiate is the Naipaulian inheritance: how Naipaul has constructed the identity of the East Indian in West Indies and the way he has projected India. They also have to negotiate Naipaul's approach, both the parody and the contempt which underlies his rejection of the past. They have grown up with Naipaul's projections which are likely to affect not only their psyche but also their narrative. One of the tasks I have set myself is to work out the relationship of the immigrant to his narrative as he/she works through the concepts of self and heritage.

Naipaul's *The Middle Passage* (1962) and *Finding the Centre* (1984) are dismissive of the West Indies and see it as a place without history, as islands where nothing is created, where there is no civilization and no revolution can take place, a place marked by distrust of the other as well as of one's own self. The island people are defined by a sense of contempt which they feel for the 'self' and the hatred which they have for the other. It is depicted as a society where alienness is welcomed by the Indian – everything that made the Indian alien gave him strength, "it insulated him from the black-white struggle" (*MP* 88). The Indian was not caught up in a one to one opposition, conflict or polarity but a triangular one. The Blacks were not his natural allies, instead they were considered social inferiors (86), while the presence of East Indians posed a threat to the Blacks.[2] The East Indian in West Indies held on to this "difference" and got caught up in a culture trapped in a time-warp and frozen at a particular moment in the past. Naipaul goes on to point out in *The Middle Passage* the obsession of the Indians with the mother-country fixation (183) leading them to recreate an India in miniature (*MP* 225-226). The Indian remained rooted in his own community as opposed to the African's desire to be part of the mainstream (*MP* 88).

The constant opposition, the sense of "alienness", used as a protective cover also subtracted from all those human impulses conducive to the growth of a national identity: the individual and the religious identities are prioritized over a common nationhood. Despite the focus on 'houses' and 'homes' in Naipaul's work, there is no emotion of belonging to the land. Instead there is a sense of temporariness, a longing for a future different from the present, and a fear of extinction. In *Finding the Centre* he refers to his father's nervous breakdown caused by his failure to see his reflection in the mirror.

All attempts at defining a self, and the subsequent efforts of the self which is thus defined, are motivated by a need to overcome this fear of extinction. It is thus an exile is born: never at home anywhere as the holding back becomes important to him. Travel as a mode of belonging, cynicism as a way of relating, satire as a way of approaching thus become the landmarks of a writing born out of this sense of alienation. But the fact remains that all alienations are not the same, and this needs to be reckoned with. For Naipaul the possibility of a dialogic relationship doesn't exist. George Lamming's sense of exile and his need for a dialogic relationship stand in direct contrast to the Naipaulian withholding of self and defining it primarily through difference. The dangers of such a self-definition are many: it encloses rather than expands, it gets anchored in a preconceived expectation rather than allow itself to change or remain flexible, it becomes self-contained and the main point of reference: the tentativeness necessary for a commonalty to surface is placed outside its reach. Insecurity is not always expressed as a hermeneutic surrender, it becomes a holding back. This defines the writer's relationship with his work and characterizes a great deal of diasporic writing – whether it is of the mutation variety as in Bharati Mukherjee, or the observer category as in Naipaul, or framed by the need to pick out the exotic, or uncover the isolated event in the past. The holding back of the 'self' does not permit any long term involvement at a deeper level. The 'self' in this case becomes a resistant 'self'.

Bissoondath in the stories in *Digging up the Mountains* is concerned with several things. His stories take on fictional constructs. Several of them are written in a female voice, the protagonist is a woman – he projects himself into the 'other' cultural situations and landscapes of the mind, identifying himself with them. "The Cage", a long short story, qualifying itself almost as a novella, is about a Japanese girl and works at several levels of migration, of belonging and alienation – constructing the self bit by bit by being buffeted about rather than defining it through location in the idea of race, an historic past or a notion of the self or through alienation and holding back.

The scene of his childhood memories is West Indies – British Guyana – and not India. His concerns are not merely personal, they are political. He does not merely observe political processes as they affect others, but explores their impact upon human relationships and on the nature of flight. In the title story "Digging up the Mountains", Hari Behary is rooted in his homeland and is reluctant to migrate. Political unrest, murders of his friends, fear stalking the streets, state of emergency, the sense of being encircled and confined in his home, finally push him to take the decision to migrate. And as he plans to leave, he is informed that if he does not return within six months, his property will be confiscated. All along images of insecurity are contrasted with Hari Behary's pride in his possessions, and his need to root himself in this present. His plan for planting the lawn – which never really gets done – is highly significant and works at a metaphoric level expressing the need to belong. India for him exists only in the remote past, "dipped into darkness" (2), his identification is with the present, "This is my land and my house" (4).

The other side of this flight is projected in another story titled "Insecurity". Alistair Ramgoolam has a deep realisation that he will need to escape and hence he carefully goes on building up a bank balance in the United States, smuggling money through business deals. The island of his birth, "on which he had grown up and where he had made his fortune, was transformed by a process of mind into a temporary home. Its history ceased to be important, its presence turned into a fluid holding pattern which would eventually give way. The confusion had been prepared for.... He could hope for death here but his grandchildren, may be even his children, would continue the emigration which his grandfather had started in India, and during which the island had proved, in the end, to be nothing more than a stopover" (72); a "way-station, a point at which to pause for a brief respite from the larger scare" (81).

But as observed earlier, the diasporic narrative is a linear one, despite its engagement with the past is so many ways. It is impossible to return. In the same volume, there is another story titled symbolically "There are Lots of Ways to Die", which is about the homecoming of Joseph Heaven from Canada to his island home with the noble sentiments of doing something for his people. But he realises that his memory had betrayed him – he had forgotten how "sticky the island could be when it rained, ... The morning rain wasn't as refreshing as he'd recalled it and the steam had left his memory altogether. How could he have sworn that the island experienced no humidity" (79). And now the nostalgia is reversed, he imagines himself on Bloor Street, he could even conjure up the sounds of a Toronto summer: "the cars, the voices, the rumble of the subway under the feet as it swiftly glided towards downtown" (80). He seems to be hallucinating all the time about the life in Canada. He begins to mistrust his memory, is unable to talk about it to his wife, walks around in search of the past – in search of the dreams which could have been realized and materialized. Joseph's house is on Pacheto Street named after an old mansion on the street, a house said to belong to a general, and one which had led to the island's mention in a book other than a history text – outside the context of slavery. This house becomes the central symbol of the nature of reality – It "was like a dying man who could hear his heart ticking to a stop" (87). Finally he seeks a childhood friend and finds that there is nothing to be said or shared,

"Frankie used to be his best friend. He was the most intelligent person Joseph had ever known." But now he works in a bank having given up his dreams of a university job. Frankie tells him "why did you come back? A big mistake" (90). Several of their friends are dead. Frankie tells him "You mean to tell me you had the courage to leave and the stupidity to come back?" (91). Overcome by uncertainties Joseph finds his way to Pachetco House, and it is here that the idealist in him crumbles – it is very different from what he had imagined it to be. Doubts assail him "Might it not have been always a big, open, empty house ... with a facade that promised mystery but an interior that took away all hope?" (95) He feels confined – "a man in an island on an island" (95) – a final signal for him to leave.

Contrasted with Bissoondath, Dabydeen has chosen different ways to shake off the Naipaulian inheritance. Not marked by rejection, his work is also not overtly located in the self. Memory, landscape and history coalesce into a continuity. The jumps are not into a historic past. But the questions of identity bother him – where does one belong? How does one root oneself? His colour, his memories of religious texts, the gods who appear in his dream project an identity he is unable to relate to. There is a story titled "Jet Lag" (in *My Brahmin Days*) which is a narrative about travelling to India on a Lufthansa flight. The Naipaulian fear of India, the distrust and uncertainty, the preconceived notions of loss and of being defrauded by Indians surface in his memory. His anxieties are reflected in a recurring nightmare he has wherein, "my luggage was quickly lost ... a cab driver kept running away with it despite my frantic efforts to hold on to what was mine." The writer-protagonist feels "I was not an Indian and may be Canada had done this to me", compelling him to approach India as a stranger. He asks himself the question, "Why go to India? We were West Indians. Then Canada, also far away, sounded like Xanadu. All shifting grounds." (76-77). There is then a disowning of India. "India seemed no longer the land of my ancestors", and as he shakes off this almost mythical past he acknowledges to himself that he was in fact a Canadian with all earlier identities shaken off, "I was a Canadian entering a foreign land. This was no mere defence mechanism. History dispensed with, Kala Pani vanished. The flux of time and change only, I was a Canadian ..... I was indeed a Canadian in a vast new land" (82-83). Ironically and meaningfully, this new found confidence is refuted by the officer at the airport who includes him in the sweeping remark "we are all Indians here".

Again and again, the Indianness surfaces. In his 1988 novel, *The Wizard Swami,* the opening sentence "Devan slowly postured himself, folding his legs Buddha-style" (5), immediately harks back to the culture of South Asia. *The Wizard Swami* is, at one level, a reworking of Naipaul's *The Mystic Masseur,* and one way of getting rid of the Naipaulian presence. Devan assumes the role of a scholar-preacher as he talks about Hinduism to the village people, reminding the reader faintly of Murthy in Raja Rao's *Kanthapura* (1938) and Raju in R.K. Narayan's *Guide* (1958). The role of a swami comes naturally to him as it does to Naipaul's hero in *The Mystic Masseur* (1957). Religion, language, myth and legend work their way into the present as the writer constructs a 'self'. Even in *The Dark Swirl* (1988) which is entirely located in the islands, the Hindu family reflects a mixed tradition. The father Ghulam has a wife called Savitri and a son called Josh. In social terms, however, there are only two divisions, the white and the colored, with Ghulam identifying himself with the Africans, which never really happens with Naipaul. As Ghulam walks along he wills himself to be one with everything:

> The insects, reptiles, animals and plants ..., It was then he felt himself to be truly Hindu and yet something else. Most times he scarcely thought about his people's origin in that distant subcontinent. Here, in this isolated part of the Guyanese coastland ... they – Indians, Africans – lived in a strange harmony .... Whatever they had been, he sensed they were becoming something else .... (39)

Ghulam has a sense of belonging to the land and against outsiders the people project a oneness (72). At the end of the novel as he looks for the white stranger and cannot find him, he remembers his face and their common search for the massacouraman. The present, uncannily, turns into memory before one can control it – memory like "an ancient, primordial imaging that surpassed the places where they had come from – Africa, India, Europe – or where they secretly yearned to return when the soil no longer accepted them" (92), but for the moment the soil claims them.

In the short-story "My Brahmin Days", the author records a visit to India when the host family immediately opens out to him an India of the past. As the young son of the family accompanies him to Agra and converses about the West, the realisation comes to him that they – he, as a person living in Canada, and Amit, as an Indian who has never travelled abroad – relate to each other's background through media projected stereotypes and static memories. The Indian from abroad has to wrestle with his "outsider-insider" status, discover the meaning of language in a different cultural context – origins, caste, family – across a varied experience while the Indian at home is lost in dreams of a distant land. India was 'homeland' to the expatriate, and Canada suddenly seemed like another planet. In between was the Caribbean background (13). The self, for Dabydeen, is rooted in all of them, not a single segment is irrelevant or dispensable. "My Brahmin Days" is not the simple, humourous experience which it appears at first sight. It addresses questions of power as well of identity, the 'littleness' of South Asians in a white country, the ego-projections of the Indians through travel abroad, a sense of apology at being Indians going hand in hand with need to identify with and be proud of the diaspora on part of the stay at home Indians. Amit and the visiting writer meet through opposing visions even as they share a common inheritance. The visitor, even as he acknowledges his Brahmin origins, uses a few words of Hindi "picked up a long time ago, from a grandmother who'd come from a part of India I'd never know" (25) realises that he doesn't belong. There is no past he can return to.

In both Bissoondath and Dabydeen it is clear that history is transmuted through the remembrance of selected events. The past impacts the 'self' through this remembrance which exists in a rootless present and which is isolated and distanced from the culture or origin both through acts willed of otherwise. Working through familial frameworks, and parodies of the past, the writers create a new self based on intertextualities. As successive generations interact with inherited frameworks, the moulds either change or crack.

This is mysterious process in itself where traces of the past linger in the subconscious and have a tendency to surface either through recognition or memory or collectivity. Holding on to the self becomes important in an alien environment, preventing a natural growth, identification and constructive relationships. But how long can or should this alienness persist and if it does so, is it able to expand the idea of self or not? How does memory relate to the intervening accumulation of details? – how does one define the whole process of relating to a tradition? It is important to note the wedge which

Naipaul has created for the West Indian East Indian towards the West Indian segment and the definition of the self which he has projected through resistance. This intertextual presence has to be realized. Then the question arises, is pastiche born out of this process of defining the self through difference or is it a defence mechanism, the result of a location on an island, a narrowing of space or falling in line with the Western position? What kind of an aesthetics is promised by a resistant self and what kind of an aesthetics is possible?

The role of imagination is also a crucial one in the whole process of creating a 'self'. Aritha van Herk in her essay "In Visible Ink" writes about the double narrative of the immigrant story. There is the overt story which relates outwards, reflects a worldly 'making of the self' as it confronts or adapts itself to the contingent forces, as it yields to the seductions of success and recognition in its search for both identity and opportunity. The second narrative is the covert one which hides in crevices and surfaces every now and then through conscious or unconscious memory. Religion or language or both may have a great deal to do with its construction. There is also, at times, a third story, the absent story which does not connect either with memory or reality but hovers between the two as a lost possibility. It is difficult to say whether the absent story has come into being or not. And if and when it is written whether it will have fantasy as a dominant mode or incline toward dystopianism.

Diasporic writers have worked variously with their material. Ondaatje has moved from culture to culture, absorbing and adopting different cultural myths[2], several others have accepted the Janus-faced hyphenated self, choosing to located themselves in the hyphen[3], yet others like Bharati Mukherjee have shed their pasts, if not as material, at least as professions about it.[4] And there are others like Rohinton Mistry who, like the Jews, wishes to locate the 'self' in a sense of community. Even as he writes about India, his cultural projection is of the Parsi life right from *Such a Long Journey* to *Family Matters*. Mistry's writing draws attention to an important facet of the diasporic self – the need to relate to a community.

Culture, history and memory interact anew for every generation. With second and third generation immigrants appearing on the literary scene, the need to explore the multiple dimensions of location and dislocation as they contribute to the making of the 'self' has become important. Even as the immigrant's narrative is linear, his relationship to the past is not in one straight line. It has many breaks, twists and paths. There can be no clean break with the past but the relationship of the 'self' towards a 'sense of belonging' can be differently governed. The 'self' may remain in constant need of an 'other' and thus adopt a resistant attitude, or it may progress from a resistant to a dialogic self, willing to give and belong, willing to transcend the ego.

II
The Difficulty of Belonging: Self and the World

How does one belong? What is it that defines that feeling of at-homeness and what defines the alien? Is belonging an individual experience or one based in collectivity? These and other related questions crop up when one explores history, the individual psyche and narratives of belonging. The 'Self' and the 'Other' in cultural terms (and not merely seen at an individual level) need to be seen as opposites in order to be visible, while merger requires surrender, change and self-annihilation. The opposition is characterised by difference in terms of appearance, race, faith, ritualistic practices, language, political power amongst a host of other elements. More often than not it is also a difference in historical relationships. How does one forget the past? What happens to memories of colonization, enslavement, forced labour, rejection and deportment, to memories of the holocaust and Hiroshima and Nagasaki? In psychological terms we do think of a collective consciousness and the feeling of guilt both collectively and individually. Treaties between nations reflect motives of revenge as well as feelings of guilt. The treaty of Versailles was one based on the idea of revenge, the US-Japan political relationships reflect American guilt about the atomic explosion. Affirmative actions and multicultural policies also reflect a consciousness of wrongs done in the past. Thus belonging is a multifaceted process.

The diasporic Indian today views it in several different ways. Ashis Gupta is of the view that usefulness to a society leads to acceptance[5], but does it really? Usefulness on what terms? Or of what kind? Immigration laws have been shaped often by an economic need of the moment and populations have been imported to fulfil the need for certain specific kinds of jobs or to balance the age factor. The highly useful slaves and railroad workers are nameless and invisible and discriminated against. Uma Parameswaran believes that belonging is a transplantation and one needs to nurture the feeling –

home is where the heart is. There is no anguished self-consciousness about any conflictual emotions.[6] For Rohinton Mistry, as he demonstrates in "Swimming Lessons", it is the ability to swim with the current, to engage in the social concern of the community, and in "Squatter" it is the conquest of the habit of the body. It is an adjustment which requires a bringing over and relocation of culture – a forward-looking attitude sans nostalgia. But both Bharati Mukherjee and Neil Bissoondath address the issue of belonging in a different way, Mukherjee by distinguishing between the immigrant and the expatriate, and claiming the status of an immigrant she writes. "I need to feel part of the community I have adopted, I need to put roots down, to vote and make the difference I can", and for this she is willing to pay the price – the trauma of self-transformation. Bissoondath seeks to define a Canadianness and focuses attention on "acceptance" rather than on belonging. The process of belonging finally culminates in the fact of acceptance, but when race and origins govern this fact, a separateness is thrust on the subject. The facts that one looks different and one's ancestors hailed from somewhere else become the basis of difference, separation and non-acceptance.[7] Problem No. 1: Ethnicity is a trap and a hindrance to the act of belonging: but the abandonment of ethnicity may erode the basis of identity. Problem No. 2. If one seeks one's self-definition on the basis of 'homeland' rather than of ancestral origins, the category homeland also becomes problematic specially in times of hostilities. For instance where does an Iraqi belong at the time of the US-Iraq war or an Arab during the Gulf War? National interest gets divided. This is the kind of situation which Uzman Alam Khan has depicted in her novel *Trespassing* (2003). The protagonist of the novel, Daanish, describes an episode when he is not allowed to enter a café:

> But at the doorway, a heavyset man blocked his entrance. 'We're closing', he said. Daanish cast a quick look inside. No one seemed to be in a hurry to leave. Walking down the street, he glanced around....
>
> Graffiti was painted across the brick wall of a warehouse: *Save America, Kill an Arab*..... All the while, bombs dropped on Iraq every thirty seconds.
>
> On average, it took Daanish twenty minutes to read each article. On average the air raids killed twenty-five hundred Iraqis daily.

Approximately thirty would lose their lives by the time he'd
finished reading how much *They hate us*. (164-165)

There is another aspect to this whole issue which surfaces when the diaspora begins to practice, what Benedict Anderson has described as 'long-distance nationalism' (qtd by Ravindra Jain, 34). This is exactly what the Sikhs in Canada did during the period of Sikh militancy (evidenced in Srinivas Krishna's film *Masala* and the crash of the Air India flight, Kaniska) and the Hindus in US are doing to fund and fan Hindu fundamentalism. Belonging has all these facets which shriek aloud for attention and are directly related to the matter of citizenship. The two focal points in the concept of citizenship are *belonging* and *status* (understood as a bundle of distinctive rights). Besides economic and social rights, citizenship also includes allegiance and responsibility. At a legal level it defines inclusion as well as exclusion (Chandra Talpade Mohanty in *Feminism Without Borders* mentions how she had to take up American citizenship as she wanted to adopt a child). Citizenship is a cognition of the fact that there is a commonalty of interests at stake. 'Newcomers' Kratochwil observes, 'must commit themselves to a new identity' (488).

I want to problematise this issue further by bringing into my discussion two other factors: (i) the question of dual citizenship; which ignores territoriality and recognizes a dual allegiance and is silent over the possibility of conflict between the two allegiances (ii) and reduction of rights or denial of rights within citizenship on account of ethnicity, religion, gender or other discriminatory positions where an extra burden is placed on the citizens to prove their loyalty. This exclusion can be on account of colour or status – a sense of rejection which is forced on the citizen. Bissoondath cites an example of Trudi Hanley, a black woman, who is rejected for modelling assignments on the ground that they have enough of ethnics (Bissoondath 116). Avtar Brah analysing the marginalization of the First Nations, categorises them as 'diaspora' within their own country.[8] These factors placed together imply that 'belonging' includes (i) recognition and acceptance, and a place in the community and culture to which one wishes to belong, (ii) that on part of a newcomer/outsider it also implies a change, a transformation, or surrender of some part of the self; (iii) the change called for affects a total reconfiguration of memory, history and cultural values even it does not call for a total abandonment. Identity – how one imagines oneself and constitutes the idea of 'self'; territoriality – place of residence and the 'homeland' in the distance – and memory – personal, childhood memory, shared struggles and history – are all equally necessary for the act of belonging. Does the individual, specially the immigrant, have to work within polarities?

We have several confessions of journeys within these two ends by eminent writers of all literatures. There is the failed *hijrat* of Intizar Husain's 'The Unwritten Epic' where the desired nationhood does not generate the desired sense of belonging. And in Josh Malihabadi's piece 'My Ordeal as a Citizen of Pakistan', where he narrates his post-Partition experiences in India. Malihabadi migrated to Pakistan in 1956. It was a sense of non-belonging which pushed him to migrate but this sense did not leave him even after he had. In his autobiography (*Yaadon Ki Baraat* 1992) he relates his meeting with Sardar Patel wherein the Sardar expressed his contempt for the Hindus who converted to Islam, Malihabadi's own respect and relationship with Nehru and finally his decision to leave in the interests of his family, in the face of the narrowing space for Muslim culture. His friends in Pakistan pointed out to him the consequences of the gradual transformation of cultural priorities (Malihabadi 200). Nehru, unwilling to let him go, suggested that he live in India and go to Pakistan for four months a year on a paid leave of absence but the response in Pakistan was:

> ... to which country would you belong? In Pakistan you will be treated as an Indian, whereas the Indians would be suspicious of you because your family members are citizens of Pakistan ..... Josh *Saheb*, you can't cross a river with your feet anchored in two boats. (Malihabadi 203)

Belonging does not only have an individual or a collective dimension but also a generational one: there are people who are born in the country which their parents had adopted or been brought to when very young, what is it that interferes with their act of belonging? Persistence of cultural memory and practices is one significant hurdle, another may be a history of past hostility, yet another their own vulnerability as subjects. In a short story by an Indo-Caribbean writer, Christine Singh, this vulnerability is articulated in many ways as the circumstances pile against the young protagonist Kris who is preparing to go for a job interview. Kris is of Indo-Caribbean origin, hails from Trinidad but was himself born in

England. He has no doubts about his Englishness but others do not accept him. His accent is different from that of other Trinidadians, they cannot even understand the way he speaks (158) but he is kept out of the white cricket team. At school 'finding friends was like fighting a losing battle' (162). When removed to the Trinidadian school he persists in believing he is English. He is pushed back into an Indianness which he does not even know (165) until he is forced to adopt a colonial response. "Your country grabbed up cheap Indian labour and stuck them in their colonies. Did your precious country not teach you that in your history lessons?" At the end of it Kris Persaud loses his sense of at-homeness. He really doesn't know where he belongs (172). A sense of belonging is something which should fall effortlessly into a pattern, somewhat like the pleasurable drinking of wine which Radhika Jha describes in her novel *Smell*:

> The wine smelt at once sweet and spicy, like cinnamon and nutmeg, and sour and earthy. There was also a slight hint of chalk that hung back, almost out of sight. The smell filed my nostrils, delicate but well-formed as a gazelle. Then I took a sip. *The wine slid across my tongue like oil, and slipped effortlessly down my throat. Underneath its silky coat, I could feel the muscle that held the various elements together.* (188, italics mine)

But exactly a hundred pages later, the reader also experiences the sense of alienation. Fear of rejection sends one into invisibility, into dark spaces, into hiding. This fear becomes a 'smell' which one is embarrassed by. The moment one holds one self aloof, one wears a protective armour. It becomes impossible for anyone to hurt the person who has already isolated and rejected his ownself, "The smell is your only defence, your revolt against powerlessness. But it isn't real. It is no more real than your defencelessness" (288).

History has thrown up some remarkable cases over the last few hundred years. One is the migration of the Parsis to India, another the spreading out of the homeless and countryless Jews all over the world, a third is the presence of Muslim populations in various parts of the world, a fourth the slaves from Africa as they were planted in different parts of the world. Each one of them raises different issues regarding the ability to belong and the integration into the national identity – a concept which it is still not possible to ignore as long as nation-states are there despite economic globalisation.

The diasporic character of those communities who have no other 'homeland' to beckon them is very different from those which continue to invest emotionally and economically in the lands which they have left behind. The Parsi community through its economic and political involvement right from Behram Malabari, Ferozeshah Mehta, the Tatas and the Wadias has participated in the development of the country. African Americans, and Indian Muslims also fall into the categories of 'native' people, people who belong, people who have been born on the land, have common political histories and whose relationship with the 'other' even when hostile has been a hostility about power, equality and visibility not about not belonging. The act of belonging has to be a willed one, not a forced one – even when it requires a partial loss of identity as in Himani Banerjee's story "On a Cold Day".[9] It is an act of balance between outward and inward movements – an overcoming of loneliness and marginality to accept the challenge of conflict.

The narrative of belonging is also a narrative of mourning and existential loneliness for the writer, and writers have, in different ways, found their own ways of handling this. At one end is a writer like Joseph Brodsky, who exiled from Russia and having lost a language, a family, and an homeland began writing in English, first critical prose, then translations and finally original poems. As the critic Adam Kirsch observes, it is the equality of 'his extremely fertile imagination' which overcomes the difficulties and hesitations of the outsider's imagination. In his essay "The Conditions We Call Exile" (1987) Brodsky wrote "the reality of (exile) consists of an exiled writer constantly fighting and conspiring to restore his significance, his leading role, his authority' (qtd by Kirsch, 46).

At the other end is a writer like Pico Iyer who moves outside citizenship to talk of the global soul. But even as he travels throughout the world, feels at home in hotel rooms and lives out of suitcases, he too realises the need to belong, even it is to put down roots amongst people who look different while sounding the same. He acknowledges, that "the country where people sound like me is a place where I look highly alien' (24). Pico Iyer writes:

> I'd often referred to myself as homeless – an Indian born in England and moving to California as a boy, with no real base of operations or property, even in my thirties.... (5)

and yet he is not an exile, or an expatriate[10] (23), instead he uses a verse of Simone Weil as an epigraph:

> It is necessary not to be 'myself' still less to be ourselves.
> The city gives one the feeling of being at home.
> We must take the feeling of being home into exile.
> We must be rooted in the absence of a place.
>
> (*Global Soul* 237)

The immigrant writer 'writes' his sense of belonging and this is worked out through retelling of the past in various different ways; it is like using the same events but each time arranging them differently in order to read them differently and to exorcise their hold – thus the preoccupation with the past, the lost homeland and the lost identity. It is through these retellings that inner conflicts are worked out and resolved, a renegotiation takes place with the self and a voice is found for self-assertion. If this memory is a mourning as Vijay Mishra has observed, an "impossible mourning", then this interiorization of memory has to be externalised: "without memory, without a sense of loss, without a certain will to mythologise, life for many displaced peoples will become intolerable and diaspora theory would lose its ethical edge" (Mishra 46). This memory has to move from recollection to imagination, hence recourse to magic realism, fable or allegory as in the works of Salman Rushdie and Suniti Namjoshi; or myth as in the work of Uma Parameswaran.

And when it is none of these but straightforward realistic narration, then what? Is it then a narrative which seeks to relate to facts and not imagination, to a rootedness in reality rather than a metaphorical recollection? Is it a return to the present? When writers frame their realities and look for parallels elsewhere, the connections are being made between the remembered, the experienced and the desired, and between the desired and the possible. If we read diasporic writers against these backgrounds it becomes possible to distinguish the stereotype from the emotionally rooted, and to work through the apparently realistic mode to its actual celebration of mourning. 'Memory', I quote Shirley Geok-lin Lim, for the newcomer, who has 'walked out of a community's living memory', becomes 'a great mourning, a death of the living'. Finally the young, immigrant forgets what it feels like 'not to be a stranger' (Lim 53). The past remains a part of the 'self' conscious of inhabiting different worlds.

The 'traces' in the Derridean sense remain, surfacing every now and then and seeking preservation.

Endnotes

1. The two epigraphs chosen from James Anthony Froude are from his work *The English in West Indies* (1887), both are damaging to the enslaved people. The first ends with the sentence, "There are no people there in the true sense of the word, with a character and purpose of their own", and the second contrasts the luxury of the imperial powers with the financial ruin of the islands. The reference to Trollope is also to a passage dated 1860. Trollope's passage praises Demerara as the Elysium of the tropics, the "one true and actual utopia of the Caribbean Seas" (*MP* 92).
2. For further details see my article on "Poetics of Exile", (*Writers of the Indian Diaspora,* Jaipur: Rawat, 1998).
3. Arun Prabha Mukherjee comments on this and there is wide acceptance of this term with reference to diaspora and diasporic writers.
4. Bharati Mukherjee in a newspaper statement titled "Two Sisters" compared her own attitude with her sister's and rejected the hyphenated space preferring to relate to her country of adoption in an integrated manner.
5. See Ashis Gupta's piece, "The Extraordinary Composition of an Expatriate Writer" and the interview given to Veena Singh titled "The Fragile Self-Image of an Immigrant writer", both in *Writers of the Indian Diaspora* Ed. Jasbir Jain, 1998. Also see Uma Parameswaran, "Home is where your feet are, and may your heart be there too" in the same volume.
6. See "Two sisters, and two ways to belong to America", Bharati Mukherjee, *Times of India,* Oct. 8, 1996. Also see Bissoondath 108.
7. In *Selling Illusions,* Bissoondath narrates how the host people are interested in origins and not in the sense of belonging of the outsider. They persist in tracing the origins of ancestry (and colour) of anyone who looks different.
8. See Chapter 8, Avtar Brah's *Cartographies of the Diaspora*, specifically the section 'The Homing of Diaspora, the diasporising of Home' (190ff).
9. "On a Cold Day" repeats the same problem of loss of identity. The young Bengali girl changes her dress and is transformed from Devika to Debbie. This happens in Bharati Mukherjee's *Jasmine* as well as in the stories by other diasporic writers.

10. Iyer writes "A person like me can't really call himself an exile (who traditionally looked back to a home now lost), or an expatriate (who's generally posted abroad for a living), I'm not really a nomad (whose patterns are guided by the seasons and tradition), and I've never been subject to the refugee's violent disruptions; the global soul is best characterized by the fact of falling between categories."

References

Alam Khan, Uzman. *Trespassing*. New Delhi: Penguin 2003.

Bannerjee, Himani. "On a Cold Day", *Her Mother's Ashes*. Ed. Nurjehan Aziz. Toronto: TSAR Publications, 1994.

Bissoondath, Neil. *Digging up the Mountains: Selected Stories*. Toronto: Macmillan, 1985.

—. *Selling Illusions: The Cult of Multiculturalism in Canada*. Toronto: Penguin, 1994.

Brah, Avtar. *Cartographies of the Diaspora: Contesting Identities*. London: Routledge, 1996.

Dabydeen, Cyril. *My Brahmin Days and Other Stories*. Toronto: TSAR Publications, 2000.

—. *The Dark Swirl*. Leeds: Peepal Tree Press, 1989.

—. *The Wizard Swami*. Leeds: Peepal Tree Press, 1988.

Gupta, Ashis "The Extraordinary Composition of the Expatriate Writer", *Writers of the Indian Diaspora*. Ed. Jasbir Jain. Jaipur: Rawat Publications 1998.

Hoffman, Eva. *Lost in Translation*. Penguin Books: USA Inc. (1989), 1990.

Husain, Intizar. "The Unwritten Epic", *Stories About the Partition India*. Ed. Alok Bhalla. New Delhi: Harper Collins (1994) 1999.

Iyer, Pico. *The Global Soul*. New York: Vintage Books, 2000.

Jain, Ravindra. "Indian Diaspora, Globalisation and Multi-culturalism: A Cultural Analysis," *Contributions to Indian Sociology*. 32: 2; 1998. New Delhi: Sage.

Jha, Radhika. *Smell*. New Delhi: Penguin, 1999.

Kirsch, Adam. "The Art of the Temporary", *The New Republic,* Oct. 9, 2000 p.46.

Kratochwil, Friedrich. "Citizenship: On the Border of Order", *Alternatives* 19 (1994), 485-506.

Lamming, George. *Pleasures of Exile*. London: Michael Joseph, 1960.

Lim, Shirley Goek-Lin. "Two Lives", *Asian American Literature*. Ed. Goek-Lin Lim. Lincolnwood, Illinois: NTC Publishing Group, 2000.

Malihabadi, Josh. "My Ordeal as a Citizen of Pakistan", *India Partitioned*. 2 Vols. Ed. Mushirul Hasan Vol.-II. New Delhi: Roli Books (1995), 1997.

Mishra, Vijay. "Diasporas and the Art of Impossible Mourning", *In Diaspora* Ed. Makarand Paranjape. New Delhi: Indialog Publications Pvt. Ltd. 2001.

Mistry, Rohinton. "Swimming lessons", *Tales from Ferozesha Baag*. New Delhi: Rupa Books, 1987.

—. *Such a Long Journey*. Calcutta: Rupa & Co. 1991.

Mohanty, Chandra Talpade. *Feminism Without Borders: Decolonizing Theory, Practising Solidarity*. Durham & London: Duke University Press, 2003.

Mukherjee, Arun. *Oppositional Aesthetics: Readings from a Hyphenated Space*. Toronto: TSAR, 1994.

Mukherjee, Bharati. "Two Sisters, and two ways to belong in America," *The Times of India*. October 8, 1996.

Naipaul, V.S. *Finding the Centre* (1984). Harmondsworth: Penguin, 1985.

—. *The Middle Passage* (1962). Penguin, 1985.

—. *The Mystic Masseur*. London: Andre Deutsch, 1958.

Parameswaran, Uma. "Home is where your feet are, and may your heart be there too," *Writers of the Indian Diaspora*. Ed. Jasbir Jain. Jaipur: Rawat Publications, 1998.

Singh, Christine. "The Job Interview", *Jehazi*. Ed. Frank Birbal Singh, Toronto: TSAR, 2000.

Singh, Veena. "The Fragile Self-Image of an Immigrant Writer: Interview with Ashis Gupta," *Writers of the Indian Diaspora*. Jaipur: Rawat Publications, 1998.

Van Herk, Aritha. *In Visible Ink*. Edmonton: Newest Press, 1991.

21

A Little About Father

Nilofer Kaul

I don't know you lying there. There are traces of blood in all those bags around you. Your leg jerks up involuntarily – once again. You look at me and momentarily there is some recognition but it soon fades. You try to say something – but the words get chewed up in the pipes. I leave because I can't bear to see you biting at them anymore.

Outside I am back in a long, narrow corridor. Some hard iron chairs. Antiseptic and phenyl blend into a familiar anaesthetic smell. The corridor is sunlit at one end, dark at the other. I take my place with the two long rows of tired, hopeless faces. From under the hard chairs poke out folded mattresses, flasks and overnight bags.

I open my bag to look for glasses, the woman next to me peers in.

"Kanga hai?"

Instinctively I zip up my bag and deny having it. She smiles painfully – "I have neither brushed my teeth nor combed my hair for three days now."

"My husband's nephew." She mumbles. Then louder she adds "Like my son."

"What happened?"

"Pehle to usko mata chad gai. Hamne mata ki puja bhi karvai" *(first he got small pox ... we even organized a prayer for that).*

"He has been given 11 bottles of blood but...uska khoon pani banta jata hai..*(his blood is becoming water).*

"What caste do you belong to?" A woman with a kind face asks her. Nobody objects to the irrelevance.

"We are Sindhi. But he got jaundice and since then he has not been able to make blood. He's only 30. Got married two years ago. His mother is so unwell we had to leave her behind in Kota. We've been on the road for so long."

"Do you have relatives here?" Somebody asks her.

"No. We are staying in the Sindhi Samaj…" She turns and retells an altered version of the story.

I turn away to write to you. I can't allow myself to be drawn into their lives. I have to guard you and can't subject you to such hopelessness.

The flame of the forest which you mocked has given way to the even more ostentatiously coloured Gulmohar. And the bridal Amaltas? I can imagine you saying that the colours are dissonant – the desert sun burns – and that the trees must soothe. But don't you see that's not harmony. In nature it's survival that counts. Only the scorching colours may survive.

I have not always loved you. When I was little I was petrified of you. You were prone to such violent rage. There was that time when you came back from Delhi and brought me a giant pen. I was so excited. It was green and monstrous. But within minutes it broke in my hand. I wept with disappointment, but I never told you. I hid it at the bottom of my cupboard. How could I tell you it was only an accident?

You were so hard to please and so easily disappointed. I remember you telling mamma that I was slow. Backward. Far too shy and diffident. Was this what the teachers told you? What was Moonface's name? Mrs. Mathur or Mrs. Joshi? I can't quite remember. She said I seemed a little retarded and you were always willing to believe the worst about those you loved. Today I understand your defensiveness because I see myself behaving like that. But then your disappointments sank deep inside me.

I don't think you ever actually hit me though you did hit Rohit a lot. Every time you smashed a plate, I cowered - and cried. Rohit and I were just children then. The bitterness between us was to come many years later. Between you and me too, things did change over the years. Slowly, I started to lose my fear of you. Maybe I just learnt to please you.

"It's your father isn't it?" Kind face interrupts my letter to you.

"Yes." I am relieved to be asked. I feel like talking to her. She listens intently.

"What about you?" I ask.

"My mother. Her lungs have stopped functioning. They give her oxygen, but she's not able to expel carbon dioxide. So these last 10 days she's been on a respirator. Everyday we are told that she'll be taken off it, but it never happens. She's fed up. Last two nights she tried to yank out the tubes, so now they've tied up her arms."

She tells me about her two grown up children studying in town, her husband posted in a far away mofussil town and her constant shuttling.

"I sit outside all day, but I hardly ever go in. I can't bear to see her."

"I know. Do you want me to accompany you?" I feel awful listening to her. It sounds bad. Her 80 year old mother. Everybody sounds worse off.

We walk in together to visit our two parents. I shrink away faster.

I studied all your expressions, your gestures, and imitated them. My friends in college recognized you when you came to see me, because they said we had the same funny walk. I didn't tell them I had copied it. On long hot afternoons when you went to nap, I would even sneak into your study and suck at your cold pipes. I still remember the mellow flavour of that tobacco.

As I grew older I learned to read your love in gestures and actions – in the way you tapped the marrow from the bones and gave it to me – the way you held my hand in your large calloused hand and took me to the market. After you finished your vegetable shopping, you'd buy me my gift. A pomegranate, jamuns, phalsas, raw mangoes, the fruit of the season. Remember the holiday in Mussoorie where you lost your wallet? We had to borrow from the guest house manager who didn't know us. Still you indulged me and bought me the bunch of jamuns you knew I craved. I never understood why you looked so happy while I ate that lush purple, sour-sweet pulp that dried the tongue and choked my gullet. But you wouldn't eat. You always invented some excuse for not eating. Children have a native selfishness, don't they?

I remember the four of us going to a hot and dusty little town. I was maybe five then. You sat down on a bench to read a newspaper while I took a fancy there to some innocuous man standing by the bench. When it was time to leave I threw a tantrum and refused to leave with you. But you picked me up and told me a story about the stork (or was it a crane?) that tried to drink soup from a flat plate. Till then even you didn't know you could weave such magic for me. Every night we would lie together - you and I – and I would fall asleep after you finished at least three stories. I liked the way you embellished them. The names of the gems that Aladdin found, the abuses that the animals hurled at each other when you translated Aesop's fables. Namakkar, Nahanjaar, millat farosh, khudai faujdar. We would laugh together and recite them. I still don't know what they mean.

The conversation around me gets animated. Two stocky middle-aged men are complaining about the hospital. I want to join in. Somebody asks them how their father is. I realize with a start that they are brothers. Chalk and Cheese.

Chalk (with an arrestingly mobile expression) points to the board outside.

"It says Intensive Care Unit. What do you think that means?" he looks around and repeats. "Intensive-Care-Unit. It means there's no guarantee given."

As he says this the door opens, a stretcher is wheeled out and taken across the corridor into the general ward. I notice I am not alone in my envy.

"If you get out from here and go across" he gestures in the direction of the stretcher "...there's a 40% chance of your survival. And if you manage to get out of there and go home you have an 80% chance. The rest ...", he purses his mouth and points upwards, "is up to Him."

His gestures have a pantomime like quality.

Everybody around nods in agreement. They start swapping tales about bills. The accounts are competitive.

"We took our father to another private hospital and after a week of deterioration brought him here. Today is his 26th day here. We have spent an average of 10,000 a day."

Cheese who is clearly the more practical of the siblings tells us.

"My leave gets over tomorrow. Then I rejoin and apply for more leave. We don't even know whether our last leave was sanctioned. We'll know tomorrow whether our salaries have been deposited or not."

Cheese speaks for Chalk as well. I envy them their harmony.
I too have a sibling...
Cheese tells Chalk that they have to get their father's ultra sound done again. Chalk shrinks.
"He fainted the first day we came here."
Chalk sits with quiet pride, then takes over the telling.
"Haalaat hi kucch aisi thay. (*It was due to the circumstances*). It was midnight. They said father was almost gone but they would make a last ditch effort and try and operate upon him. We wheeled him into the O.T. and were told to arrange for three bottles of blood. Immediately! It was the first time I had seen the inside of an O.T ... I passed out. But my brother here, he can stomach anything."
This time Cheese looks around with quiet pride.
A newcomer who is eager to join in nods eagerly.
"I too fainted once. I have a friend who knows somebody who does post-mortems. I begged him to let me see one. He tried to dissuade me, but finally relented. The patient was brought in..."
"Patient or corpse?" Chalk mocks.
"OK. Corpse...I just couldn't say it. They took a ballpoint and began to draw lines on it. Then they picked up a scalpel and started incisions. I just blacked out..."
Kindred tales pour forth.

As you can see I am trying to write you a real letter – something that I have not done for years. Not since I left home. Whatever else there may have been, honesty was never the strength of my relationship with you. Earlier it was out of fear of your displeasure. Later it became a habit – a desire to protect you from any possible hurt. I don't know how it changed. Maybe it had to do with seeing you so close to dying that time when I came back from school. That moment governed my life and I have lived with the constant dread of losing you ever since. Every time I left home and you stood waving goodbye, I would notice your fragility and feared that it would be the last time. Somewhere I imagined I alone was responsible for your happiness – or the absence of it.

Still, there are no excuses for dishonesty. Yet you too never tried to break that pattern. Whenever you sensed a crisis brewing in my life you couldn't bear to ask me, so you would mail me a poem. When I told you about the time I felt betrayed and had lost faith, you said nothing but sent me Hopkins with a note for an excuse.

One line from there remains in my head ...
"That night, that year of now done darkness when I lay wrestling with (my God!) my God."
In much the same fashion I replied to you later by which time I hoped you were less anguished on my part.

I have desired to go
  Where springs not fail,
To fields where falls no sharp and sided hail
  And a few lilies blow.

And I have asked to be
  Where no storms come,
Where the green swell is in the heavens dumb,
  And out of the swing of the sea.

Its about a nun's vocation – one of your early grouses against me was my lack of vocation. That's where Rohit scored above me. When he went on to study zoology, you admired him. I remember that. I too wanted to do something – to set your approval. I thought I might do something wildly different like advertising or mercantile law. But knowing how far away this would take me from you, I couldn't. So I stayed close, following your footprints, fitting my small feet where your large ones had been. Sometimes I think I am your form without the content. I am competent, but insincere. I know that even though, like yours, some of my students too appreciate my lectures. But the relationship is distant, formal, functional. I would have liked to have inherited your passion but know that I lack your ability to inspire. You, on the other hand don't know my hollowness because in your presence I dissemble. I have learnt to mask my cynicism and have by now built up my rationalizations. Luckily this is something you couldn't understand. Not you with your earnest faith

You were admired for your integrity, your spontaneous lack of worldliness. I remember the swell of pride every time people asked me my father's name. I can't remember anything else. Not even when you sold off all the precious heirlooms one after the other to run the house. Ma and Rohit couldn't understand why you spent your time writing books that got you no money. But it wasn't our poverty that I held against you.

Because I suffered your indignities too – it hit us together when I went to study in your old department. You were invited to teach again. I began to notice how you felt out of step when you met your old friends. They no longer spoke the same language as you. You had studied alongside them and then you all went your different ways. They came back deconstructing narratives and decolonizing minds. They only talked oral history and self-reflexivity. From your otherwise inexplicable rage directed at me, I understood you were upset. Its true I admired some of them. It's also true that there is no old fashioned rigour anymore. Nobody plods through the classics. Shakespeare is just another writer to be deconstructed and inspected for all his racism and anti Semitism. If all categories are equally valid for everything, wherein lies the magic of poetry? I don't know Papa – I am as always, split in the middle. Trying to negotiate a compromise.

A lot of your anger with me was because of what you saw as my complicity with them. With those who argued with your certitude.

I plead guilty. Maybe I did it because I suffered your humiliations. And I wanted to protect you. I also wanted to share the excitement of a new world with you. For once, I wanted the roles reversed. But you were always too proud for that.

I begin to understand your sense of betrayal now. Earlier it was different. Whenever I expressed an opinion you would stamp me out. It hurt and I did not find it in me to forgive you. Naively I believed that loving was easy. Now I see how hard it is to let go. Your alienation then, helped me to make my choices without the burden of guilt.

"Your father wants you inside". The newcomer tells me.

I go in and find you grimacing continuously. You point to the cardiac monitor and want me to switch it on. You want to hear the news. Bombs may have fallen on Iraq. Why nobody has given you tea even though it is past noon. You want to know whose birthday it is and how much it costs to have all this air-conditioning. For your part it is a criminal waste – all these birthdays and air-conditioning and five star hotels. You want to be in your own home. But why can't someone give you tea...

Around you patients look irritated. The attendants are amused. They exchange knowing glances and look at me. One white coat says dementia, the other says, it's only anesthesia. Either way they will sedate you.

You sounded so changed before your hospitalization. Despite your professed waiting when we come to visit you, you remain withdrawn – your face mask-like. Still immersed in your large vault like library, always dark and smoke-filled, where windows have never been opened or curtains drawn. I now dread visiting you. But guilt nudges me on ... you show no joy except when you shuffle across to greet us. The long, hard bony embrace. And then I know you'll disappear. Inaccessible as ever. Why do you want me to come, I always complain? You look uncomprehending. You don't understand this need for companionship. Never. Not after living with Ma for decades. What does it mean to spend time together? You took care of her through her illness and sobbed like a baby. But when she recovered you never told her how much it had mattered to you. She still doesn't know. In any case she hardly comprehends things anymore.

More than ever you sound alienated. Terse. The laugh in your voice that I am used to has faded. When I press you, you only mention physical pain.

Then the old retainer calls us. You've refused to eat or drink. Ma is uncomprehending and eerily calm. You have not woken up. Your pulse is feeble. We hurtle across. I don't expect to make it in time to see you.

I feel myself crumbling. Is it possible that today I am begging you silently to live on, as you did years ago when you sensed me slipping?

But at home everybody is composed. Ma actually smiles in recognition. Something she does only now and then. She tells me I look haggard. Why? Papa will be fine.

I notice the garden looks pretty in a disorderly way. Calendula and Snap-dragons and Salvias all growing wild. When you neglect them they always disregard order.

At the hospital, the doctors will not commit. You are too old. They will just cut you open. You have bled a lot. You are slipping away. The childhood nightmare always comes true eventually. But I am older now – mother and wife. You will cease to be, while I will go on. I no longer think of your death as the end. Still it hurts. More than you could ever imagine.

A stretcher is brought out. One big-built man accompanying it crumples suddenly. The young man from Kota was his brother. He's gone. Kind face and I recoil, almost huddle into each other. There's a hush.

"Every day since I have come at least one dead body …" she whispers.

"Yesterday the Bengali boy next to your father left. They had been here for two months. He was also on the respirator. He had polio and there was septicemia, which just kept spreading. Finally, he took out the tube and left. His father carried him back. Everyone has limitations." It's the newcomer.

We have a secret community here. The community of the living. We know the fragility of belonging here. But we cling to each other. We don't want to be talked of in hushed whispers tomorrow. We want to triumph and feel sorry for those who couldn't.

I plead with the guard to let me see you. You are a hollow mask. Your face darkens when you see me. Menacingly you wag your finger. You try to swallow your pipes. The doctors have sedated you again.

We may be able to take you home eventually. But it won't be you as I want to remember you. I fear that the frail image I have saved of you will disappear. I can't reconcile you two. I am filled with longing to be freed of the bond that tugs me to this scarecrow. It might have been easier if I had loved you less and I could forget the taste of raw mangoes, the magic cave of Aladdin's treasures and the warm assurance of your calloused hands. All around people are only too willing to advise. Be detached and caring, is their *mantra*. I don't know what that means. Neither do you for all your espousal of stoics … I want you back.. but I am afraid of what that means. Then there is a call from the white coats.

"Your father has had a cardiac arrest", they said. When I go to see you in the hospital knowing it to be the last time, I see Kind face outside. She is beaming with joy. Her mother is breathing without the respirator. I feel a passing pang of envy.

At the ward they are waiting for us. You have gone finally. It's late at night when we come back from the hospital for the last time. There's a haze. It's a strange night – I can't tell whether it's foggy or dusty. Its almost springtime. The flame of the forest outside is in bloom. The end of March is wrongly reckoned spring, you once wrote. For a long time all I can feel is an unreality. The long day's task is done and we must sleep… In the distance I hear the cry of a hungry child.

Someone is shaking me to say it's my boy.

Contributors

Shiv K. Kumar, Padmabhushan awardee, eminent poet and novelist. Lives in Hyderabad.

Sudhir Chandra an eminent writer, at present lives in Delhi, and is engaged in research on the religious conversions in the upper castes.

Santosh Gupta, Professor of English, University of Rajasthan.

B.C. Upreti, is Associate Professor in the South Asia Studies Centre, University of Rajasthan, Jaipur.

Dorothy M. Figueira is in the Department of Comparative Literatures at the University of Georgia at Athens.

Tej N. Dhar currently teaches at Asmara University, Eritrea.

Vijay Lakshmi, creative writer, teaches in Community College, Philadelphia, USA.

Malashri Lal, Professor in the Department of English, Delhi University, Delhi.

Veena Singh, Professor of English, University of Rajasthan, Jaipur.

Supriya Agarwal teaches at Khandelwal College, Jaipur.

Sudha Shastri is at the Indian Institute of Technology, Mumbai in the School of Humanities and Social Sciences.

Mini Nanda, Associate Professor, Department of English, University of Rajasthan, Jaipur.

Ila Rathore is located at Government College, Bilaspur (Himachal Pradesh).

Harish Narang, Professor at Jawaharlal Nehru University, New Delhi.

Alka Kumar teaches at Shyama Prasad Mukherjee College, Delhi University.

Anisur Rahman is Professor in the Department of English and European Languages, Jamia Millia, New Delhi.

Sudha Rai, Professor of English, University of Rajasthan.

Veena Jain teaches at Government College, Alwar.

Anu Celly, Associate Professor, Punjab University, Chandigarh.

Jasbir Jain is Honorary Director, IRIS.

Nilofer Kaul teaches English at Han Raj College, Delhi.

Index

Achebe, Chinua 41, 160
Ahmad, Aijaz 102, 215
Alvarez, Julia 91
Alvi, Moniza 190ff
American Indian Movement 18
AMriiKA 160, 162ff, 168ff
Anderson, Benedict 62, 116, 175, 241
Anger of the Aubergines 105
Arasanayagam, Jean 138ff, 142ff, 146
Aristotle 161
Atwood, Margaret 128ff, 138, 142, 147
Ayodha 4

Babri Masjid 4, 8, 15
Bangladeshi Muslims 19

Bannerji, Himani 11, 12, 18, 20ff, 25ff, 203, 207ff, 212
Bano, Gulzar 197ff
Beauvoir, Simone de 149
Because of India 180, 181, 185ff
Bedi, Kiran 101
Bhabha, Homi K. 62, 125, 215
Bhatt, Ela 101
Bhatt, Nasreen Anju 195, 196
biculturalism 18
bilingualism 18
Bissoondath, Neil 230, 231ff, 240
Blind Assassin 128ff
Book of Secrets 162ff, 168
Bowl of Warm Air 190
Brah, Avtar 215ff, 241
Brennan, Timothy 215
Brodsky, Joseph 244

Brooks, Brenda 179
Butalia, Urvashi 146

Canadian identity 12
Caribbean writers 70
Chandra, Vikram 102, 110ff
Change of Address 216ff
Chatterjee, Partha 150
Chatterjee, Upamanyu 102, 110ff
Chauduri, Nirad 104
"City of Sorrow" 114ff
Close Sesame 71, 86ff
"Clothes" 152ff
Codrescu, Andrei 91, 92ff
colonial discourse 65
community, communities 15, 17ff, 19, 23ff, 26ff
Comparison between Canada and India 14ff
"Conditions We Call Exile" 244
"Confessions" 152
Conversations of Cow 178ff, 181ff, 186
Country at My Shoulder 190

Dabydeen, Cyril 230ff
Dark Side of a Nation 203ff
Dark Swirl 236
Dawood, Attiya 199
Derrida, Derridean 62, 246
Desai, Anita 102, 105
Deshpande, Shashi 102
Dhondhy, Farukh 102
diaspora, Indian 148
diaspora 175ff
diasporic consciousness 178
diasporic studies/sensibility 174

diasporic writers 37
Digging up the Mountains 231, 233
Dissent to Nowhere 166
Distant Music 216ff
Divakarani, Chitra Banerjee 150ff
"Double City" 191
Duncan, Sarah Jeannette 122ff

Eliot, T.S. 93-94
English, August 110
Enlightenment 11
Equal Music 107
Estavez, Sandra 93
ethno-religious conflicts 52
exile 69ff
 five-star exiles 103
 inner exile 91, 103

Family Matters 238
Farah, Nurruddin 67, 71, 81ff
Fasting, Feasting 105
Feminism Without Borders 241
feminism 204ff
feminist political theory 205ff
feminist politics 25ff
feminist 39
Finding the Centre 231ff
Forster, E.M. 124
Foucault, M. 62
Froude, James Anthony 230

Gandhi 2, 6, 26
Gandhian traditionalism 28
Gazdar, Saeeda 198
Ghosh, Amitav 102, 103, 106ff
Gill, Lakshmi 204, 208, 209

Index

Glass Palace 107
Global Soul 245
God of Small Things 107ff, 109
Guide 236
Gujarat 4ff, 7ff, 24ff
Gunny Sack 161ff, 168
Gupta, Ashis 239

Habib, Shaista 198ff
Half a Life 22ff
Hariharan, Githa 102, 107, 109ff
Herk, Aritha van 238
Hindu (negative description) 20
Hindu nationalism 24
Hindu Personal Law 20
Hindu Right 16
Hindu sensibility 184
Hindu-Indian equation 7
Hinduism 178, 184
Hindus and Muslims 4, 14ff
Hindus and Sikhs 4, 14
Hindutva 4ff, 7, 8, 27
historical metafiction 78
House in Pondicherry 216ff
Husain, Intizar 113ff, 242
Hutcheon, Linda 78
hybridity 62

Idea of India 102, 106
identity/self 21ff, 174ff
identity, Canadian 12
Ilaiah, Kancha 28
Imam, Hina Faisal 198
immigrant narrative 231, story 238
immigrant writer 24, writing 90ff

immigrant 149ff, 155ff
immigrant's language 93ff
In the Garden Secretly 139
In Visible Ink 238
India, tribal population 17
India:From Midnight to Millennium 106
Indian identity 4
Indian modernity 27
"Into the Garden." 139ff
Ishiguro 93
Iyer, Pico 103, 244

Jha, Radhika 243
Joyce, James 70, 83, 230

Kalsey, Surjit 204, 206ff, 211
Kanaganyakam, Chelva 177, 183
Kanthapura 111, 236
Khan, Uzman Alam 240ff
Khilnani, Sunil 102, 106
Kingston, Maxine Hong 91ff
Kundera, Milan 92

Lamming, George 230
Langley, Lee 216ff
Law of the Threshold: Women Writers in Indian English 109
"Legal Alien" 90
lesbianism 178ff
"Letter from India" 114ff
"Life at the Margins" 171
Lim, Shirley Geok-lin 245ff
Love and Longing in Bombay 110

Malihabadi, Josh 242

Index • **263**

"Management of Grief" 152ff, 155ff
Meaning of India 106
"Meeting Mrinal" 152ff
Mehta, Gita 102ff
memory and reality 92, 93
memory 237ff, 241, 245
Middle Passage 230ff
Midnight's Children 76ff, 80
Mishra, Pankaj 102
Mishra, Vijay 210, 245
Mistry, Rohinton 238
modern self 28
Mohanty, Chandra Talpade 205, 241
Moodie, Susanna 122ff
Morrison, Toni 39
Mukherjee, Arun 40, 42, 206
Mukherjee, Bharati 150ff, 156, 238, 240
Mukherjee, Meenakshi 141
multicultural context 177
multiculturalism 1ff, 10ff, 18ff, 23ff, 203ff, 215ff
Muslim fundamentalism 23
Muslim leadership 22ff
Muslim Personal Law 22
Muslim women 22ff
Muslims (Indian) 24ff
  migrants from Bangladesh 24
My Brahmin Days 230
"My Ordeal as a Citizen of Pakistan" 242
Mystic Masseur 236

Naheed, Kishwar 199
Naipaul, V.S. 93, 230, 231f, 235ff
Naked Needle 82

Nandy, Ashis 11
Namjoshi, Suniti 174ff, 180ff, 245
Nandan, Satendra 214
Narayan, R.K. 236
national identity 24
Nehru 101, 242,
Nehruvian modernity 28
No New Land 168

Occidentalism 67
Ondaatje, Michael 238
Oppositional Aesthetics 40, 42
Oppressive Present: Literature and Social Consciousness in Colonial India 6, 7
Orientalism 65
Orientalism 65ff
Orwellian nightmare 85
Other, 'other' 1, 11, 12ff, 62ff, 148ff, 151ff, 239, 244,
others as looking glass 12
Out of Place 69, 71, 73ff

Pakistani women poets 190ff
Pan-Indian Hinduism 6
Parameswaran, Uma 204, 208ff, 210, 211ff, 239, 245
partition 113
Passage to India 124ff
"Persistence of Memory" 146
Persistent Rumour 216
personal law 20, 21ff
Philoctectes 90
Playing in the Dark: Whiteness and Literary Imagination 39
Pleasures of Exile 230
Poetics 161

Politics of Dispossession 72
Postcolonialism, My Living 42
Postcolonialism 62ff, 111
   criticism 61ff
   postcolonial critics 62ff
   subject 63
   theory 60ff
"Presents from my Aunts in Pakistan" 191
Proustian memory 92

"Quail's Nest" 142ff
Question of Palestine 72

Ramanujan, A.K. 143
Rao, Raja 106, 111, 236
"Reflections of Exile" 72
refugee problem/refugees 44ff, 54ff, 69, 139
Representations of an Intellectual 72
Requiem for a Rainbow 214ff
Riaz, Fahmida 191, 198, 199
"Ring of Memory" 143
Rothstein, Edward 67
Roy, Arundhati 101ff, 107ff, 109, 110
Rushdie, Salman 70, 76ff, 80, 82, 84, 9, 102ff, 177, 214, 245

Said Edward 62, 65, 67, 69ff, 72ff
"Sanctuary" 138ff, 143
Sara, Shagufta 199-200
Sardines 71, 85ff
Satanic Verses 91
Satchidanandan K. 111
"Search My Mind" 14ff

self 1ff, 12ff, 19, 22ff, 27, 222ff, 226f, 231, 232
   conceptualization of the self 9
   modern self 28
   necessity of community 12ff, 19ff, 148ff, 239ff
   secular self 26ff
Selling Illusions 231
Sept 11 67, 160, 172
Seth, Vikram 102, 106, 107
Shah Bano case 22ff
Shame 71, 76ff, 81
Sharma, Bulbul 105
"Silver Pavements, Golden Roofs" 151ff
Simple Adventures of a Memsahib 122ff
Singh, Christine 242ff
Singh, Khushwant 103
Smell 243
Snakes and Ladders: A View of Modern India 103ff
Sophocles 90
Spivak, Gayatri Chakravorty 62, 215
"Squatter" 240
Stevens, Wallace 148
Such a Long Journey 238
Suitable Boy 107
Sweet and Sour 71, 83ff
"Swimming Lessons" 240

Tharoor Shashi 102, 106
Thiong'o, Ngugi wa 93, 160
Third World 62ff, 65
Thousand Faces of Night 109ff
Trespassing 240ff
Trollope, Anthony, 230

Uhuru Street 163, 168
Uniform Civil Code 16, 27
Universal Man 27
"Unwritten Epic" 114ff, 242

Vassanji, M.G. 160ff

Wehner, Monica 92ff
Weil, Simone 245

White, Hayden 79
"Wife's Story" 152
Wilson, Edmund 90
Wizard Swami 236
women of colour 11, 25ff
Wound and the Bow 90

Yaadon Ki Baraat 242

$30